PLUG

THE HOLES

FILL

THE BARREL

A BEGINNERS GUIDE TO
BUILDING WEALTH WITH REAL ESTATE

JASON M. KOGOK

INVESTORS WEALTH EDUCATION, LLC

PLUG THE HOLES, FILL THE BARREL

©2022 Investors Wealth Education, LLC & Jason Kogok

ISBN: 978-0-578-35717-1

Disclaimer

BEFORE READING THIS BOOK, please review the critical information below:

All investments, including real estate, are speculative in nature and involve substantial risk of loss. Investors Wealth Education, LLC ("IWE"), and Jason Kogok, encourages investors to invest carefully. The information provided in this book is intended to be a source of valuable information for the reader; however, it does not replace or serve as a substitute for direct expert assistance. Investors should always do their own research and due diligence, and seek advice from a professional investment or financial advisor, accountant, real estate agent, and/or attorney, as appropriate, prior to making any investment, including those related to information published or discussed by IWE or Jason Kogok in this book or elsewhere. We do not in any way warrant or guarantee the success of any action you take in reliance on our statements or recommendations.

Past performance is not necessarily indicative of future results. IWE offers no guarantee that systems, indicators, signals, spreadsheets, strategies or opinions will result in profits or that they will not result in losses.

Investor's Wealth Education, LLC, Jason Kogok and its officers, members, affiliates and assigns are not registered investment, legal or tax advisors. Although best efforts are made to ensure all information is accurate and up to date, unintended errors and misprints may occur. The author and Investors Wealth Education, LLC, disclaim any and all liability in the event that any charts, data, opinions, or other information presented in this book are found to be inaccurate or incomplete, or result in investment loss.

Under no circumstances should any material in this book be used or considered as an offer to sell or a solicitation of any offer to buy an interest in any security, investment or real estate, or the rendering of personalized investment advice.

Table of Contents

Preface

OVER THE PAST TWO decades I have worked with thousands of people in the real estate world, from clients to investors to brokers to students, all wanting to learn more. Through the years, I've noticed a common thirst for knowledge and a never-ending interest in using real estate to build wealth and financial freedom. I could hardly attend a social gathering without the topic coming up in one or more conversations with eager people wondering how to get started or take the next step. And I loved having those talks and being that resource. But, as often accompanies popular interests, I also noticed the *thousands* of books, seminars and classes teaching the same number of different ways to be successful in this space, many of which were convoluted and leaned on rare or unrealistic examples, some even trying to upsell the reader to buy more of the same resources. With so much information available, the true novice investor can be overwhelmed and lost on which direction to head first. That is what led me to write this book. My hope is to simplify the process and cut through the noise by distilling my decades of experience into an easy to understand, step-by-step resource that provides practical guidance to a beginner or intermediate investor. While doing that, I want to give smaller investors hope, motivation and encouragement that they too can build a financially secure future and can do so without needing to buy 20 homes or an entire apartment building. So often real estate investing guidance comes in the flashy forms of buying more, more, more! The bigger, the better. There's nothing inherently wrong with that strategy if it's right for you. However, the simple truth that's not discussed enough is that these large projects also come with increased risk and the need for significant up-front capital. While those projects may sound exciting, the statistical reality is that most investors will never build to that scale. Here's the good news: In order to achieve significant wealth through real estate, you don't *need* to grow to that scale. I wanted to write a book that doesn't sell the dream, but rather helps investors build their own.

As a real estate investor myself, I have done all types of residential real estate investing, from your basic, run of the mill rental homes to large-scale renovation projects and flips. I've been teaching real estate investing on many levels for over a decade, and I work hard to incorporate the lessons with an easy to learn and approachable teaching style using real-world examples and not cherry-picked samples that are impossible to find in reality. My goal is to help the average person build wealth with just a few investment homes that can set them on the right path to reaching their goals.

If you already own 20 homes, an apartment building or a commercial building, I didn't particularly write this book for you. But if you're new to real estate investing, or already own a property (or a few!) and are seeking experience-based guidance on how to build and maximize your wealth, then I welcome you to your next step in that journey. My hope is that this book inspires you and gives you the confidence needed to take action in your journey to building wealth through real estate investing.

Chapter 1 - *Why this Book?*

"Real estate cannot be lost or stolen. Nor can it be carried away. Purchased with common sense, paid for in full, and managed with reasonable care, it is about the safest investment in the world."

~ Franklin D. Roosevelt

This statement has been proven true time and time again.

I SHOULD PROBABLY SET some expectations for you before we get too deep into this book. I am not a writer by profession. I'm a real estate broker, teacher, coach, and investor. Writing is not my specialty, but real estate investing, growing wealth, and helping people get on the right track are my forte. I divulge that information early on because as you read this, you won't see too many fancy words or long-winded explanations that seem to go in circles with no end, or at least, I hope you won't.

Instead, you will see straightforward, insightful examples and instructions that prove productive to you. I'll also presume this isn't your first real estate investing book. People have written about this subject since landlords rented out the first home. I do hope it's one of the last ones you ever need to read. Some real estate books talk in generalities and not specifics, or they talk about large-scale projects and huge investments. However, most people don't have the time, money, know-how, or motivation to tackle these projects. My strategy for writing this book is a little different.

I'm a goal setter and believe that sharing my goals out loud keeps me committed to reaching them. So, I'll share my goals for this book.

I have two goals in writing this book. First, I want to share my love for real estate investing in a way that hopefully manifests itself into some motivation for you to start.

The second, and most important to you, is that I want to teach you how to build wealth with real estate but do so in a *simple* way, without the need to own 10, 20 or 100 homes. While real estate investing is the basis of this book, I'm hoping that some of the lessons taught here can be used in other areas of your life.

I should probably explain what I mean by *simple*. There are so many ways to make money in real estate, which is one of the significant parts. On the other hand, because there are so many ways to partake in real estate investing, it can be overwhelming, confusing, and downright intimidating. I could go online right now and invest $10,000 in some company buying apartment buildings in a no-name town in any state in America, even in the world. Would that make me a real estate investor?

Technically, yes. I could go and buy an office building and rent out the space to different businesses. Would that make me a real estate investor? Yup, sure would. I could buy a plot of vacant land and allow a solar company to lease the land to install a solar farm. You guessed it; I'd be a real estate investor. I could even call up all my family and friends, raise some money, buy a piece of raw land, and do a land lease back to a restaurant franchise. Yes, real estate investor once again.

The list of examples is almost endless, but here's the rub. While those items can seem relatively simple when described in one short and sweet sentence, the reality is that the ins and outs, risks involved, and overall 'Where do I start?' questions usually place roadblocks and obstacles before the average investor.

Now that I've reviewed some reasons for writing the book let me shed a little light on who I am. I think subject matters are sometimes only as good as the people teaching them. There are many excellent writers who are poor real estate investors and unbelievable real estate investors who can't articulate all their knowledge effectively. I hope to fall somewhere in the middle of those.

Originally born in Washington, DC, I grew up in Maryland. This isn't an autobiography, so I won't bore you with the details, but we'll sum up my youth as 'average to above average.' I had hard-working parents who always ensured there was food on the table, a roof over our heads, gifts under the tree at Christmas, and at least one family vacation to the beach every summer. It was by no means a struggle in my world, and I won't pretend it was. We had our share of financial hardships and struggles, but things were pretty good by comparison. As a kid and teenager, I had a genuine affection for building stuff, taking things apart, and in my later adolescence years, I found an odd passion for home improvement!

My parents weren't handy, but like most people, they weren't helpless either. We had an uncle for those tasks that required a saw or electrical tools. I soon replaced that handy uncle as our go-to repairman. One of the greatest gifts my parents gave me was something they probably didn't even know they gave me until they read this. That gift was the permission to try and build or fix stuff in our house. It seems simple on the surface, but if my father had been super-handy, I probably wouldn't have had as much 'trial and error' under my belt.

I likely wouldn't have been given so much leeway in doing things so imperfectly. My parents allowed me to build a deck on our house, my grand finale project. I was 16 or 17 years old at the time and had never been so excited to create this 10x12 deck that was two feet off the ground.

I spent countless sleepless nights planning in my head how I was going to dig the footings, bolt the beams to the posts, strategically lay the joists, and miter cut the handrails. It was worth being exhausted the next day due to the lack of sleep. Several decades later, I experience the same joy and sleepless nights when I am in the middle of a fun project. The point is that my hobby grew into a passion because no one stifled it. So, when my love grew from tinkering on decks into real estate investing, I attacked it with the same drive and searched for similar support from other investors and people in the industry.

Now, back to my point (see, a true writer would stay on task). Sometimes my parents had a few extra bucks, and most of the time, they were careful about where they spent each dollar. Until my early teen years, I observed things related to our family's financial situation, but I didn't understand it. The shift from just *watching* to *truly understanding* was monumental for me.

It was a blessing when my father lost his job, our only source of income. Hang with me – I know saying you were *blessed* when a parent lost a job seems odd, but it's true. It shaped who I became during those formidable years, and in many ways, helped form some of the foundations I'll share throughout this book. I learned five lessons that I'll pass on to you. While you probably know these lessons already, a little refresher is always helpful before diving into real estate investing lessons.

Lesson #1

The first lesson is that the old saying "Money doesn't buy happiness" is only true to a point. Money pays your bills and puts food on the table. Money puts cleats on your child's feet so they can play soccer. So, while money won't add time to your life, cure an illness or give you true love, it sure as hell is brutal to move through life if bill collectors are hounding you, you are price-checking every item in your grocery cart, or trying to find the money to get your kid on the soccer field. From a life perspective, I understood the underlying theme behind "Money doesn't buy happiness," but I fully understood what money did buy.

> ➤ **I learned the power of money and what it controls.**

Lesson #2

The second lesson I learned is that hard work only goes so far, unfortunately. I know that's not true in every case, but the reality is that even the most successful, hard-working people need to catch a break occasionally. Someone opens a door for them, or they get an opportunity to move forward. My parents worked very hard. My mom was the captain of the ship. Honestly, if it weren't for her, my three siblings and I would be fools lost without direction.

While it was tough to understand all those years ago completely, she had to be the 'bad guy' during those years to make sure we did our homework, ate decently, stayed active, made our beds, used manners, and did all the other things that as kids we didn't see as beneficial.

Many mothers perform this work and don't get the due credit (my wife is on that list). While my mom may not have brought in a lot of money during those years, her value went well beyond any measurable monetary value. Having money won't make you a good person with polite manners who aims to do the right thing. My dad, on the other hand, played more of the traditional father role that you'd see in the '80s and '90s. He went to work, stayed there long hours, didn't want to talk about his day afterward, and would catch one of our soccer games when he could. No blame given. He had to make money. To make money, he had to be *at work. That last sentence is so important; I want to repeat it - for him to make money, he had to physically be somewhere, which meant he couldn't be in two places at once.* That is why real estate investing can be so crucial for so many people - if done correctly, it allows you to make money but *not have to be there in person.*

While my father was searching for a new career when I was in my late teens, he worked two jobs. He worked jobs back-to-back, and while he didn't talk about it, you could tell that working so hard was beating him down. He worked all night, came home, and tried to manage a family while pretending all was OK. Some of you can relate.

As the years went on and my father found a new career, it wasn't always enough to consistently pay all the bills. This is why he took a night job delivering pizzas. Ironically, I did the same thing at the same time at a different pizza shop. I did mine in our hometown. He did his job about 20 minutes away in another town. I've never asked, but I've always thought he worked in the next town over so he would be less likely to have to deliver pizzas to someone we knew in our hometown. I gained a tremendous amount of respect for him during those years. He wasn't delivering pizzas because he liked the way his car smelled for days after. He was doing it out of necessity.

> ➢ **I learned that your ability to hustle, even in the toughest of times, is a critical differentiator in the level of success you'll have. While hard work needs to be accompanied by opportunity, opportunity without hard work will go nowhere.**

Lesson #3

The third lesson in all those experiences was not to be at the mercy of others for your entire well-being. Many people express the desire to work for themselves or own their own company. As someone who does, I can tell you that there are many days when I would like to walk into a nine-to-five job, punch the clock, do my thing, and leave some of the responsibilities in someone else's hands.

I'd be lying if I didn't also say there were some great perks. One of the biggest perks became glaringly obvious to me during those teen years as all the money issues unfolded. If you're in charge of writing your own paycheck, and everything rests on your shoulders, then it's hard for someone else to bring you down.

Of course, things can happen in the economy outside of your control. *(Look at what the COVID pandemic shutdown of 2020-22 did to many restaurants)*. Maybe you own a store selling a product, and someone creates a better version of that and puts you out of business *(Think about what Netflix did to Blockbuster Video)*. Yes, those things can be outside of your control, but at least, if you're the owner and not the employee, you'll always be the one collecting the last paycheck.

One of the things that are often overlooked in "being your own boss" is the degree to which you take that idea. For instance, you may have a great paying job as a technical code writer at IBM, and it comes with wonderful benefits, and you enjoy your job; maybe you don't necessarily quit that job to "be your own boss." You could use real estate investing as your backup plan or future income. That way, if you lost your IBM job or just grew tired of it, you already have a business in motion where you would be in charge.

> ➤ **I learned always to have some control over my income security, even if just part of it. Write your own check for at least something you do.**

Lesson #4

The fourth lesson I learned was relying on savings to save you in a long-term financial crisis is bullsh#t. Too often, we're taught to focus on savings and not more sources of income. We're taught to be defensive instead of offensive.

A common question that is asked, through any financial disruption, is, "How much have I saved?" Everyone is supposed to have a safety net of savings of some sort, even if your nest egg just covers a few months of your expenses. Most financial consultants recommend that you save somewhere in the range of three to six months' worth of expenses. If you lose your job, it may be because of a company or industry issue and not an overall macroeconomic concern, such as a recession. However, if you lose your job in a recession or even because of industry disruption, getting a new job may not be easy. During our family's tough economic times, my parents drained the little savings they had, then expanded their efforts into asking family members for a bit of help. Combine exhausting your savings with having to ask family for money, and you can imagine the extra layers of stress they endured. As I watched this unfold, I thought, "I better save money, I need to save money!" That message was very real during those tough times. If I didn't save, how would I help myself in times of financial crisis? How could I help my family if they needed something? To this day, I believe that those years turned my siblings and me into big believers in savings. Here's the issue that I came to learn about years later. Savings is stagnant. Savings is a minor band-aid in your arsenal of tools if you have a financial disruption in your life. However, in many households, it's taught to be your saving grace. It's not.

Because savings is stagnant, it does not grow. In essence, if you have $10,000 saved, in six months, even with bank interest, it's probably only worth $10,010. It doesn't move the needle. You're exchanging the potential growth of that money for its security. If you invested every dollar you had and the market crashed (*pick your 'market' that you may have invested in - stock, real estate, cryptocurrency, oil, etc.),* then your immediate safety net could be quickly and severely diminished. Even if my parents had saved double the money they had, the same result would have occurred, just two to three months later than it did. In some circumstances, that extra two to three months may have made all the difference. In many cases, financial troubles can take much longer to resolve than initially anticipated. What took me years to grasp completely was that if I can get paid by multiple sources, even if they were just hobbies, I can withstand almost any financial crisis. If I lose one source of income, I have others to supplement. Here's an example: When I was in my late teens, I worked part-time at a hardware store. And two nights a week, I would also deliver pizzas. I didn't work 40 hours at just one of those. Instead, I split the same hours into two different sources of income.

Then, I turned my hobby into some extra cash on the side. I did minor fixer-upper projects for people I'd meet at the hardware store, such as hanging a ceiling fan, painting a fence, or putting up window blinds for someone. I was always cautious that I didn't turn my hobby into a full-time job and lose the joy that a hobby can give if it becomes a requirement. I wish I could say I was savvy in those early years and knew how vital multiple streams of income were, but honestly, I wasn't.

My local hardware store closed at 5 pm on the weekend, and I learned some friends who delivered pizzas were making good money, so I thought I'd try it out. I did the same thing making a few extra bucks on my hobby of fixings things. Someone would come into the hardware store and ask if they knew anyone who could help with a task, and I'd say, "I can do that for you." It was very unplanned, but the lesson was very impactful as those small sources of income added up. I never lost a wink of sleep saying to myself, "What if the hardware store shuts down?" or "What if suddenly people hate having pizza delivered?" or "What if everyone in the world starts to paint their own fence?"

The point is that all my eggs have never been in one basket. To this day, I have multiple streams of income. I sell real estate, I teach investing at some local colleges, I teach continuing education for real estate brokers, I do some fix-and-flip renovations, and I collect income from rental properties. Of all those things, earning money on rental properties is something that can be done without me being physically there in person.

> **I learned that savings are a good starting point**
> **but that the real <u>key to financial security is having</u>**
> **<u>multiple sources of income</u> that can grow, even if at**
> **first, the work is just a hobby.**

Lesson #5

One of the most difficult parts of watching my parents struggle through those years, outside of the pressures that you would expect with financial hardships, was the fact that they felt "stuck." You can probably relate if you've ever been in this situation. You can experience the same kind of grief over losing your only source of income that people feel after other challenging life events, like a death or divorce. Like it or not, your job in many ways defines you. While some people may not admit it, losing a job can make you feel 'lost' in the world. When my father lost his job, we all were impacted. That job loss had many downstream effects. I remember very clearly trying to better understand money because of this experience. I would think to myself that *money* caused all these things and that I would treat and learn about money in a different way than my parents had known about it. I would teach my children about it differently than how my grandparents taught their children. As I mentioned before, I recognized that money didn't buy happiness - money bought freedom. That was kind of a light bulb moment for me at that age when I finally realized that money isn't bad. Money doesn't cause issues that weren't already underlying there. Money is just a tool, not the actual toolbox. Once I realized that even if you have money saved, things will not always be OK, I could start to grow my financial toolbox to ensure that I would never repeat what my family went through during those years.

> **I learned that money buys freedom, but only if used properly.**

I always knew that those experiences impacted me today. I think it's also why I have a passion for teaching others. It's why I hope this book motivates and educates people about improving their financial freedom.

There is a saying I pass along often in my teachings: *Plug the holes, fill the barrel.* It's also the title of this book. I think it's a great time to explain that. You'll see me use that same slogan several times through-out this book. Please do me a favor and imagine a rain barrel at the end of a gutter on a house. Imagine it is like one of those barrels that collects rainwater to use later to water plants, etc. As it rains, the barrel fills up. There is a small hose spigot at the bottom of that barrel that you can open when you need water. This, in my opinion, is a perfect image to describe how people should view their finances. The rain gutter is my job supplying income into the barrel, which is my bank account and retirement funds. When the bills come in, I turn on the spigot to get some money out to pay them. Sounds pretty good if it were only that simple.

Now, imagine that very same rain barrel, but instead of just one hose spigot at the bottom, there are a few holes in the barrel of varying sizes; some just a pinhole size, some the size of a golf ball, and some the size of a baseball. This comparison reflects our reality. If we consider those holes as all our expenses, we don't have just one. We have many of varying sizes. That pinhole is the cup of coffee I pay for on the way to work or the quick lunch sandwich I grab. By themselves, they're simple pinholes in our budget, and most of us consider them inconsequential. What about the golf ball-sized holes? Those are our car payments, student loans, credit cards, etc. What about the baseball-sized holes? Those are more like our rent or mortgage payments; large holes that could really take a chunk of water out of the barrel if not managed properly. I like that imaginary picture better than just the singular hose spigot at the bottom of the barrel because it's more accurate.

Typically, most novice investors learn to master the "plug the holes" part of their business first. Reducing and fine-tuning expenses is usually easier than creating new sources of income. You come to understand that the fewer holes you have in your barrel, the more money you end up having in the barrel. What we end up with in the barrel will help us buy houses, build wealth, and hopefully, continue to *fill the barrel*.

While we're there, let's talk about the *fill-the-barrel* part. Most people have one large gutter dumping into their barrel, which is their full-time job. It seems fine if more comes in from that gutter than out of those holes, right? Wrong. What if it stops raining? What if I get a clog in the gutter? Those can easily be translated to, what if I get laid off, my hours cut, or decide to quit one day? What if my company goes bankrupt or gets bought out, or my job gets outsourced or is replaced by a computer or a cheaper, younger version of me?

If you've worked anywhere long enough, you know that these aren't far-fetched ideas at all. So, how do we fix that? It goes back to some of the lessons I mentioned above of my late teens and early twenties. I need more gutters dropping income into my barrel, so if one goes away or slows down, the barrel is still being filled.

You should feel comfortable imagining this picture by now, so do it again. You have your rain barrel attached to the house, but instead of a hose spigot at the bottom, there are various holes throughout it. Now, instead of just one gutter downspout dumping water into the barrel, imagine that there is still one downspout, but there are also two or three other hoses that are pouring into the barrel. There is my full-time job as the large gutter downspout, but now there are two the size of a garden hose and one just the size of a tiny IV tube, all of them adding more water into the barrel. Even the IV tube, which is just dripping water in, has an impact. If nothing else, it's helping to offset that pinhole in our barrel: our morning cup of coffee on the way to work. Now, if a drought impacts that main gutter downspout, i.e., if we lose our job or it's negatively impacted, guess what - we have other sources of income. No, these sources aren't as significant as the main downspout, but we can last much longer having those other hoses there to help. Sometimes, the most challenging part of adding the extra hoses into our barrel is getting any sort of financial flow out of them. Still, once we do, we can focus on growing those garden hoses of income into a fire hose of revenue. If I lost my job today, I'd be better off increasing something I already have than trying to create something from scratch and then grow from there.

Most people I talk to feel comfortable with the idea of plugging the holes. After all, a large part of most finance teachings revolves around watching your expenses. Still, very few of those teachings talk about increasing your income simultaneously with several streams of income, not just one. It's diversifying your income, just like you diversify your investments. A question I get often is, "What should those secondary hoses be?" I'll share what I have with you to give you an idea.

1. My main downspout is real estate sales as a Realtor. I am a co-owner of a real estate team and make deals for clients, which is my main downspout of income.

2. I have smaller garden hoses filling my barrel: these are rental homes that give me some cash flow every month.

3. I've also got a hose off to the side that doesn't run continuously but rather is turned off and on every few months when I renovate and flip a house.

4. My IV-sized hose is my teaching at the local community college. If you've ever been a teacher, you know the income is not why you get into it, but it is income, nonetheless.

5. Occasionally, I sell one of my rental properties, which, while slowing down the hose providing cash flow, does put a more significant lump sum of money into the barrel.

Who knows, one day, this book may represent another hose. That's mine. For others, it may be as simple as turning your hobby into income - maybe you buy stuff at yard sales and resell it, or like to refurbish furniture or can help tutor kids, etc. Remember, we're not trying to replace our main downspout just yet, so the hose size is almost irrelevant. This book is about real estate investing, so my goal is to help you add a bunch of rental house hoses into your barrel.

It's about having as many hoses as you can fit, so if you decide to, or are forced to, replace that main downspout in the future, you already have some backup plans in place that you can help grow into more extensive hoses.

Plug the holes. Fill the barrel.

Chapter 2 - *Why Real Estate?*

MANY NOVICES, AND EVEN intermediate real estate investors, underestimate the benefits and risks of real estate. Any real estate investment consists of costs that can be calculated at any given time, such as my current mortgage balance, or my expenses. However, real estate investments are also littered with variables that we must estimate. If you are buying a home to rent out, you must forecast for possible repairs to the rental home, both in the near and long term, as well as how many periods of vacancy you may encounter when you don't have a tenant in a home. You must forecast future appreciation and where property values may go. Some investors just guess those numbers while others try to calculate an educated forecast.

Any good investor also sharpens their tools on the economics of their market so that they are up to date on housing inventory, consumer confidence, employment levels, inflationary concerns, and interest rate forecasts. These can directly affect the real estate market and its impact on the rental market and home prices. The list goes on. The good news is that you don't have to be a pro at those items, but it would be wise to have a basic understanding of them. I think most investors underestimate the power of having a grasp of macroeconomics, which is considered the broader market as a whole. I live in Raleigh, NC, so my "micro-market" is in Raleigh, and my "macro-market" would be the entire state of NC and even expanded to the US. I need to have a good idea of what our local market is doing and possibly where the nation is headed, too, as it may trickle down to me. You need to understand that the best investors know their local market very well and have at least a basic understanding of the economy.

Let's start with what is great about real estate investing.

There are items that we may consider somewhat apparent benefits, such as house price appreciation. Over the historical long-term trend, homes go up in value. So, for a very simplistic view, I could buy a house today for $300,000, and if I get a modest 3% appreciation increase over the next five years, the home's value would be $347,782. Here is how that looks:

Year	Value + 3%
0	$300,000
1	$309,000
2	$318,270
3	$327,818
4	$337,652
5	$347,782

While real estate values do ebb and flow up and down, historically, any dip has rallied back. Consider the people who bought at the peak of the market in 2006 and sold during the descent in 2008. Many people got stung on their values, but that's because they didn't give the market enough time to rebound. I fully understand that then, not everyone had the luxury of waiting on the market and had to make tough financial decisions for their families. However, those people that bought in 2006 and sold in 2021 did well by holding. The downturn of 2008 had no impact on them because they held on to the asset and didn't sell. Some people chose to turn their homes into rental properties during that time instead of selling at a loss. That was a great 'plan B' that proved to be financially beneficial for many.

The only price that matters is the price on the day you sell that house.

If I look and see my retirement account go up in value, I may feel very confident in my future financial security, but honestly, it's *fake money* because I haven't sold anything. I haven't *realized that gain*; it's just paper gains. The account could go down the next day. I can also look at that same retirement account when the market is down and think, 'I'm never going to be able to retire,' but once again, it's fake money - I haven't sold anything. The same mentality applies to real estate. One significant positive about real estate is this *appreciation factor* and that holding the asset through tough times can prove beneficial in the long run. A stock that goes down may never rebound, but real estate, on the other hand, has a much better track record of recovering over time.

Another great perk of residential real estate investing is *cash flow* and *principal pay down*. While your mortgage payments usually dictate principal pay down, cash flow can vary wildly depending on your market, the actual asset, how you financed the property, and a host of other variables. These variables include maintenance, saving for future capital expenditures or improvements, and other variables we'll discuss.

Let's take the principal pay down first. As you may know, when you make a mortgage payment, the two main components are 'Principal and Interest.' We typically label that combined amount as simply P&I. The interest is how the lender makes their money for giving you the loan, and the principal starts to reduce your balance owed. You may also know that most of the payment goes towards just the interest in the early months, or years, of the loan. However, as you make more payments and time goes on, more of your payment is allocated towards the principal. The easiest way to look at it is that every single payment you make, from month #1, more amount goes towards principal every month. Therefore, the longer you hold a property, the faster you chip away at the balance.

Here is a simple way to look at this. Let's say I get a mortgage for $300,000 at a 4.5% interest rate for 30 years. That would give me a Principal & Interest mortgage payment of $1,520 per month. Here is a chart of those P&I payments for the first five years:

Total Payment	Month of Payment	Interest	Principal
$1,520	1	$1,125	$395
$1,520	12	$1,108	$412
$1,520	24	$1,089	$431
$1,520	36	$1,069	$451
$1,520	48	$1,049	$471
$1,520	60	$1,027	$493

Of that $1,520, on my very first payment, $395 goes towards paying down the amount I borrowed (we call that principal pay down), and the other $1,125 goes towards interest. Fast forward three years and that same $1,520 will have a breakdown of $451 per month that goes towards the principal and $1,069 towards interest. And on month 60, the split will increase to $493 for principal and $1,027 for interest. During the entire time, your P&I payment of $1,520 remained steady, but as time went on, more of that payment went towards paying off the loan, which is a benefit to you.

Some people reading this book may already know this P&I breakdown. However, I do think it can be overlooked as part of the investor's strategy as it relates to your holding time. We can see that there is benefit in our principal pay down the longer we hold an asset as the payment remains the same, but I receive more benefit by chipping away at what is owed as time goes on without paying more per month.

Now to the famous 'cash flow' portion. I jokingly call it *famous* because many investors live and die by the idea that cash flow is the only thing that matters in real estate investing, and I disagree on that always being the best benefit. Cash flow is simply the difference between what rents we collect from our tenant and our outgoing expenses. Using the same P&I payment above of $1,520, let's also add in the following:

P&I:	$1,520
Property Taxes (Monthly)	$350
Property Insurance (Monthly)	$117
HOA Dues (Monthly)	$45
Total Monthly Payment	$2,032

Our total payment, which we'll call our **PITIH** (Principal, Interest, Taxes, Insurance, HOA dues) is the monthly sum of all of those: $1,520 + $350 + $117 + $45 = $2,032.

If we rented the home for $2,450, on the surface, our cash flow would be $2,450 - $2,032 = $418. Now, most people I know would love an extra $418 per month. However, these are surface numbers on a singular month that don't account for any expenses or repairs that may occur during the year, just not in that month. They also don't account for any savings for future big repairs like replacing the HVAC or roof. Investors call those items *capital expenditures or Cap-Ex*. The IRS tax world refers to those as "capital improvements." Don't be concerned if you see those terms interchanged. For this book, we'll refer to them as capital expenditures, except when we talk about taxes. And what about saving for when you must repaint the entire house or put down new flooring? How about the periods when the home is vacant in between tenants and you need to pay the mortgage payment yourself? Those items aren't meant to scare you. If you can estimate some of these items, you'll be much more prepared and have fewer surprises.

Initially, that $418 per month looks great, but you need to examine the numbers much deeper. I'm going to teach you how to estimate some of these items later. Still, I just wanted to point out that other items may reduce that number, so while some investors may run a quick analysis like we just did and tout a certain amount of cash flow, it can be misleading without factoring in all the actual expenses.

While the actual net cash flow, after expenses, of a single property may not get your blood flowing, the cash flow of many properties can be impactful. You can increase your cash flow in various ways too. Here are a few quick examples of how to improve your cash flow:

❖ Put down a larger down payment and borrow less.

❖ Try to get a lower interest rate or refinance your mortgage in the future to a lower payment.

❖ Find ways to run your property more efficiently, from the way you approach repairs and vacancies, to how you deal with tenants.

❖ Try to maximize what you can ask for in the rental amount.

We'll dive deep into strategies on how to increase cash flow, but for now, understand that cash flow is a benefit of real estate investing and there are ways to improve it over time.

Before we move on, I'd be doing you a disservice by not mentioning why I don't think cash flow is the "end-all and be-all." I believe that real estate investing offers many benefits, some of which we're talking about now, and some of the other benefits can outweigh the cash flow portion. There is a case to be made that in some circumstances, breaking even or even a slightly negative cash flow on the right asset can still be overall a good investment in the *long run*. Lastly, cash flow can be very dependent on the market. In some parts of the country, home prices may be relatively low compared to their rental prices and thus, deliver an excellent cash flow, but you may be giving up on long-term appreciation in those markets. While other markets that appreciate faster than rental rates increase may have a more challenging time providing excellent cash flow, you may get great appreciation rates in those markets long term instead of the cash flow today.

Now that we've talked about cash flow, as well as principal pay down, it's a great time to talk about '*equity and leverage*.' Equity and leverage are some other positive things about real estate investing. Sometimes, they don't make it into the top three reasons to invest. However, using equity and leverage with your properties can significantly impact your ability to grow your portfolio of homes quickly. An easy way to view equity is to consider the difference between what the home is worth and what you owe on it. In the most simplistic example, if I owned a home worth $350,000 and had a mortgage balance of $210,000, I would have an *equity* position in the property of $140,000. The ability to use that $140,000 in various ways is what we call *leverage*.

There are two types of equity. I'm in love with homes that I can get both.

Natural Equity: If I bought a home for $285,000 and had a mortgage of $225,000 @ 4.5%, at first and my only tangible equity in the home is the money I put in - my down payment. On day one that would be my $60,000 down payment. As I pay down the mortgage with regular payments, that $225,000 is reduced. After two years, I would owe $217,573. Even if the home did not appreciate and remained at $285,000, my equity would have grown from the original $60,000 to $67,427.

If the home has appreciated 3% per year over each of those two years, the value would go from $285,000 to $302,360, and my loan balance of $217,573 would give me an equity position of $84,787. I call this "natural equity" because it is just a byproduct of the market and owning real estate; you did nothing to the home to increase the value. The market, along with your regular mortgage payments, did the work. While that equity isn't in a cash form in my pocket right now, I can *leverage that equity* for my next property purchase without selling this home. This is a common investment strategy that we will evaluate in the upcoming chapters.

Sweat Equity*.* This is typically the harder of the two types of equity to accomplish. Sweat equity can be the part that some people, like myself, consider being more fun to obtain. This type of equity is when you do something to the house to increase the value. In the previous example, the home's value increased because the market simply appreciated at an average rate. The saying "a rising tide raises all boats" is an excellent way to think of the first type of appreciation. If the market went up, and you owned a home, then your value increased. Sweat equity, however, is particular to your individual property, and that's the difference. There are a few different ways to create sweat equity and not all will require your actual sweat! The term sweat equity arises from the idea that you do the work yourself to save on some labor costs thus your effort is creating the equity. Probably the most two common examples of sweat equity are as follows:

1) You purchase a home that needs work and is priced accordingly for that work. You do the job, and the value increases.

The math does have to work to make the equity. If I bought a home for $300,000 and it needed $25,000 worth of work to be valued at $325,000, unless I do all the work for under $25,000, I would have broken even with no extra equity. However, if I buy that same home for $280,000 and put in the $25,000 of work, now I have built-in equity because I have spent a total of $305,000 for a home now worth $325,000. The same math applies if I pay $300,000 for the house but could do $25,000 worth of work for $15,000 because I did some of the work myself and saved money, then I would have some equity built-in, too.

2) Another typical example of this equity is as follows: The neighborhood I buy is in a mix of homes that have been updated or renovated, along with many homes that haven't been touched since they were originally built. I'm sure you can think of neighborhoods in your town like this. We have a few great examples in my market. One was an indoor mall area, just north of our downtown. Eventually, the mall wasn't viable as a business, so it shut down. Surrounding that area was access to our major highways, downtown, and offices. The location had a lot of potential. It was also surrounded by large neighborhoods built in the '60s and '70s which consisted of small ranch-style homes or split levels. A developer bought the mall, tore down most of it, and rebuilt a beautiful new outdoor and indoor shopping center with great restaurants, hotels, higher-end shops, and apartments. In just a few years, the entire area was the new hip spot to live. The people who lived in the surrounding areas before, during, and after

this development were beneficiaries of the "rising tide lifts all boats." They didn't have to do anything to their homes for their values to increase. However, the neighborhood improvement also encouraged many people, not just investors, to invest in their homes and give them stunning makeovers from their original older versions. Due to the new activity, the people who lived there didn't want to move, but rather improve their current homes. In just a few years, the range of home prices in that area at that time went from $150-200,000 to up to $1,500,000 for a larger, new home. When that was happening, if you had bought one of the originally built 1960s or '70s homes, you could update or renovate it and it could be worth much more than your investment. You got sweat equity for the work you did to your home because the market was so desirable in that area that appreciation was outpacing the original purchase price plus renovation costs. This type of equity still falls into the sweat equity category because it wasn't just the location of the home that was increasing the value. The buyers purchasing in those areas were paying top dollar for more desirable homes, so to maximize profits, renovations and updating were necessary.

There are a few challenges that investors may face when trying to search for types of equity opportunities. First, some investors will over-improve the homes and therefore, it will eat away from the very sweat equity they're trying to create. I've seen investors dump thousands and thousands of dollars to get nicer tile or upgraded kitchen counters, when, the market is valuing your home for just having any new tile or basic counters. The end price doesn't always go up because you put in nicer upgrades; there is a ceiling on pricing, in most circumstances. A singular buyer may decide to pay you a little extra for those nicer upgrades, but, as investors, we need to focus on what the mass of buyers thinks. All those high-end features sound nice, but it doesn't mean that the everyday buyer will pay for them at the same cost you paid. When you are doing those updates to get sweat equity, make sure you understand the profile and expectations of your future buyers or tenants, and what your competition is doing, to make sure you maximize your available equity. We want to appeal to the masses. Remember, this is not your personal house. This is an investment, so your overall goal should be to capitalize on the largest return possible.

Another misstep that investors tend to make, and this one admittedly is tougher to get right all the time: they overestimate the future forecast of development into the area. Think about whatever city you live in, there may be an example of parts of town where development and large commercial investment had started or was proposed, but it just never really hit the grand plans as hoped for. Sometimes, the city or developer caused the issue, and sometimes, the economy changed, and plans were scaled back. If you're investing early on during this type of development, you may feel like you are ahead of the game, and you might be, but there is a higher risk you're taking on because the development is not completed yet. In this circumstance, having a backup plan is vital for that asset. If you're investing after almost all the development is completed and the risk of non-completion is minimal, you'll probably be paying a premium for those houses because the risk is reduced. If the development is just proposed or in the early stages, the prices of the surrounding homes may still be reasonable, but the risk is higher based on the development still left to be completed.

I look for desirable areas with years of consistent appreciation. I don't need 10% a year, but if I look back at least 5-10 years, I want to see appreciation just about every year, as well as I, like to see how quickly homes sell in those areas. Do they always sell faster than other areas? The icing on the cake is finding a home in those consistently desirable areas that also need work in which I can invest some sweat equity. I'm certainly not saying that you should only buy homes where you can create sweat equity. If that was the case, you may be waiting for that opportunity and miss out on other great homes that are out there.

The next positive factor is the ability to *leverage*. Many novice investors miss this item but realize it later in their portfolio building. When looking to buy more homes, there is the option to try and save a new down payment for each home, but that can take a long time to save that much money and may stunt the growth of your portfolio. More experienced investors, as they grow, are doing so by utilizing the equity in their current rental homes to leverage their next purchase. As we just saw, we have various types of equity we can earn or create. When you have equity in your rental property, there are ways of pulling that equity out in the form of cash to buy another property. This leverage is how many investors grow their portfolios. As the portfolio grows, so does their ability to pick and choose which homes they use to leverage for their next purchase, which gives them more opportunity. Another great point about utilizing this equity to leverage the purchase of more properties is that most methods have no tax consequences to the IRS. You'll be able to pull the equity out and not pay taxes to the IRS for that cash at that time. We'll examine various leverage strategies later, but I felt compelled to keep piling on the positive factors here!

Leverage and equity can ebb and flow, especially when we look at the appreciation of the home. In some hot markets, the house's value may go up rapidly, giving more opportunities to leverage it, and in cold markets, the opposite may occur. Having a long-term plan in place and understanding the market will allow you to capitalize on those times when the most leverage may exist in your portfolio. The interest rate environment also impacts how and when we decide to leverage. For instance, in an environment with higher interest rates, we may choose to leverage less than in a market with lower interest rates. Lastly, real estate itself is typically all about leverage, even when purchasing your primary home. If I can put down $70,000 on a $300,000 house, when the home appreciates, it's doing so as a percentage of the overall value, not what I invested. For example, if the market appreciates 3% over the next year, the value of that home should be $309,000; a potential equity gain this year of $9,000. I invested $70,000 and after one year was looking at a gross return of $9,000, so the return on my investment is almost 13% ($9,000 appreciation / $70,000 investment).

One of the other benefits of real estate that I like is that it's a physical asset. I enjoy the ability to change and adjust that physical asset if I need to help increase its value. As time progresses, the market changes, and the needs and wants of buyers, as well as tenants, change, and having a physical asset can allow me to change that asset at the same time. On the inexpensive side, you may just add a new coat of paint, refresh flooring, or update appliances to give it a unique look. Therefore, you may rent the home quicker (fewer vacancy costs) or increase rents by getting a tenant who is looking for something really nice (more rental income). You can also update the home on a larger scale, such as new kitchen cabinets, redoing one of the bathrooms, or even possibly adding a fence or a lovely outdoor space for a future short-term clientele who specifically wants to stay in a luxurious rental for a few days. The possibilities are endless when you own a physical asset. If I were to hold stock in a company, I wouldn't get any input or ability to change that asset; I am simply an investor on a level that has no real impact on the direction of that asset. With owning a physical asset, not only do I get input on adjustments I want to make, but I also can manage it however I like. I may choose to self-manage the tenant or use a property manager. I may decide to do a more traditional lease of one to two years or short-term vacation rentals or even corporate leasing. While some people shy away from the responsibility of owning a physical asset, I enjoy the ability to adjust based on my portfolio needs or market conditions. On the other hand, holding a physical asset does have its pitfalls, such as it's a non-liquid asset meaning you can't just press the "sell" button and have your money within a few minutes - it takes time to sell real estate. It also can be time-consuming to own, as you usually need to be actively involved to some degree. Understand that the options for investments that you can touch and feel and directly adjust the value to aren't that wide-ranging. Real estate is one of the leaders in that category.

Another benefit to real estate investing is that there is a level of security with the customers. If you imagine your rental home as a business that sells something, the success of that business is usually directly related to the number of customers: simple supply and demand. What our business sells and how much of it we can sell is based on the demand for that product, the competition by other stores that may sell similar products and the length of time that product lasts before they need to come in and buy another one. Let's compare our rental house to the business of a grocery store. With a grocery store, competition is high - there is one on almost every corner, but no matter the economy, people need to eat. It may seem as though there are many rental houses out there, but everyone needs a place to live. In our business (our rental home), the customers are renters. We're like a grocery store because rental homes are readily available, and there isn't a ton of loyalty with our tenants. Just like a shopper may go to the closest grocery store to buy bread, irrelevant of the store itself, many tenants will rent from anyone if the house meets their needs. For the most part, except in very tight inventory markets, you can always find a home or apartment to rent. We're not talking about affordability or prices here, but if you can afford market rents in your area, you can probably find a place to live. A large pool of customers exists. Your real goal is to get them to shop at your store. As a landlord, if you can create some sort of value or loyalty, you'll have more tenants than you can handle. Ask yourself some simple questions as we try to relate this to rental houses:

- ❖ Would you prefer to shop at a clean grocery store or one that is dirty and unsafe?

- ❖ Would you instead like to go to a store that has some level of customer service to assist or one with no one around to help?

- ❖ Would you like to shop at a store that is gouging you on price or one that seems to price their products by what you're getting in return?

These may seem like simple questions with obvious answers, but many landlords can't relate successfully to their customers. Little things still can go a long way. We know as landlords we have competition from other homes available for rent, so we need to price our home within reason, keep it clean and safe and when there is a repair that is required, get it taken care of promptly, and provide decent customer service. Many landlords treat their tenants like second-hand citizens or manage as a dictator. I disagree with that method. There are always customers because people need a place to live, however, you still must manage your business to get the best customers who will pay top dollar and create loyalty. Despite all the innovation we've had in this world, no one has ever found an alternative to people needing a roof over their heads.

The last benefit I'm going to talk about is the tax benefit. There are two commonly utilized tax benefits to rental properties. Before discussing this, I'll remind you to talk to your CPA or a tax professional prior to making any investments.

The first is Depreciation. Rental properties are depreciated on your annual taxes, as an expense, and usually, that depreciation can offset a large portion of the rental income you receive as gains. For instance, if I made $6,000 this year on my rental property as cash flow after expenses, and had $4,500 in depreciation, I would be taxed on $1,500 in gain this year, not the $6,000. As you probably know, taxes are never that simple, especially when claiming a *loss* to the IRS. We dive deep into depreciation later when we discuss our cash flow analysis. The flip side to this tax benefit is what we call Depreciation Recapture. Depreciation recapture is the IRS tax provision that allows the IRS to collect taxes on any profitable sale of an asset that the taxpayer had used to previously offset taxable income (i.e., the depreciation you took per year). Depreciation recapture has many rules. The rules are based on things like income, or if you took a loss, how you sold the property, whether a 1031 exchange was involved, or even if it was sold as part of an estate.

I won't go in-depth here because truly every situation can be unique to the person and property, but know that the taxpayer is getting a benefit while owning the property by using depreciation to offset rental income. When we look at our complete cash flow analysis in a later chapter, I'll show the complete depreciation schedule and its impacts.

The second tax benefit currently in place is the rate upon which capital gains are taxed. When you sell your property and make a profit, there is a tax on part of that gain called Capital Gains. Most real estate capital gains are separated into two categories for residential homes – short-term or long-term gains. These profits are taxed at different rates. If you owned the property longer than 12 months, most sellers would fall into long-term capital gains, and that tax rate can be less than your ordinary income tax rate, which is the rate for most short-term gains. If you were to 'flip' a home in less than 12 months, you would probably pay a higher tax rate due to the length of time you owned the property versus if you held a house as a rental for longer than 12 months. This is important because understanding the rules around taxes as they correlate to the length of ownership will impact what some investors do with that property. Several times I wanted to 'flip' a property, but instead, decided to rent it out for a year or two so that I could reduce my tax liability by 10-20% on the gains.

Finding your benefits in the tax code can be challenging. After all, the IRS is designed to collect taxes. Always consult a CPA on any tax strategy because not only are IRS rules ever-changing with various amendments and new legislation, but the IRS bases many of the rules on the individual. Person A may have an identical house to person B, but their income or other tax inputs are different, and thus have different applicable rules.

I'm very passionate about the positives of owning real estate, but I'd be remiss if I didn't also talk about the negative items.

Two negatives related to real estate investing are the fact that real estate is not a liquid asset, and the cash required can be significant (that is why *leverage* becomes so important). Selling a home, even in the hottest of markets, typically requires time, and if you happen to be trading in a slower time, or in a buyers' market, it could take even longer. Real estate is not one of those assets like stocks that can sell in a matter of seconds and your money is back in your hands. It does take time. Personally, while it's a negative on the surface, I see that the best investors are also the best planners and forecasters, so rarely do they have to unload a house quickly anyway. Seasoned investors know months, if not years out, which property they plan on selling next. When you plan and pay attention to the market, you can typically adapt so that you don't have to sell the home so soon. That doesn't mean you may not want to sell quickly, but you don't necessarily have to. There are times when a slow sale could negatively impact you for sure. Some of those examples where I've seen slower sales sting some people are in situations where there may be a divorce, and the unloading of assets needs to happen faster than usual, or there is some sort of emergency or loss of a job that requires the investor to scramble for cash, some of which may be tied up in the real estate. If at that time, the market is slowing or declining, you may be in a position where you can't weather the storm of the market fluctuations for too long, and therefore, timing becomes even more critical.

The second common negative about real estate investing is the cash required to get involved. A truly savvy investor tends to use outside sources of money and not necessarily their own cash for every purchase. Later in this book, we talk about strategic finance and how to use various money sources. Still, for this example, we'll use the presumption that your down payment and any upfront vacancy costs are coming out of your pocket directly.

Purchase Price:	$300,000
Down payment:	$60,000
Closing costs:	$6,000
Money for vacancy until rented:	$4,000
Total Money In:	$70,000

Real estate can certainly be cash-intensive, especially initially; in this example, we'd have to have at least $70,000. There is a counter to this negative, however. While the initial purchase can be cash-intensive, you can't ignore two factors. The first factor is the cash you invest, in this case, $70,000, which gives you leverage, unlike any common asset investment. Like we looked at previously, if that $300,000 home that took $70,000 to purchase, appreciates $9,000 in the first year (3%), then you made $9,000 on a $70,000 investment. That is almost a 13% return. If you wanted to buy $300,000 in stock, which is more liquid, you'd have to have $300,000 in actual cash. In our real estate example, we could buy a $300,000 asset with only a portion of the cost.

The second factor not to be ignored is what we mentioned earlier as well. You can use your equity to leverage another purchase in the future. There are a few ways to tap into that $70,000 to help purchase another property at a later time. We have complete examples of how to do this later in the book. However, I need to mention this again because of its significance to your potential growth.

Speaking of cash, real estate can require *continual* money. Again, let's use the $300,000 house v. $300,000 in the stock example. With a $300,000 stock purchase, it runs itself in the fact that no one is going to call me from the stock company and say their HVAC is broken, so can I buy more stock, right? However, real estate does require continual maintenance and occasional vacancy. Even if you're a terrible landlord and rarely improve or maintain your assets, there will still come a time when you must do some repairs. There is the apparent nickel-and-dime type of stuff such as dripping faucets, broken lights, and running toilets, but the actual costly items can be the capital expenditures. Big-ticket items, such as roof replacements, new HVACs, and things like that can weigh heavily on your returns. A good investor continually saves for capital expenditures and is calculated about how they are committing a portion of their cash flow from tenants for future repairs. Unfortunately, many investors don't hold the money, or at least don't save enough of it, and those significant repairs, while rare, can sting the investors' pockets. While there can be continual required cash for the property to run correctly, I view this as a 'cost of doing business.' My gains and the ability to leverage have always outweighed these costs, but I'm also a prepared investor who plans and anticipates these business costs. While I never like cutting a $7,000 check for an HVAC, I don't lose sleep over it, because I'm always taking a portion of my cash flow from the tenant and setting it aside for these items. Also, when you sell the home, you may have to put some money into it to get top dollar. When I sell a rental home, often I find myself really making it lovely right before I sell - almost as if I was *flipping* it. It allows me to squeeze everything out of the house depending on the neighborhood. I will have enjoyed the years of cash flow, principal pay down, appreciation, and tax benefits. Then I'll get it in tip-top shape right before selling to maximize my return. For me, that is just another way to get the most out of the home. It also requires the house to be in an area where I can get out more than I invested, so I do this on a property-by-property basis.

Another negative consideration when buying real estate is the time involved. I always laugh a little at the term "passive income" when investors talk about rental properties. Real estate can be somewhat passive, and if you hire the right team, owning homes can be passive, but I never view it as totally hands-off. As a matter of fact, many novice investors are hands-on, for several reasons. First, their initial rental property purchase may require a huge chunk of their savings, so it can be nerve-wracking. Being very involved in the property can settle some of those nerves because they feel they are in control of their money. Secondly, some novice investors don't realize the time savings that a good team can provide them. They don't want to pay a property manager to assist with the day-to-day operations of the home or hire a general contractor to manage repairs - they want to save every dollar and do it themselves. And then what about finding the actual house? I know many investors will rely on Realtors to assist or attend many investor networking events, but all of that still takes time. Once the rental property is up and running, the owner's time involved should dramatically decrease. Time and money are always factors that tend to discourage people from getting started in real estate investing. I would strongly encourage you to look to the benefits of tomorrow instead of the work today. As with most long-term wealth-building strategies, there is usually upfront legwork and expenses, but it can pay dividends in the long run.

One of the ways I look at real estate is by creating a personal *Scale of Passivity*. Think about the *"Plug the holes. Fill the barrel,"* image we talked about earlier. Remember how the end goal was to have multiple hoses going into the barrel simultaneously, some of varying sizes producing various amounts of income? Well, what we didn't talk about was the time required to keep each one of those hoses pumping. That is where I like to look at my scale of passivity. Let's do another visualization. Imagine just a straight line, and on that line are tiny dots spaced out evenly. Each one of those dots represents a source of income or a hose in the barrel - one might be your full-time job, another might be your current or future real estate investing, one is your retirement accounts or 401K. One may be a hobby that produces income or something that you do here and there that pro-vides a few bucks. Now, put those dots in order based on the amount of *time* they require, not on the amount of *money* that they provide. Here is an example:

On the left side are the items that require less time. The items on your right side are the ones that need the most. For most people, the items on the furthest left will be something like your 401k that someone else may manage, and on the far right is your full-time job, as it requires the most amount of your time. This diagram is only a *time scale for income-producing activities*, otherwise known as your **scale of passivity**. This scale is imperative to managing multiple hoses in your barrel because, let's face it, we all only have 24 hours in a day, so just like we must have financial management skills, we must have time management skills as well. Anytime I'm considering adding a hose to the barrel, I plot where it falls in my scale of passivity - is it on the left side where it won't take a ton of my time or on the right where it is time-intensive. Ideally, we're stacking income-producing activities on the left side where it takes less time. A new rental home I buy may start on the right side, but slide to the left after a tenant is in the home. I would strongly recommend you create your own scale of passivity even if you only have one income source currently. You can use this type of scale for other non-income producing activities in your life too. It's a great visualization of how I invest my time. You *buy things with time, not money*. Typically, your time is what creates your income. Money is just a reward for your time spent. If you didn't go to work, you most likely wouldn't get paid. I want you to think about this as you progress forward because we tend to put all the weight on the money aspect of things, and seem to discount our time, which is the most precious asset of all. If you utilize, value, and appreciate your time, you can better manage your income streams and grow them quickly. **You buy things with time, not money.**

Another item that can be negatively associated with real estate investing is the impact of market conditions. When the market is hot, investors may say 'values are inflated,' and they want to wait for prices to drop. If we're in a down market, investors tend to say they are scared to invest with the economy doing poorly, and want to hoard savings or wait to see how far prices may drop. The best investors can make money in any market. Most of this is attributed to what we call *Paralysis by Analysis*. In essence, you're overthinking something that doesn't need to be. Sound familiar? It's probably the most common sticking point for novice investors, even beyond the financial and time part. Novice investors tend to use the market conditions as an excuse not to look for opportunities. Time can fix most things in real estate, whether buying at a peak or in a valley. Just as your financial advisor may adjust your 401k holdings based on the stock market conditions, you should do the same with your real estate investing. Blaming the market for not investing is usually an excuse that makes you feel better for being too scared to do anything. The reality is that real estate is usually a long-term investment and trying to time the market or finding the perfect spot to enter or exit is simply never going to happen. If it does, it's probably just luck. The most successful investors make moves all the time; they adjust to the market and refocus their strategies, but they rarely sit on the sidelines. Here is a quick breakdown of how I explain the market to people who are afraid to invest:

If the market is 'hot'…then supply is typically low, and buyer demand is high (this can be referred to as a 'seller's market'). That high demand drives the prices up and absorbs available supply. Increased demand can be driven by a few factors, but one of the most common is below-average mortgage rates. Rising prices can deter investors from wanting to buy as they fear prices may be inflated, so they sit and wait for the market to cool down.

What cools down the market? Typically, less demand will slow down the market and create more supply. That reduction in demand and increased supply can cool off prices. This is typically referred to as a 'buyer's market'.

What may cause the demand to slow? Demand is typically cooled off by increasing interest rates and a lack of affordability. As mortgage rates increase, affordability decreases, demand slows, supply increases and prices will sometimes lower as sellers make price reductions to be more competitive. Investors may be more excited about the prospect of lowering costs. After all, we all want to pay less for something.

What was the trade-off? In exchange for lower prices, we received higher interest rates, which is many times the catalyst for slowing the market. Both 'hot' and 'cold' markets had their flaws.

If we bought a house for $325,000 and put down a 20% down payment ($260,000 mortgage) at a 4% interest rate in a 'hot' market we'd have a Principal & Interest payment of $1,241. Now, let's say over the course of two years that interest rates go up to 5.0% and cool down the market. As a byproduct, the value of that home goes down to $310,000. If we were to have purchased the house at that price and still put down 20%, our mortgage would be $248,000 (the loan amount is less since the purchase price is less). At the increased interest rate of 5%, our Principal and Interest payment would be higher at $1,331 even though we borrowed less ($248k v. $260k). If we compared the two scenarios, the home *in a hot market at $325,000 @ 4.0%, would have us paying $186,861 in interest over the life of a 30-year loan, and if we bought the home for $310,000 @ 5.0%, we would pay $231,272 in interest. In the scenario that we paid <u>less for the home and borrowed less;</u> we would actually pay $44,411 <u>more in interest</u> over the life of the loan. That extra $44,411 in interest is more than the $15,000 we would have saved on the purchase price by waiting for prices to come down. Furthermore, we had to wait 2 years for prices to come down and in that time, we lost rental cash flow, principal pay down, and possible tax benefits.*

The point of sharing that example is simply to show you that there is a reason prices go up and down, and many times what you think you're gaining in one bucket, you may be giving up in another, and all the while, you're deciding which bucket is more critical, you're wasting time. The time you could be getting a tenant to pay your mortgage down. The time you could be earning cash flow from the rents. The time you could be getting some tax benefits.

I want to end this chapter with a quote from the Hall of Fame NFL player, Jerry Rice: *"Today I will do what others won't, so tomorrow I can do what others can't."* It has always resonated with me when discussing some of the items in this chapter. Opportunity exists for the people willing to find it.

Chapter 3 - *Setting Your Goals*

IF YOU'RE ONLY GOING to take away one thing from this book, I hope it comes from this chapter. I genuinely mean that. I believe that too many investors, no matter their experience, don't set enough actual goals. I can be guilty of this, too. When things are rolling along, I seem to enjoy the ride and not challenge myself as much as I should. Challenging yourself to set more goals is critical to being truly successful, not only in real estate investing but in life. I also think posting your goals in places where you see them daily is very important. As I write this very sentence, my goals are taped on the edge of my computer monitor, screaming at me, 'I'm still here!' I think it's also vital that you share your goals out loud with others. That task is challenging for many because they fear revealing a possible failure, but I seem to push harder to reach my goals when I feel as if I have accountability to others.

As we progress through this chapter, we're going to talk about how to look at goals related to real estate and analyze real examples of how to set up our plans. I'm not naive to the fact that most real estate investing projects are monetary based — we do it for the money. Money, however, can be viewed in many ways.

- ❖ How much money do I need?

- ❖ What am I going to do with it?

- ❖ Am I passing on any to my heirs?

- ❖ What do I need to save for the future?

- ❖ When am I going to retire?

- ❖ What will my retirement look like?

❖ Do I need continual income throughout retirement, or can I live off savings and the sale of my real estate assets?

❖ What are the tax consequences of that income or sales?

❖ Will any of my current sources of income continue through retirement?

❖ What costs will I have during my later years that aren't prevalent now?

These questions regarding proper planning and setting goals for our future aren't even the tip of the iceberg. It can be daunting. It can be scary to find out you're not where you want to be or even where you *think* you are.

As with many goal-setting exercises, you need to start at the end and work backward to today. So, let's start there!

What is your end game?

Let's start with the word *retirement*. I'm not a fan of the idea of retirement, as many people perceive it. To me, when someone says they retired, I imagine someone who worked for many, many years and has now reached an age, or financial point, where they have stopped doing any work altogether. It seems like the point when movement and income creation stop. I choose to view retirement a little differently. I view retirement through the lens of still producing income, yet in a more passive fashion. Retirement's mantra should be '*because I want to, not need to.*' The most significant disconnect with retirement is the lack of income expected to be produced. There is a presumption by many that you'll just live off what you have saved when you retire. By retirement, you should have several hoses filling your barrel. Personally, I never plan to stop creating sources of income for myself, my family, and my heirs, but that doesn't mean I'm going to continue to dedicate the same amount of time to those sources. Remember our Scale of Passivity? During retirement, we should load our left side of the scale much heavier than our right side. The first thing we need to do is change the mindset that when you retire, your income stops. Setting goals to create long-term cash flow will be a challenge if we think like that. We must develop a mindset of earning income in retirement, but not at the expense of time.

Task #1

Your first task is to decide **how you envision your future**. You can't figure out how much money or income you need if you don't know how you're planning to live and what you expect to be doing. Paint your picture without a monetary value attached first. Don't half-ass this either. Everything we do and plan moving forward will revolve around this image you create for yourself.

Part of imagining my future is living at the beach most of the time. Real estate investing allows me to do that. I don't have to live where my investment houses are. I also imagine renovating properties. I love the rental side of investing, but if you remember, I get a lot of enjoyment from home renovations, so I plan on doing them for many years to come - because *I want to, not because I need to*. As we talk about goals, that will be a recurring theme; what do I *want* to do and not *need* to do? Start to envision your future with measurable goals and the time-frame to achieve them. For instance, if you are like me and want to live near the beach, you need to know how much a beach house may cost at the time you want to move there. Our desired future — or retirement target — should be results-oriented, observable, measurable, and time-driven even at this early stage. If we don't set any quantifiable guide to our goals, our dreams may turn into unrealistic fantasies.

Write down how you envision your future. I will show you some sample future goals at the end of this chapter.

Task #2

As you continue to progress through your real estate goal setting, I think it's important to **recognize who you are at your core regarding your other investments and risk thresholds**. Are you conservative by nature, or do you lean towards the riskier side of things? Do you have any desire or know-how of construction, renovations, updating houses, etc.? Are you comfortable with the thought of pouring a sizable amount of money into a singular investment? Do you get queasy when your 401k ebbs and flows downward based on market conditions even though you're not selling anything at that time? Are you one to set a path and stick to it, or do you tend to chase the next big thing? These are just a few of the essential questions to ask yourself when deciding how aggressively you may want to invest and into what type of real estate assets. Your task is to look deep inside who you are and analyze your risk comfort level.

Multiple real estate television shows that glamorize real estate investing trick novice investors and newcomers who are always searching for the *home run* of deals. The truth is that those home runs can be rare and are typically over the skill level of beginners. Big deals typically require an enormous scope of work for which the novice is not experienced. That inexperience can destroy their budget. Even worse, they may never actually buy anything because they are always just looking for a home run of a deal. If we're sticking with a baseball analogy, did you know that, on average, less than 3% of all baseball games are won with a walk-off home run? Most of the games are won slowly by accumulating walks, singles, and doubles. That doesn't sound glamorous, though, so that's not what is on the TV highlight reel. The straightforward rental houses that just need a little fresh paint and carpet don't excite anyone. However, most investors will win by buying these types of properties over time. The point of all of this is to recognize who you are at your core. When you set your goals within that framework, you start to establish an early idea of how many investment properties you may need to hit your target goals by a particular time. In my experience, the investors who stray too far outside of who they are deep down end up not reaching their goals, and if they do, it can be a painful process. Instead, I suggest starting your portfolio within a comfort level of who you are and what doesn't freak you out too much. The experience will allow you to expand your core comfort level and dive deeper into those riskier projects that may produce a more significant payoff. I wouldn't buy a 100-unit apartment complex if I've never owned a single-family rental house, but that doesn't mean I can't hold that apartment complex later in my investing career.

Slowly, your are building your path to setting tangible goals for yourself and getting down to brass tacks with the actual numbers. *You should be exploring how you envision your future and thinking about who you are at your core, especially with your other investments.*

Task #3

The next thing to consider is **your time**. I used this quote earlier in the book: '*you buy things with time, not money*.' Think about your 'scale of passivity' that we envisioned earlier, along with the multiple hoses filling up the barrel. On the surface, when we think about those things, we typically only think about the money they may produce. The biggest challenge is managing those various hoses, no matter how passive we want them to be, with our available time. How do we manage them now and as we move into the future when we may desire more personal time, too? The nice thing about real estate investing is that even the most successful investors have one thing in common with novice investors — each only have 24 hours in a day. The way we use our time is critical to the success of our portfolios.

We need to know when to hire someone to assist, even if that person costs money, or when to pay for knowledge or information that can save us time, even though it may put another pinhole in our barrel. These are all things that will prove critical to your success. The old saying 'you can't do it all' is accurate when investing. Of course, in the early stages, when every penny counts, you must be very wise about how you spend your money. I think it's essential to look at the expense factor as a direct correlation to your time and what you can be doing with that time. If you're doing nothing productive, then yes, it's burning money unnecessarily, but if you spend that time more effectively than whatever task you hired out for, it is a smart move.

Here's a simple, personal example. I used to always cut the grass at my house. I did it as a kid for my parents and have cut my lawn since I bought my first house decades ago. I actually enjoy pushing that mower around for an hour or so. I also have a landscaper who will mow it for $40. Over the past year or two, as our family has grown and I've gone deeper into different ventures, my time has become more precious to me. So, to gain an hour, I've paid my landscaper $40 to cut it. I had to ask myself, is that hour worth more than $40? It's a straightforward question and the answer was obvious to me.

Here is another time strategy I use. I decide if whatever I need to do for that day or week must be done in the light of day and if that task is impacted by weather. For instance, as I sit here and write this book, it's 6 am, dark outside, and I can write no matter the weather outside. So, every day, I reserve this time for writing. I have no interruptions. None of my real estate clients are calling me, no tenants are asking me questions, and none of my students are expecting a lesson delivered from me. Some people may view this hour I spend writing as any other hour within today's 24, but they couldn't be more wrong. I chose this hour specifically to efficiently utilize it.

On the other hand, the landscaper can only cut the grass when it's not raining out and there is daylight. They require specific conditions to do their job. When you start to view your time more in detail, and choose to be methodical about it, it becomes more precious and productive. My wife jokes that I plan out every minute of every day. I explain that you can do certain things at specific times more efficiently. The keyword here is *efficiently*. **I want to stop wasting time.**

Your task here is to *Audit your Day!* Write down everything you do every day for an entire week. Be very detailed. When you're at work, just don't write 8am-5pm "at work." Instead, during that time slot, write when you're being productive, when you're surfing the internet or when you're talking to co-workers. Most people who do this exercise realize they aren't truly using their time efficiently. No matter how efficient you are with your time, you'll probably need to make some sacrifices when starting your real estate ventures. These sacrifices might mean skipping the TV shows you watch after dinner for a few nights a week or waking up earlier to get 30 minutes to do real estate research. I fully understand that in the beginning, as you are starting all of this, time will be one of your most significant challenges, but it's just that, a *challenge*. It's not impossible to find the time. I once read, "stop using your weekends to escape the life you have and start using that time to create the life you want."

It's just a choice. Maybe, like me, you decide to pay someone $40 to cut your grass to gain that hour. Perhaps you order some premade meals for a few nights a week to earn an extra 45 minutes of your time instead of cooking yourself. Maybe you plan your grocery shopping around times when the store is less busy to save you that additional 10 minutes in line, or even better, do an online grocery pickup. You must **give your time the respect it deserves,** and until you know where every minute goes and what you can only do at certain times, it's tough to use your time more efficiently. Start to train yourself to relish the idea that you buy things with time, not money. When you do, you'll start to get more passionate and appreciative of your time and find ways to carve out time for yourself to start investing.

Don't think of your car payment as $500 per month; think of it as how many hours you need to work to earn $500. Don't think about buying an $80 shirt as just $80 from your barrel. Think of it as how many hours you had to work to put that money in the barrel. The most intelligent investors value time over money, and if you start that process early, it will pay you dividends later! Speaking of later rewards, after you do your time audit, ask yourself, *"Of all the tasks I've completed with my time this week, how many of them will pay me residuals?"* Is there anything you did with your time today that will pay you tomorrow and into the future? Have you done anything today to create more sources of income? If not, you need to start to shift your mindset into evaluating your time not so much as it equates to payment today, but instead, in the form of continual gains into your future without more time invested? **You want the time you spend today to develop residual income later.**

Task #4

This last task to complete before diving into actual real numbers is to **evaluate your current financial situation**. This task may seem relatively common sense. Before considering making a significant investment in real estate, know what you currently have. I never cease to be amazed by the number of people who want to start investing in real estate and have very little understanding of their personal finances, or already carry immense amounts of lousy personal debt, or have no risk threshold. Real estate investing can require a decent amount of money to purchase properties. However, no one says that money must be your own. Many novice investors choose to partner with someone who is financially stronger than themselves. That could be family or friends, contractors, or even private lenders. Before exploring those options, it's best to make sure you have your finances in order and have a comfortable grasp on your risk tolerance for borrowing money and partnering with someone. We'll explore *how* to do this later in the book. For now, you need to determine *if and why* you need to have a partner. The only way to accomplish that is to have a full breakdown of what you currently have, what you produce in income, what you can save, and what your liabilities are.

Furthermore, you need to evaluate those items to see where you can improve them. Where can you *plug the holes and fill the barrel?* There is no shortage of borrowable money for real estate investing, and there are endless creative ways to finance a property, but before diving into those, it's best to know what you have first. You can't set a clear path if you don't have a starting point. You need to identify your financial starting point. When evaluating and securing your finances, start to make practice cash flow statements and consider possible homes for sale. Even though you may not be financially able to purchase them at that time, don't waste your time by not at least practicing and running sample investment houses.

These four tasks will force you to think about your future, determine your risk tolerance, examine how you value your time and consider your current finances. These will be the foundation for your goals. If you don't have these items firmly ingrained in your long-term goals, it may prove challenging to reach them when we get into the numbers. Some people are hesitant to sit down and honestly address all four tasks for various reasons. A leading one is they just don't know the answers to these questions. I tell them to answer what they do know for sure, then continually ask themselves deeper questions based on those initial answers. It's a process that takes time and will continually evolve, so get comfortable with that.

Before we get into the actual financials, it's crucial to talk about the difference between being *rich* and being *wealthy*. I bring this up before determining actual numbers because I think many people get into real estate to be *rich*, and I'd prefer that you strive to be *wealthy* instead. The words themselves may seem similar, but honestly, they are far from it. I'll give you my opinion on how the two differ. Being rich is more about money and job income. Being wealthy is about having assets that produce income and create time freedom.

Being rich is more centered around having a lot of income, spending a lot of money, and even showing off that money. You could be rich and in debt at the same time. That's a simple "spend more than you earn" equation. Ever hear about doctors that make $250,000 per year and carry $200,000 in student loans? It's like being rich and in debt simultaneously. A key factor to being rich is not only money-based, but also time-based. Most high-income earners must dedicate a lot of time to earning that income. That same doctor who makes $250,000 per year must work 60 hours a week to earn that income.

However, most wealthy people have the luxury of valuing time over money. As I previously mentioned, the worth of your time is enormous. Wealthy people tend to have more time to do the things they want, the time to spend with the people they desire to spend time with and aren't living paycheck-to-paycheck. Wealthy people have usually created something long-lasting that does not depend on a salary to produce income. They have several hoses in their barrel that don't require much time, such as real estate. They have created assets that provide income for them passively, which frees their *time*. Their assets usually perform two functions. One function is they provide continual income, such as cash flow from rental properties. The second function is the security of owning the asset, so they could always sell the asset for extra money. Wealthy people usually have multiple streams of income, whereas many rich people rely on one source: their jobs. Many rich people are one unforeseen disaster away from being broke, whereas wealthy people have set up security layers based around *assets other than cash*. In many of the classes I teach, I say, "Rich people equate their financial status to cash in the bank, and wealthy people equate it to the number of assets they own."

Would you rather have $1M in the bank or own four rental homes, each worth $250,000 producing income? The rich take the cash; the wealthy take the houses.

On the surface, both concepts revolve around money, but it's only true wealth that will give you long-term financial and time freedom. Another perk of wealth versus rich is that wealth provides the leverage to buy more assets that produce more income and appreciation. Wealthy investors focus on growth. To grow, you need leverage to purchase more assets. Owning assets provides that leverage differently instead of draining cash in your bank account. Don't lump cash and asset leverage in the same bucket, as they're not the same. Using money to purchase each asset drains your barrel, and you need to turn up the hoses to refill it. Using your assets to leverage allows you not to use nearly as much cash. In essence, it adds another hose to your barrel without touching the level of money inside the barrel.

Imagine having financial freedom and the time to enjoy it! Driving a brand new Mercedes to a job you hate isn't success. As we progress through this book and goal setting, let's change our mindset from wanting to be rich to wanting to be wealthy.

"Being rich is having money; being wealthy is having time."

There is a level of risk in any investment. By and large, most people agree that real estate is one of the most effective and trusted ways to double dip on an asset class; cash flow + appreciation. Of course, nothing is guaranteed, that's why it's an investment, and it's also why the banks pay terrible interest rates. Your money in the bank is secure, and your reward is pennies.

By now, you should start to understand some of the critical, big picture questions you need to ask and the decisions you need to make to begin to set some real goals. Later in the book, we will do a full portfolio review of an investor and pull together all these questions to formulate real goals and targets to hit. That is where we'll take the information from our tasks and translate them into real dollars and actual targeted goals.

Everyone will have different long-term visions of their future, but here is the synopsis of the sample investors we will go through later in the book to analyze how much money they will need, down to the penny.

❖ James and Cindy Smith want to buy a condo in South Carolina in a golf/beach resort complex. They want to buy the condo now and use it for short-term rentals until they retire. They only plan on owning a few rental homes in their local market to help reach their goals. They don't want to be big landlords and own many properties, but rather just a few to supplement their future net worth and retirement. Buying the condo is a straightforward long-term goal they have, and we'll go through all the variables needed to ensure they can do it comfortably. When we get to that chapter, you may be surprised how much goes into the plan!

While there are endless examples of what future goals may look like, here is my personal long-term goal:

My wife and I would love to retire at the beaches of North Carolina. After running our goal and financial breakdowns, we decided to continue to invest in our current Raleigh, NC market with rental properties for the next three to five years instead of buying the beach home today. At that point, based on our financial forecasting, we should have enough income from our rental properties to support the purchase of a beach home. We would use the home sporadically as a short-term rental and enjoy it for ourselves and our family until we retire. Upon retirement, we will probably sell one or two of our local rental properties to help pay off the mortgage on the beach house and maintain our three to five rental properties for long-term cash flow through retirement. We hope to leave at least one or two rental properties to our children through our estate.

I have heard many people's future goals through my many years of working with investor clients, coaching novice investors, and teaching at various educational institutions. I'll share a few of my favorites here.

- ❖ I had a student who was an HVAC tradesman. He loved his career, made decent money, and had no genuine desire to "be rich." However, he wanted to make sure that his two daughters could go to college without taking student loans, which he could not afford to do by just saving. At the time, he had one daughter who was two and another who was four years old. He knew he wouldn't save enough money from his salary to pay for college for both. Therefore, his goal was to buy only two rental properties. He would buy them both within the next two years and hold them for 12-16 years until his daughters were ready for college. Then, he would sell them to pay for their education. His goal has stuck with me for many years. I've repeated his story to hundreds, if not thousands, of students along the way. So many people get into real estate investing to make a ton of money, and that's great. However, to do that, you must sacrifice both time and finances, take on debt and continually grow in the face of markets that you don't control. This father's goal was beautiful, simple, and very targeted. Most of all, it was reasonably obtainable.

- ❖ Another student of mine simply wanted to create generational wealth for his children. He took one of my courses with one of his sons to get his son started early. While his son, who was in his early 20's, was interested in making lots of money, his father understood that the start could be just as important as the finish. They worked together to formulate a goal that

would leave his estate with a fair number of rental properties, divided up among his children to give them a kickstart
with their financial futures upon his passing. The father also
planned to put some of the properties into a trust. He wanted
to protect the gains until his children were at an age to use
the money wisely. I respected the father wanting to leave his
children a level of wealth that could change their lives early on. He also wanted them involved in the process, so they
understood what it took to get there. Too often, heirs are just
given a lump sum of money or property via inheritance, and
they don't entirely realize what it took to build that. In this
situation, the father ensured that his children came along for
the ride in creating what they would eventually have. While
the father never would truly financially benefit from his hard
work, he felt confident that he would be changing the course
of all his children's financial futures.

❖ Another investor I taught was planning to grow as big as he
could, as quickly as possible. At the time, he was single and
not 100% sure what his long-term future held for him. He
was in his late 20's, and it's tough to know what you may want
20, 30, or 40 years down the road. However, he knew that he
would need wealth and cash flow as part of his goals, whatever they ended up being. Instead of trying to pinpoint a clear
long-term goal, or even a long-term dollar amount, he chose
to invest in as much as he could as often as he could. That
meant he would have to take risks beyond many people's risk
thresholds, borrow a lot of money, and leverage many properties. Those things are riskier than most people reading this
book may want to do. At his age, he realized if he didn't take

risks at that time, while unmarried, without children, and untethered to any significant responsibilities, he may never take them. Since then, he has built a massive portfolio of single-family homes and large multifamily projects in our market. His current cash flow and asset worth opens many more doors for his future goals. Many more than what he could have thought of a decade ago when he started.

Your goal may be crystal clear or murky as muddy water, but you must start to formulate what your goal will be. At first, you may feel limited by your current income, how much you have saved, or your risk tolerance, but try to put your fears aside and set your goals. Honestly think about what you want, and then go backwards. Maybe you'll realize you're not as far off as you think. Perhaps you'll find out that you have a lot of ground to make up. One thing is for sure, though. You won't know unless you dive into these tasks and dedicate the time to analyze these things. Your goals may change along the way, which may cause you to adjust your portfolio along the way, too. I once had a professor tell me, "Some things are written in sand, and some are chiseled in stone." You may have some firmly ingrained core beliefs and goals; however give yourself permission to change some of your plans along the way.

As I previously mentioned, later in the book, we're going to do a deep-dive into the actual numbers behind goal setting for our investors, James and Cindy Smith. For now, I want you to focus on the tasks we evaluated in this chapter. They are critically important to your long-term success. While some people take the attitude that they *must do these tasks,* almost as a chore, I find it more productive to think you *get to do this.* Your mindset to reaching your goals is equally important as your actions to achieve them. Exchange your "*I got to*" with "*I get to.*"

Consider this analysis an opportunity to create your secure financial future.

I want to conclude this chapter with a quote from Franklin D. Roosevelt, "A smooth sea never made a skilled sailor." Expect some bumps along the way when you try to firm up actual numbers and targets behind your goals. Don't skip the goal-setting process, and don't cheat yourself from diving deep into these questions. You may find that the answers surprise you. As with almost everything in life, we learn more from trying and failing than never trying at all.

Chapter 4 - *Understanding the Economy & Markets*

BEFORE WE CAN PUT actual numbers behind our goals, we need to forecast and estimate certain factors within our finances and real estate holdings so we can put together our long-term path. We need to have some basic understanding of the economy and how it impacts us.

I have been perplexed over the years by many serious investors' lack of knowledge of economics and how well they know their markets. I'm a firm believer in quality over quantity when it comes to real estate investing, so while some investors will buy just about anything, I'm more inclined to buy homes with better long-term potential. Sometimes that means it can take longer to find the right property. Sometimes that also means I pay a premium for those properties. However, if done correctly, I believe you can make as much money with fewer homes, as the investor who buys lots of homes but with less long-term thought behind the decisions.

In this chapter, I want to visit some of the economic factors I think all investors should have a basic understanding of. I'm not an economist, but I have enough knowledge and experience to share my opinion on a few factors as they impact real estate investing.

Here are some of the items we'll explore:

❖ Mortgage interest rates

❖ Supply and demand for housing

❖ Inflation as it relates to real estate

❖ Forecasting home prices

❖ Understanding our economic past

❖ Why people rent v. buy

❖ Understanding your local market

❖ How we should treat our rental homes as businesses

Let's start by addressing mortgage interest rates and just getting a basic understanding. A few variables impact these interest rates, such as what policies our Federal Reserve sets in motion (the Federal Reserve, aka the FED, does not directly set mortgage rates). The Fed sets the Fed Fund Rate, a target *range* that banks charge to one another for lending excess cash on an overnight basis. Banks must maintain a certain level of reserve money, and when they fall short, they borrow money from other banks, which charge them interest. Let's review where this rate has been. In the early 1980's it was as much as 20%, and during our Great Recession in 2007-2009, the rate was down to pretty much 0%. The Fed looks at inflation, recession risk, and other issues affecting growth when evaluating where that targeted rate range should be. If they want to spawn growth, they keep the rates low to make it more affordable for people to borrow money.

If the banks borrow money at a lower interest rate, consumers will benefit. If the banks must pay a high-interest rate to borrow money, the consumer will, too. So, while the Fed doesn't necessarily set specific interest rates, there is no doubt of the direct correlation between the rates they do adjust and the rates consumers pay at the end of the day.

Another rate to understand is the Discount Rate, which is the rate at which banks borrow from the Federal Reserve (instead of another bank). This money is lent on a very short-term basis, usually just under

24 hours, and is made for a specific shortfall or emergency purposes. Banks usually only borrow money from the Fed, instead of another bank, in rare circumstances, so you don't hear about the *Discount Rate* as often as you do the *Fed Funds Rate*.

If you notice, there is one thing in common in these types of interest rates - they are short-term interest rates, that is, the length of time that the bank is borrowing the money is relatively short. Mortgage rates, on the other hand, are longer-term and impacted by other factors, not just the Fed's actions.

Regarding mortgage rates, it's essential to understand that there isn't just one source determining the "mortgage rate," but rather each bank and lender is determining their rates. Of course, to stay competitive, they usually stay within a similar range of each other. How is that range determined? Before we go into that, we need to understand what happens to your mortgage after you get it. Many people just think that whoever they write their mortgage payment to is the actual owner of the mortgage. Large investors, such as insurance companies, annuities, pension funds, and other large institutions buy mortgages. These institutions are looking for specific asset-secured returns. Thousands of mortgages are pulled together into a Mortgage-Backed Security (MBS), and various investors buy that MBS on what we call the *secondary market*. Besides the previously mentioned investors who purchase mortgage securities, the predominant purchasing investors are two companies - Fannie Mae or Freddie Mac. They are the largest purchasers of mortgages when this book was written (and they have been for quite some time). For instance, you could write your mortgage payment to "ABC Mortgage Company," but the mortgage may be owned by Fannie Mae, Freddie Mac, or various insurance companies, pension funds, or annuities that purchase these MBS.

They buy these MBS as an investment and a way to get consistent returns. In the above-mentioned example, ABC Mortgage Company may just be the servicer of that loan - they keep a small portion of the interest payment as their fee to manage the charges, but someone else owns the mortgage. Think of them as the property managers of mortgages.

We need to understand what a MBS does because the appetite or demand for MBS's influences interest rates. We could quickly go down a rabbit hole of information on this subject, but let's say that a large pension fund wants to buy a MBS to help earn interest on all the money they are holding. That way, they have money to pay pensions long-term. If they pay $10M for a MBS and that MBS is offering a 4% return, then they would get $400,000 in interest that year. Now, using that same example, let's imagine that the economy is facing inflation or some other negative impact, therefore purchasing large amounts of mortgages may be considered riskier.

In that case, to buy another MBS, the investor will want a higher rate of return, more than the previously mentioned 4%, because their risk is higher in those new economic conditions. If the MBS is composed of mortgages with interest rates, the only way to get a higher interest rate for that MBS is to have mortgage rates go up. Thus, mortgage rates go up to increase demand for the buyers/investors of MBS's. On the flip side, what if the risks are lowered for mortgages or the other available investment choices become riskier? That same pension fund may choose to take a 3% return instead of 4% simply because they can't find any safe returns and therefore, mortgage rates may go lower since demand for MBS's are higher. In essence, it's simply supply and demand.

If there is a lot of demand for MBS's, consumers typically will have lower interest rates. If demand is low, then to entice buyers of MBS's to come to the table, the mortgage rates will need to come up. One main factor is supply and demand for these MBS's, which are affected by inflation, growth, and future expectations. Mortgage interest rates are typically set in the morning and as the day progresses, the stock and bond markets adjust, and the mortgage market changes accordingly.

While the demand for MBS's may impact the mortgage rates, the demand itself can be impacted by many variables, such as risks to the unemployment market, increasing/decreasing consumer confidence, inflation forecasting, and even things like energy pricing and political instability. The MBS rates need to be competitive in the overall investment landscape, and if the rates aren't competitive, large investors will look for stable returns elsewhere.

Some real estate investors watch the 10-year US Treasury bond as that investment option sometimes competes with the same investors buying MBS. If the 10-year bond price is reduced, which means the yield or rate of return increases, then sellers of MBS's must typically follow suit since they are often searching for the same buyers. The 10-year bond typically does not impact the mortgage market as much as the factors previously mentioned and is usually viewed more as a 'benchmark' and less of a variable of impact. However, they tend to rise and fall in similar ways over time. It's essential to understand that just because the bond and MBS prices and yields can rise and fall in similar patterns, many factors impact one and not the other or affect them at different rates of change. The 10-year bond pricing and yield are more of a barometer of the overall market.

I know these items can be confusing at first. However, an investor needs to have a basic knowledge of these things. If you're buying three, five, ten, or more homes, just think about the impact the interest rates will have on your cash flow and ability to pay off the mortgages. If you had a $300,000 mortgage, a difference of ⅛ of 1 percent in interest rate is over $5,600 during the life of the loan. Imagine if you have multiple properties or could save ¼ percent on each. It may not seem like much, but *it's real money that you're giving away to the bank or can keep in your pocket!* If you know enough about this topic, forecasting for your portfolio becomes more accessible and more accurate.

Next, I want to talk about housing prices. One of the biggest things real estate investors talk about is appreciation gains. For instance, I bought a rental house for $250,000 in 2016, and five years later, it was worth $310,000.

That is almost a 5% appreciation return.

Final Sales Price:	$310,000
Original Sales Price:	$250,000
Gross Gain over 5 years:	$60,000
Per year again:	$12,000

If we made $12,000 per year on an initial investment of $250,000, that is 4.8% per year.

We spoke about the various types of appreciation earlier; natural market and sweat equity. Here, we're talking just about natural market appreciation. The market raised the price over time. If we're building a portfolio of houses for a specific goal over a particular period, then forecasting future appreciation is critical. What happens if we predict a 6% per year appreciation return and it turns out to be 2.5%? All our numbers will be off. What happens if we presume it will be 2.5% and it turns out to be 6%? We may end up buying more homes or doing various leverage strategies unnecessarily. I'll be the first to admit that forecasting appreciation is like having a crystal ball or knowing tomorrow's lottery numbers today. However, we can do a few things to become more accurate.

The first thing I would suggest is to watch the market and neighborhoods closely in which you own property. While the market in your city will produce an average rate of appreciation, that is, unfortunately, inaccurate for your particular property. Utilizing just a city's average appreciation rate is like using the national average appreciation to dictate how one city does. There are too many variables. Think of your city or town - are there areas or neighborhoods that always seem to be popular? Areas where homes always sell quickly? Rarely do homes come up for sale, and when they do, they always seem to feel pricier? And how about the opposite - neighborhoods or parts of town that seem less desirable? Sit on the market for longer? More homes for sale at any given time?

We can't apply an average appreciation figure to our portfolio when, in fact, appreciation can depend on the neighborhood. I may have one home that I think will get 6% and one that is going to earn 2%. That is an average of 4% - should I just be lazy and apply a 4% forecast?

Not if I want to be a good investor — scratch that — a great investor.

Great investors look at their portfolios on a closer level. Admittedly, investors that own many homes will tend to use more of a city average, but that is because they hold so many houses that they can use the law of averages to level out most errors. For most of us investors who will own fewer than ten homes, and the vast majority that will own less than five, it would be prudent to look at each home individually and do so annually.

Of course, we will apply long-term forecast estimates when we buy, but we should be updating them each year. We should be updating both to what the home did appreciate this past year and if we see any *future changes* to our original forecast. It's not that time-consuming if you're paying attention to your specific homes and neighborhoods and only own a few houses. You can go to any one of the hundreds of real estate websites and set up searches for your area, and every time a home is listed for sale, it will notify you. You don't have to do any legwork. Keep an eye on those listings and sales, and I promise you'll quickly know what that neighborhood is doing which will significantly assist you in the forecasting. If you want to be great, you should pull past data for the neighborhood and compare the annual appreciation for the past three, five, and ten years to other neighborhoods you're considering.

I suggest going back ten years for the simple fact that going back a decade typically allows you to see various types of economic markets which impact supply and demand, and in turn, may have affected values.

When writing this book, it's 2022, and the market has been red hot over the past 18 months due to an increased demand for homes and a reduced supply of listings. Part of this increase is attributed to the Covid pandemic, which forced people to spend much more time in their homes. Consequently, many people realized they needed more space or could work remotely and have more location options. There was also an added layer of demand created by below normal mortgage interest rates. If I were an investor doing forecasting and only looked back one, two, or three years, the average appreciation would be above average quite a bit.

If I applied that rate to my future forecasting, I'd be making the presumption that the past will equal the future. Any good economist or investor will tell you markets adjust, and more data is better. If I were to get the past 10 years of sales data, I'd have the Covid housing explosion rate included in that data. I'd also have the time in 2017-19 when mortgage rates were starting to increase, thus reducing some affordability and more reasonable appreciation levels. The tail end of the Great Recession and the recovery of 2008-2015 and those impacts would be included in those ten years as well. All in all, appreciation rates would have ranged due to the various, broader economic conditions. My average appreciation rate per year would be lower over the past ten years than the past two years and probably give a more accurate forecasting projection for the future.

Consider these main things when forecasting future home prices:

❖ Adjust the value of every house in your portfolio once a year, based on what has happened over that past year. Decide if you should change anything for the future. I may have been misguided in my forecasting when I purchased the home, or some economic/market event has happened since, but that doesn't mean I can't adjust my portfolio to be more accurate now. If I calibrate annually, it reduces the risk of being off by too much over the long haul.

❖ When purchasing a home or looking at the future, I want to see as much past data as possible. It's essential to look at each year's appreciation within that data and see what was going on in the economy. It's one thing to know that my neighborhood appreciated 4.5% in 2016, but almost as important to understand what was going on in the broader economy. Those two pieces of information will help me be more accurate in the future.

❖ Pay attention to what much more intelligent people say. You don't have to be a total economic nerd with this, but reading what a few of the most respected economists say about the future is extremely helpful. You can still make your own determination about the future, but I think hearing various intelligent opinions is critical. This does not mean the person on social media ranting about where our economy is headed, but someone who based their conclusions on facts, the analysis of past data and has a certain level of experience within the field.

❖ Pay attention to what activity you see in your immediate local market. For instance, I live in Raleigh, NC. Over the past few years, we've seen an influx of prominent companies opening sizable operations in our area. Those employees need housing. Many may want to rent before deciding to buy. That increases demand, which typically increases prices. As that residential market demand rises due to more employment, the auxiliary infrastructure is also affected. The businesses affected include grocery stores, schools, and public transportation. It's all connected; so pay close attention to those items in your market. Typically, when large-scale investors build shopping centers or office buildings, or cities build schools or widen roads, they are doing so to meet *demand*.

Next, we need to have a good grasp on supply and demand, along with their impact on home prices, as well as affordability. Many variables impact supply and demand, but overall, it's vital that we understand *why*. Why is there the number of homes for sale on the market and not more or less at any time? Why is there the number of buyers out there and not more or less at any time? Factors like availability of skilled labor, cost of materials, supply of those materials, employment, and inflation all influence the supply and demand conversation, and as an investor, you should be familiar those. After all, supply and demand directly impact prices. Let's evaluate some of these factors.

One factor that affects supply and demand is the actual number of homes for sale and the number of buyers. This is probably one of the more accessible items to understand when discussing macroeconomic factors - simple supply and demand. You may remember the early days of the Covid pandemic. Finding toilet paper, gloves, masks, and disinfectants was challenging. All the grocery store shelves were bare, and people were going to extreme lengths to get a hold of them. The question here is: were too few of those products making it to the grocery stores, or were people buying way more than they usually do?

Was it a supply-side issue that made demand look high, or was the demand so high that normal levels of supplies weren't enough? In the early stages, there was more demand - people were buying those items at higher rates than average. After that initial demand subsided, why was there still a lack of some of those items? Later, it became a supply-side issue due to manufacturing plants closing, limited transportation, and playing catch up to the early demand side.

We saw the same thing in the housing market where things turned red hot, and prices were rapidly rising during this time. The question was, were there fewer homes for sale because sellers didn't want to list their homes during a pandemic or couldn't find a suitable replacement property? Or, was demand so high because interest rates were low, and people could now work more remotely, thus allowing more freedom on location?

It's like the old saying, "Which came first, the chicken or the egg?" Sometimes, it can be difficult to pinpoint the real driver. The novice real estate investor needs to watch the inventory of homes for sale (supply) and the rate upon which they sell (demand), known as the absorption rate.

Supply and demand are common factors in determining where home pricing may go, so it's essential to have a pulse on where the housing market is with regards to those. In terms of real estate, supply and demand is sometimes described as a *buyer's market* (oversupply of houses) or a *seller's market* (limited supply). During our Great Recession of 2008-2009, we had a surplus of housing and not enough demand, which pushed pricing downward. During the Covid pandemic, we had an undersupply of housing, which drove prices up.

Another factor that impacts real estate prices is interest rates. It does so by affecting the buyer's affordability. When interest rates are abnormally or government-induced low, borrowing money is less expensive. Simply put, if I had a $300,000 mortgage at 5% or 3.5%, the one at 3.5% would cost me less interest, and thus, I would have a lower monthly payment. That seems relatively straightforward and common sense, but how do interest rates affect pricing? Lower interest rates appeal to buyers in several ways, e.g., they encourage them to act. We call a buyer who is considering buying real estate but not taking real action as 'being on the fence.'

That means they can't decide if they should buy or not and having the opportunity to get a lower than usual interest rate can push that buyer off the proverbial fence and get them to buy. In essence, it brings more buyers into the market (demand). As we already noted, if demand increases but supply does not keep up, that typically pushes real estate prices up and creates a seller's market. If, however, the supply of homes for sale keeps up with the increased demand, we usually see less upward pricing pressure.

While interest rates may not directly impact pricing, they can influence demand, and demand can push prices up. Lower interest rates can also increase the buyer's price range. If I'm a buyer and want my principal and interest mortgage payment to be no more than $2,000 per month and interest rates are at about 5%, I can borrow around $375,000. That would give me a P&I payment of about $2,000.

However, if interest rates are at 4%, I can borrow almost $50,000 more and have the same P&I payment. Therefore, the buyer can buy a more expensive house, maybe a larger one or a house in a more desirable area, all because the rates are lower. The lower interest rate also has a multiplier effect regarding sales because of this affordability factor. It allows first-time homebuyers who may not afford a home at 5% to become genuine buyers if the rates were at 4%. When they buy that first home, it allows those sellers to buy another home and probably at a higher price because the rates are low. The lower interest rates simply open the door to allow more buyers into the market, while allowing some buyers to borrow more at an equal cost as if the rates were higher.

When we get into strong seller markets, where homes receive multiple offers, buyers can offer the sellers even more than their asking price to win the house with less impact on the buyer's payment. For instance, if a home is listed at $400,000 and there are multiple offers, the buyer may be more willing to offer $430,000 to that seller to win the home. If the interest rates are relatively low, the buyer may give that seller more money with less impact on their overall mortgage payment. Lower rates make things more affordable and allow more buyers to participate in ownership - including investors.

Using this same example, if the buyer who offers $430,000 gets their offer accepted by the seller, when that home closes, and the sale is recorded at $430,000, other sellers with similar homes in the neighborhood will now want at least $430,000 for their home (instead of possibly the $400,000 they thought their home was worth). That is the perfect storm of high demand, low inventory, and relatively low-interest rates, which can push prices up quickly. And yes, the opposite is true when rates are higher, and there is more supply! Due to supply and demand, plus lower than average interest rates, the house worth $400k but sold at $430k has created a new benchmark.

Another consideration in forecasting housing prices is the cost of labor and materials. Material pricing can be impacted by many variables such as demand increases, acts of God (such as hurricanes), cyberattacks, supply chain hold-ups, transportation issues, energy costs, workforce participation, and inflation. Some of these items are obviously easier to forecast than when the next hurricane or cyberattack may cause problems with supply chains. Most large builders and developers, who control vast swaths of land and homes for sale, can hedge themselves against some risk by buying in massive quantities and buying materials in advance.

Just as airlines may purchase large amounts of jet fuel at one time to hedge against fluctuations in future pricing, the average investor does not get the luxury of buying massive quantities. Most investors typically do not buy hundreds of 2x4's and store them at their house for six months until they need them. In most circumstances, small material price increases won't drastically affect the smaller investor; however, labor pricing, labor availability, and lack of supply could cause significant impacts. For material and labor costs to increase and have a meaningful impact, we usually need to have those issues exist for an extended period.

We're more focused on longer-term and more significant scale demand issues, where prices go up and stay up or come down slower than they went up. For instance, home prices typically don't go up just because a hurricane in the Gulf of Mexico disrupted fuel lines and prevented lumber trucks from delivering their material for a week or so. It may affect the actual cost of lumber or fuel for a few weeks afterwards, but the length of time that the supply was impacted would be relatively short.

The last variable I want to talk about is inflation. You may not know it yet, but inflation impacts a good portion of what we've discussed above. Inflation affects home prices, supply and demand, and materials costs. Inflation can be defined in many ways or shown in many examples. A straightforward case is buying a sandwich. Let's say I go into my local deli shop, and I buy a 6" sub for $7.50. Then, I go back six months later, and that same sub now costs me $8.50. That is an increase of $1 in six months. That is 13%! I think we all can accept that things have naturally increased in price over time, but there are also times that the increase happens at an abnormal rate.

In 1975, that same sub may have cost $3.25. The difference between the two scenarios is how long it took the rate of increase to occur. The increase from $3.25 in 1975 to $7.50 in 2022 is slower. It's still technically "inflationary," but at a rate that does not affect the average person. The reason is that most employee wages have also increased from 1975 to 2022 thus the impact on the consumer is relatively unnoticed. However, in the first example of the $1 in 6 months, or 13%, the consumer's wages did not increase by 13%. The rise in the sandwich costs outpaced the increase in my income over that same period, which in turn makes the money in my pocket not go as far as it once did. That is inflation - a devaluation of money.

Inflationary causes are not always crystal clear, and the best economists sometimes disagree on this topic. During periods of rising inflation, some will argue that it is just temporary, while others will sound the alarm, saying we're heading towards a financial cliff. Some will say the Fed must get involved to slow down inflation by increasing interest rates, and slowing down the economy. It is a very complex subject so we won't get lost in the weeds on the topic. As an investor, you want to pay attention to inflation for a few reasons:

- ❖ Could interest rate increases be on the horizon if inflation is increasing?

  - ➢ If yes, what does that do if I have one of the following financing tools:

    - o Adjustable-Rate Mortgage

    - o Home Equity Line of Credit

    - o Cash-Out Refinance in the near term

- ❖ How does the average consumer feel about inflation?

  - ➢ If they feel their dollar isn't going as far, will they:

    - o Slow down on purchasing goods?

    - o Scale back discretionary spending?

    - o Hold off on purchasing homes?

    - o Not invest money into their current homes?

- ❖ If the FED does or doesn't take any action during a presumably inflationary period, what could that action (or inaction) do to the ability to buy affordable housing?

- o What buyer pool will be most affected?

- o Will demand for homes slow down?

- o Will inventory of homes for sale increase?

- o Will that increased inventory result in more significant price reductions?

❖ What could increased inflation do to the rental market?

   ➤ If inflation increases:

- o Will the rents I charge increase as well?

- o Will tenants choose to move more often if rental rents continue to increase?

- o Will I trade maintaining the same rental amount for a lower vacancy by having fewer tenants move?

- o At what point would a tenant choose to become a buyer based on increasing rental amounts and increasing interest rates?

These are just some of the items that we should think about in order to best build and protect our portfolios. The decisions that impact inflation are above our pay grade; however, we need to understand the consequences of those decisions. I like to think about these topics in the format I just displayed – more of a Q&A type of analysis.

There aren't clear answers to many of these questions, but understanding what impacts could come into play will allow me to think about my portfolio differently. I analyze it in a way that acknowledges the economic impact that could arise out of things beyond my control, such as inflation. One of the easier ways to keep an eye on inflation is to pay attention to the Consumer Price Index (CPI), which examines the weighted average of prices for various goods and services that consumers need and use. Some of those industries include transportation, food, and medical care. As that weighted average increases, so too does inflation.

Now, inflation to real estate investors is not always bad. Real estate itself can actually help hedge some against inflation. Here are two quick examples:

Example #1

As explained earlier, increasing inflation can devalue your money, but if you're collecting more cash due to increased rents that extra money helps offset its devaluation. If I own a rental property with a fixed rate mortgage, even if interest rates increase due to inflation, my principal and interest payment stays the same. If I can charge more rent for that property due to inflation pushing rental prices up, I have increased my cash flow because I'm charging more, but my mortgage payment has remained the same.

Example #2

Let's say I own a rental property and because of inflation pushing prices upward, the value of that home goes up. When that value goes up, it gives me more *equity* in that property and opens the opportunity to implement more *leverage* strategies to help grow my portfolio. If I take advantage of that equity as prices increase, I will continue growing my portfolio.

Hopefully, you understand factors that affect housing prices, and that knowledge can assist you in forecasting where prices may go. One of the key factors to both examples is time. You would want to take advantage of those increasing prices and rents as inflation pushed them upward, but not react too late that inflation is coming back down and could bring prices with it.

In addition to the CPI report, I'd like to share a few other reports and indexes valuable to you. These can affect interest rates up and down, as they could indicate the economy's health.

Report	Results	Typical Action to Rates
Consumer Price Index (CPI)	Index consistently rises	↑
Gross National Product	Increases (shows strong economy)	↑
Producer Price Index	Index consistently rises	↑
Unemployment Rate	Report shows increased unemployment	↓
Home Sales Report	Report shows a large increase in sales	↑

Many economic indicators and reports can affect how people feel about our economy and whether it's growing, slowing, or at a standstill. The above-mentioned reports are probably five of the best ones.

Here is a quick cheat sheet about what those reports mean:

CPI - prices that affect the consumer directly

Unemployment - ability to earn income and pay for things

Gross National Product - how much our economy produces as a whole

Producer Price Index - the prices that sellers of goods receive over time

Home Sales report - the strength of the housing market based on sales

Once again, having at least an understanding of these reports will help you as an investor in forecasting more accurately. You don't need to be an economist with this stuff. Since I'm a proponent of owning fewer homes, but better homes, making educated decisions that include the impact of the economy are critical to timing purchase and sale decisions. I believe that you need to sell some properties from time to time, take your gains and clean up your balance sheets. It's challenging to accomplish that if you don't understand the outside factors impacting your portfolio. A basic understanding will go a very long way!

We also need to understand <u>why people buy</u> or <u>why people rent</u>. You can understand this information on a national level with some of the information we've talked about previously and by having an excellent grasp of your local market. Here are just a few items that impact buyers' decision to buy v. rent:

❖ Interest rates are low, and they can buy something for a competitive monthly price on mortgage payment v. rental price. Inversely, where mortgage rates are on the higher end, their mortgage payment may outpace the price they could get by renting.

❖ Housing grants, loan programs, and tax credits can impact the decision-making process. When government-sponsored down payments or tax credits are offered, they may entice an average renter to buy. These things may not always affect a buyer who wants to purchase no matter what, but it can attract a renter to become a buyer and lower the pool of available tenants. Programs that reduce the minimum down payment, credit score, or income levels can benefit renters in an oversized proportion.

❖ Opportunity to capitalize on the real estate market for future gain. A seasoned investor may see an opportunity where a less experienced person may not. Either way, if more people see opportunities within the market, they are more likely to buy. That could mean that prices are increasing, and they see a chance to get some future appreciation if they buy. When more opportunities for gains exist, more buyers will emerge.

❖ When home prices increase at an above-average rate, it may be harder for some buyers to purchase homes that they desire, so they may continue to rent. Some buyers will jump in to a hot market to partake in the potential of future gains, but some buyers will be pushed out of that type of market.

❖ FOMO - Fear of Missing Out. We see this in markets that are usually riding the extremes. If the market appreciates at a very high pace and people are bragging about how much their home has increased in value, and you are renting, you may feel like you're missing out on something that everyone else is doing. On the same note, buyers may feel the same way if there is a ton of inventory on the market, and people are bragging about how great a deal they got on a home. Of course, each buyer has a different mentality to all of this, and their experience and finances will weigh into their decision, but this type of purchasing happens all the time.

When you find yourself in extreme markets, you need to be careful about whose advice you take. Personal factors, of course, impact these buy/rent decisions.

- ➤ How secure is my job?

- ➤ Do I need more space?

- ➤ If I owned before, what was the experience?

- ➤ If I have always rented, how has that experience been with landlords?

- ➤ Am I married? Am I starting or growing a family?

- ➤ Do I like the city where I live, and do I see my employment staying there?

The list of personal considerations can go on and on. There is a plethora of information about the economics and psychology behind why people choose to buy an asset as significant as a home versus why they may decide to rent.

As investors, we need to understand what is most common in our markets and price points. In addition to the economic reports we've discussed, networking with other local experienced real estate investors in your area can be a massive wealth of knowledge and opinions that could be beneficial to you when exploring these topics. Furthermore, understanding things like *is this neighborhood over-saturated with rental homes* or *wow, there is nothing for rent in this area* all impact your long-term ability to keep vacancy low within a rental home, as well as increase rents at a faster rate.

A truly great investor is always looking for possible impacts to their portfolio and potential opportunities. Here are just a few ways they are doing that:

- ❖ They are watching competitive rental homes in the same neighborhoods and areas where they already own properties. They see how those homes compare to their property and how they can stay competitive as the #1 option for the next renter.

- ❖ They start to watch for rental homes and sales in the areas they are considering purchasing in and do so before making their purchase. They pay attention to how quickly those homes rent and if prices seem to be stable or increasing. They don't enter a neighborhood or market haphazardly. Instead, they possess confidence based on knowledge and research.

- ❖ They are reaching out to investors who own those rental properties and inquiring if they would ever consider selling. Instead of waiting for the next home to come up for sale that you can turn into a rental, why not explore buying one that is already a rental?

You must do the research and ask questions to grasp what is happening on the ground level of your local market. You will often discover something that stats and reports can't show you. You may be amazed by what you find out with a few conversations with fellow investors or with neighbors in places you're considering for purchase.

Attending local investor networking events is an easy and productive way of getting ground-level information from investors. In my market and most others, several investor meetings occur monthly. The key to having a successful outing is getting your butt out of your chair, introducing yourself, and talking to people. If you just sit there quietly and put nothing in, you'll typically get nothing out.

Social media sites also have many online investor groups that can add great value to you as well. Many are national, so I prefer finding the ones in my local market. In the beginning, I'd join them all to learn as much as I could. My only disclaimer to these meetings is that you're listening to someone else's opinion, so don't always take it for a fact. Make sure that if you're putting faith in someone's opinion, you have some facts behind it. That is why understanding some of the items we've spoken about in this chapter is so important. It's easier for you to put more stock in one opinion over another if you have some factual knowledge about the subject.

I like networking in-person events better because you can turn them off. Social media is on 24/7 and can create 'paralysis by analysis.' You can receive too much conflicting information or hear too many 'investment rules' and end up searching for a needle in a haystack that may not exist. You can also listen to too many experiences from other people's markets. Real estate is very local, so what one investor may do in their market may seem silly or next to impossible in another market.

There is one last concept I want to talk about before we learn about financing and how to make the actual numbers work. That is the concept of building your real estate portfolio similarly to a retirement investment portfolio. I mentioned this earlier with the example of running your rental home like a business, but this concept goes a little further and discusses your entire portfolio. Something that intrigues me as an investor, a teacher, and a real estate broker is the different ways people structure their retirement portfolios with stocks, bonds, mutual funds, and real estate.

Think about your current retirement investments, such as a 401k or any other similar type of investment. Most individuals don't go out and put all their money into one company or one stock. Nor do they usually put it all into just one mutual fund or a singular investment. Most people diversify. People don't invest in an 'all or nothing' strategy because it is perilous. A large portion of your financial future depends on that money, so it wouldn't be wise. The further away you are from retirement, you may be more willing to invest in riskier stocks and funds, but they are usually still diversified. It would be foolish not to build our real estate portfolio with a similar strategy of diversification to help hedge against future risks, such as interest rates, inflation, soft rental markets, and depreciating prices.

The best method to hedge against future unknowns is diversification. However, some investors consider all rental houses the same, which is to say, they are interchangeable, and I strongly disagree with that mentality. They think that just having real estate within their overall financial portfolio is being diversified, which is accurate to a point. However, they don't diversify the real estate portion itself. And I'm not talking about diversification based on buying single-family residential, multi-family, and commercial, although that is one way. The typical investor isn't going to invest in all those classes.

I want you to reformulate how you think about buying houses. You should no longer view the houses you buy just as dwellings. **Think of each home you purchase as a company.** Our real estate portfolio, just as our retirement investment portfolio, should be a blend of risk and safety.

Let's look at an example. Review these four sample mutual funds and what they have to offer. Then we're going to use the same type of structure to formulate our real estate holdings.

Future Growth Fund: It comprises stocks like Tesla, Bitcoin, Facebook, and Apple. All are high-priced, high-powered investments that will continue to grow if they develop new technology that people use. However, these pricey investments come with quite a bit of risk as a good portion of their pricing is built upon the idea that they *will* create those technologies, not that they have already. This is our higher-risk investment because if those companies don't continue to develop new and groundbreaking technologies, their stock prices will fall.

> The task for you: Try to think of a part of your town or city that you live in that demonstrates high growth potential; a place that may seem underdeveloped now, but seems like an excellent location for future growth. If those areas are invested in, the property values could rise quite a bit. If there is no future, large-scale, investment in that area, the values may not increase much at all.

Consumer Product Fund: This fund comprises companies that support the consumer with needs always in demand. The fund includes companies such as Procter & Gamble (soap, shampoo, etc.), Pepsi (water, sports drinks, and soda), Colgate-Palmolive (toothpaste, deodorant, cleaning supplies, etc.), Costco & Kroger (places we buy the goods mentioned above). This fund is nothing glorious and probably will never shoot to the moon. Still, it is consistent in growth and security because consumers always use those products no matter the economic landscape.

> The task for you: Think of parts of your town that have always been relatively always desirable. The area doesn't necessarily have to be *hot* but, more importantly, *consistent*. A place where the schools are always decent, the price points typically fall within the median home value for your city and a place that, while it may not seem glamorous, would present a consistently safe investment.

Medical/Biotech Fund: This fund comprises various health systems and pharmaceutical companies. Examples of companies in this fund are United Health Insurance, Anthem, Johnson & Johnson, Pfizer, and Bristol Myers. These companies have been around for quite some time. Like the consumer product fund, they provide a service or product that consumers will always need. This fund is a little riskier than the consumer fund because these companies are more likely to be impacted by government restrictions, new legislation, patents on medicines, rising R&D costs, and a host of other issues that can directly affect the consumers.

The task for you: This part of your town should be more *up and coming,* unlike the part of town that is currently undeveloped. When looking at the Future Growth Fund comparison, this part of town has had some investments, and it is starting to make some changes. Think about the aspects of the city that maybe have new commercial construction, where developers are building new large multifamily apartments, and the transportation department is creating road extensions. Money has started to be invested into this area, but it has not reached its full potential yet. The risk is less than the undeveloped area but more than the area that has been around for a long time and been consistent.

Dividend Income Fund: This is a fund composed of various companies that take their profits and divide it up to whoever owns shares in their company. We call this divided profit a *dividend,* and dividends can be paid monthly, quarterly, or annually to the shareholders. Traditionally, these stocks don't rise in value quickly because instead of taking profits and trying to grow their companies, they give those profits back to the shareholders. This fund includes companies like AT&T, General Mills, Dominion Energy, and Chevron. These companies have various dividend rates, but they always pay the investor (us) some of their profits, so even if the stock prices go down, as long as we don't sell, we're always getting income.

> The task for you: This part of your city would be what we call your **cash cow** area, which means they offer opportunities to make decent cash flow every month, but the long-term appreciation may not be there. You're exchanging long-term growth for today's payment. These areas could be a little on the outskirts of your town or city. This area may be one where property values typically remain steady, don't usually appreciate at a rapid pace, but tend to have long-term tenants that start to rent and rarely leave. You get consistent and decent cash flow with little vacancy, but you give up the potential of a future significant appreciation gain. Of course, those homes could have a catalyst for a significant appreciation in the future, but as of now, you don't see it in the works.

I'm not suggesting that you buy any of the stocks mentioned here. I am citing them merely to give an example of how people diversify their retirement savings. Hopefully, as you read through these four funds, you can think about different areas of your town. If you did, then you are in the right place to start diversifying your future real estate portfolio. You may buy a single-family home in each of those areas. Even though they may all be single-family-style homes, you have created a very diversified real estate portfolio to accompany your diversified overall financial portfolio.

If an investor is 35 years old and is not planning to retire for another

25-30 years, they can take on more risk. Therefore, if they are considering investing in those four sample funds, they can invest a more significant percentage in the risker companies because they will have more time to make up for any losses, if any. On the flip side, someone investing at age 55, who is closer to retirement, may invest their largest portion in the consistently secure companies, even though their overall returns may be lower. Each investor will put money in all four funds but at different percentages. Both are diversified; however, they are doing so differently **based on their risk threshold.**

Real estate should be treated no differently when building a portfolio.

If you were building a retirement account using homes instead of stocks, what questions would you ask yourself?

❖ Do I invest in all riskier areas of town regarding future appreciation and growth, or am I only investing in the areas that have proven desirable over the years?

➢ Suppose I only invest in areas that have proven to be desirable. In that case, I'm probably going to pay more for those homes, so my future appreciation, while probably consistent in the rate of return, may not ever really take off.

➢ Suppose I invest in riskier areas that haven't yet developed but could be the next desirable area. In that case, I may be able to buy at a much more affordable price now before said possible development. We can do both and hedge our risk, but it depends on our goals as they relate to our <u>time</u> to hit those goals.

❖ Do I need a home that will give me more cash flow today, like our Dividend Fund? Or am I less concerned about a few hundred dollars extra a month and want to focus on a more long-term play with appreciation growth in a transitional area lacking current development? Which homes and parts of town in my city will give me those unique characteristics? Paying attention to city development plans and request, and commercial development will help you gauge which areas fall into those categories.

❖ Watching various property styles of homes for rent, what they rent for, and how quickly they rent will help you assess rental decisions. Do I buy a more traditional style three-bedroom and two-bath home on ¼ acre or a less common modern or contemporary style, where maybe I'll have a smaller rental pool of people who want that style? Still, since there may be fewer of those homes in the market, might I get renters who will pay more and stay longer because supply is lower? Understanding what your market offers and the demands will help you formulate that answer.

As you work through some of these items, you should start to create Key Performance Indicators (KPI). KPI's are a measurement of performance that you can quantify. For real estate, some KPIs could be as follows.

❖ What are my monthly and annual cash flow goals for this property?

❖ What appreciation rate do I need on this property to hit my long-term goals?

❖ What measurable factor exists within this home or location that I can use to support those obtainable cash flow and appreciation goals *(such as population growth in the area, new job creation, commercial construction, etc.)*?

You need to train yourself to develop measurable variables that will support your forecasting. As you understand more about your particular goals and your local market, it becomes easier to create KPI's that you will want to use when analyzing a property.

If you start to change your mindset of how you view homes, and how you build your portfolio, you will probably end up with a diversified portfolio of homes that will help hedge you against some of those previously mentioned risks. Adding in the layer of time you plan to hold your portfolio will also assist in when you may enter and exit those properties.

The last market factor I want to mention in this chapter is the Median Home Price for your market. The median home price is different from the average home price. Average home values are calculated by adding up recent sale prices and divided by the number of home sales in a given time period, thus giving you an average. The median home price is simply the middle home price of the homes sold. If a particular town had 501 home sales this past quarter and you ranked them from the least expensive to the most expensive and looked at the house that was #250 on that list (right in the middle), that price would be your median home price.

Most investors prefer to look at the median price instead of the average is because the median helps eliminate extreme sales. Having a few very expensive or inexpensive homes in your sales list could make the average a little more inaccurate; therefore, using the median helps eliminate those extremes. Depending on your market and the investors you talk to, varying weights are put into the importance of median home prices. The median price is supposed to give you a good indication of the average buyer for your area and their price point, and as an investor, when we want to rent or sell in the future, we want to *market to the masses*. Knowing the rental and sales median price points in our area can be helpful when determining if our homes, at least from a price standpoint, will appeal to the masses. Of course, median and average prices are constantly fluctuating because sales are continual, but it would be a good idea to know the median price point of your state, city, and even neighborhood.

Some investors are very strict about median home prices as they relate to what they will purchase, but for most of us, we should focus more on the house itself and future potential. While I wouldn't get too hung up on the cost of your home as it relates to the overall median price, I would certainly know that information, especially as you grow your portfolio. Personally, I wouldn't want to be too far away from the median price point, unless I had a specific reason to do so.

As we cite other examples in this book, I use many cases of homes in the $300-400k price range. In my market, that is where our median home prices typically fall. In your market, that may be $150k or $500k, but those have no impact on the formulas or examples we use. The numbers in each of the models we use will simply adjust based on the particular property you may be evaluating.

Also, when selecting examples, it was essential to show that I wasn't using cherry-picked examples. I wanted to use more realistic models. While people in Northern California may dream of a home only costing $400k, there are usually some options in that range for the rest of us. However, had I used examples in the $150-200k range, it would have been tough to find in most US cities.

This chapter revolves around forecasting and what tools we use to predict the future accurately. Forecasting always reminds me of Peter Drucker's quote. Drucker was a well-known author on management who said, ***"The best way to predict the future is to create it."*** Markets will change. Real estate values will change. Your goals and plans will change. Change is all around us, all the time, but our futures are in our control if we allow them to be. Don't make excuses for how change is impacting you. Prepare for change and react to it while keeping your eye on your goals.

Chapter 5 - *Financing and Leverage*

UNQUESTIONABLY, ONE OF THE more challenging parts of real estate investing, especially for newer investors, is how they will acquire the money to pay for it. Many investing books out there don't dive deep enough into the inner workings of how the average investor can get started from the financial aspects. There are also many books that explain complicated and risky financial tools to help purchase properties. Many of those tools will simply be too risky or complex for most beginner investors. This chapter will go over the more common financial components available for the average investor.

Most real estate investors will start by purchasing their first rental property with a traditional mortgage loan, so we're going to start there. We'll talk about other strategies and options for financing and growing your portfolio as we progress.

Let's start with a few terms that we're going to use moving forward.

Loan-to-Value (LTV) - I've mentioned this earlier in the book and have explained it, but this is just a simple ratio of how much you're borrowing (loan) to the value (purchase price). Very simply, if I buy a $300,000 house and borrow $240,000 with a loan, my LTV is 80% ($240k/$300k = 80%). The remaining $60,000 typically comes from the purchaser, and we call that your down payment, which is 20%.

Not always, but usually, to receive the best interest rate for an investment property, the buyer would need to put down 20-25%, resulting in a 75-80% LTV. I know saving a 20-25% down payment for some investors can be challenging, so going back and evaluating your Chapter 3 task of *assessing your current financial situation* is very important. It may require you to partner up with someone or look at some of the alternative financing options we'll talk about if you're not close to that amount of money.

Credit score - This score is compiled from financial institutions that report on your borrowing histories, such as car loans, credit cards, medical collections, past mortgages, and student loans. Your credit score is a number that is created using various data points and reporting to help lenders determine your creditworthiness or risk level. You may have heard of a FICO score, which is a relatively common score used by lenders for mortgages. FICOs range from 300 on the low end to 850 on the highest end. If you're at 850, your risk to that lender is very low that you won't repay based on your history that has created that score. The opposite is true if you land in the 300-500 score range.

If you're purchasing your primary home, you may be able to get loan approval in the 600+ range based on other financial factors. If you're looking to purchase an investment property, you'll probably need to be in the upper 600's at a minimum and at least 700+ for the best rate options.

It should be noted that while FICO is a company that produces this report, there are several credit agencies that have their own scores that operate on a similar system. Depending on which report the lender uses will dictate your score/risk, however, most run in a similar number range. The higher the credit score, the lower the risk to the lender and thus, the better the interest rate you'll receive. There is more to the story than just the score, as with anything. What is in the report is just as valuable. Here are some things within the actual report that the lender will evaluate:

❖ Have you ever been late on any payments? If so, how many

times, how long ago, how late, and which type of loans?

❖ Are you borrowing most of your allowable credit lines? For instance, if you have a credit card with a $10,000 limit, is your balance $9,500 or much lower at only $500? The person using $9,500 of their $10,000 balance may be short on cash or living outside of their income means, and that could hurt their overall credit score.

❖ Do you have many credit lines open? Are you one of those people who always open a credit card at a department store to earn an extra discount? Open lines of credit show the lender that even if you're not using those credit lines now, you may use them in the future, so the future risk is increased.

❖ Do you have several car loans or just one? Are you driving a Honda with a $400 payment or an expensive Mercedes with a $1,000 monthly fee? Those things may matter to a lender as they describe how you may value your cash, income, and debt levels, even if you're never late on your car loan.

❖ Do you have a lot of fun toys, such as a boat, ATV, or side-by-side off-road fun buggy?

❖ Do you have student loans, and if so, have you put them into deferment, or are you paying consistently? How much do you owe on them?

❖ Do you have medical bills, and if so, are any in collections?

❖ Have you ever had a foreclosure, bankruptcy, short sale, or judgment against you?

Keeping an eye on your credit report and pulling at least one type of report annually so you can review it and make sure you don't see any incorrect reporting is very important. It takes very little to decrease your score but can be a long process to increase it. Remember, it's not always about the overall score, but also about the picture it may paint of your financial stability and financial decision-making process. If you make $35,000 a year, you probably shouldn't own a Porsche SUV towing a boat behind it!

Bank Statements - Most lenders will want to see two complete bank statements when applying for a home loan, if not more of them. These bank statements help tie the picture together regarding the expenses you say you have, as well as where your disposable income goes. It's a way to track things that may not appear on your credit score report. It may feel invasive to give the lender all your bank statements to see where your money is going, but they need to ensure that you have enough money consistently to pay back the money you're borrowing. Think about it this way - if you have a car loan, student loans, credit card payments, and a mortgage on your primary house, then those things should all report to your credit score. There's no real hiding from it. However, what about all your other disposable spending items, such as eating out, putting gas in your car, buying new clothes, etc.? Those things don't report to your credit because you're typically not 'borrowing' money to pay for them. You're using your cash.

The banks want to ensure you have enough money to pay for this new home mortgage, and even though you're going to rent it out as an investment, they know there will be some vacancies and repairs over the years. Other items that may be hidden on a bank statement that wouldn't show up on your credit report are things like child support, alimony, and things of that nature - those can be significant expenses.

Seasoned Funds -The term 'seasoned' refers to how long money has been in your account. For instance, the bank may want your down payment money to be *seasoned* for at least 60-90 days in your account. They want to try and ensure that money is yours, not a loan or gift from friends or family, etc. The presumption is that if the money has been in your account for a few months, it's most likely yours. Verifying this is another reason for them checking two to three bank statements. That doesn't mean that investors don't get personal loans from family, friends or business partners to help with the down payment. They just usually do so at least 3 months in advance of going under contract on a property. That way, when the bank looks at 2-3 months of bank statements, that money will have always shown in the account.

Reserves - Think of the term 'Reserves' as your backup money that you could have access to if you needed it. Typically, lenders want you to have access to six months' worth of mortgage payments for the property you're getting the loan on, plus two months for all other properties you own. Let's say the new rental home you're looking to buy will have a mortgage payment of $1,800. We'll also presume your primary home has a mortgage payment of $2,700 and you have one other rental home with a mortgage payment of $1,400. The bank may want you to have access to the following amount of cash, beyond the down payment and closing costs to buy the rental home you're currently looking to purchase.

New property:	$1,800 x 6 months = $10,800
Primary residence:	$2,700 x 2 months = $5,400
Other rental property:	$1,400 x 2 months = $2,800
Total cash access of:	$19,000

Please note I kept using the phrase *access to*. This does not mean you need to have this cash in your bank accounts, but rather you just need to have access to that amount. Lenders will look at your available cash in the bank, retirement accounts, any stocks, or bonds you may own, or any other sort of liquid money you can access.

Amortization Schedule - This is a simple chart that breaks down any loan scenario regarding how much of each monthly payment goes towards the principal and the interest. It also calculates the reducing loan balance after each payment. As you make a mortgage payment, part goes towards reducing the loan balance (principal), and another part goes towards the fee the bank makes for lending you the money (interest). While the total payment itself may remain the same over time, the proportion that goes towards the principal and interest changes monthly, thus why an amortization schedule is essential. We utilize these continually while examining the financial decisions we must make. Luckily, hundreds of phone apps and websites will run these numbers for free and spit out the results instantly. You just need to know the loan amount, interest rate, and length of the loan. Here is a sample of how one looks for a $280,000 loan with a 4% interest rate on a 30-year mortgage analyzed on an annual basis (they can be run monthly, too):

	Beginning Balance	Interest	Principal	Ending Balance
1	$280,000.00	$11,110.26	$4,930.86	$275,069.10
2	$275,069.10	$10,909.35	$5,131.77	$269,937.30
3	$269,937.30	$10,700.28	$5,340.84	$264,596.43
4	$264,596.43	$10,482.69	$5,558.43	$259,039.96
5	$259,037.96	$10,256.22	$5,784.90	$253,283.04
6	$253,253.04	$10,020.54	$6,020.58	$247,232.42

After Repair Value (ARV) - This is a prevalent investor term, and it usually goes just by the acronym ARV. This term means, "What is the home worth after it has been fixed up?" Here is a simple example and how the acronym would be used. If I bought a home for $285,000 and it needs about $30,000 worth of work, however, if I do that work to the house, it then should be valued at about $335,000. My *After Repair Value (ARV)* would be $335,000.

Adjustable-Rate Mortgage (ARM) - An adjustable-rate mortgage is a type of mortgage that, instead of having a fixed interest rate for the entire life of the loan, typically 30 years, has a rate that can adjust. The acronym ARM commonly refers to it. ARMs can change at various time intervals, and have the adjustments based on varying indexes. People ask, 'why would I ever want a loan with a rate that can adjust up, if I could get one that is always the same?' ARMs typically start with a lower rate (teaser rate) than a 30-year fixed rate mortgage, so, at the beginning of the loan, they can be more affordable, increase your cash flow and help you qualify for a mortgage with lower payments due to that initial lower interest rate.

Lenders offer ARMs because the hope is that after that initial lower interest rate expires, the new adjusted rate will be higher, and they'll make more money on interest at that time. If that rate increases, the original lender may suggest you refinance that loan with them. In doing so, they can earn more in fees and possibly interest versus had you selected the 30-year fixed mortgage originally. Deciding on doing a fixed-rate mortgage or an ARM typically comes down to this - how long will you hold the <u>loan?</u> If you're going to keep the loan for less time than it takes for the rate ever to adjust, you may be on the winning end of the deal with an ARM.

Please note that I once again referred how long I'll hold the loan for, not the actual property. There are times that I may keep the house but get rid of the original loan. A common example would be if I do a mortgage refinance; my original loan is replaced, but I never sold the home.

Here is an example that may be easier to understand:

<u>Scenario:</u> I'm purchasing a $300,000 home with a $240,000 mortgage and am looking at a 30-year fixed mortgage at 4.5%. The lender has also offered me a 5/1 ARM at 4.25%. I just threw a new part to the ARM, which was the 5/1 part. All ARMs have a notation of how long the initial interest rate is locked for (in this case, five years, the first number) and how often the rate adjusts after the initial period (in this case every one year, the second number).

Please note, some ARMs second number is the number of months, not years, that it can change. A 5/6 ARM could adjust every six months, so always read your loan terms. There are also 5/5 ARMs that are fixed for the first five years, and then adjust every five years after that.

We're going to go over a real example with actual numbers later in the book, but for now, I just want you to understand the concept of an ARM and when it may come into play. Here is a quick comparison to a 30-year fixed.

30-year fixed at 4.5%

❖ Years 1-30: Interest rate permanently fixed at 4.5%

5/1 ARM at 4.25%

❖ Years 1-5: Interest rate fixed at 4.25%

➢ Please note for the first five years of the loan, I am paying .25% less in interest with this ARM versus the

30-year fixed loan option. We can calculate the first five years very accurately as we have the fixed rates for both options at that time.

❖ Year 6: Rate can adjust based on a particular index or treasury

❖ Year 7: Rate can change again

❖ Year 8: Rate can change again

❖ And so on, every year, up to year 30.

Where might be some good places to use an ARM?

❖ I'm only planning on holding this home for a few years; ideally less than the first rate change opportunity of my ARM. If I only plan on holding for five or fewer years, than the future year six possible rate adjustment may not matter to me.

❖ I'm going to refinance this mortgage in less than five years and get a new mortgage, so I might as well save money with the lower interest rate for those early years.

❖ I'm going to sell other properties or assets and keep this home, but pay off the mortgage before that first adjustment period.

All of those are somehow related to **time**. My finance decisions should be dictated by the length of time I plan on holding the mortgage or property.

The other essential item to understand about ARMs is my rate's index. Many ARMs use the SOFR (Secured Overnight Financing Rate) or some sort of Treasury note, as their index to adjust. All the indexes that could be used are very easy to find with a simple internet search or daily financial publication. Within your ARM loan terms, it will lay out how much to add to the index at any given adjustment period.

For instance, if my loan term agreement says my ARM will adjust as follows in year 6: "SOFR + 3.5%," and as of today, the SOFR is only at 1.5, then if it changed today, my rate would go to 5.0%. If my ARM agreement says that it changes every year after the first five years, then the same process will occur in years six, seven, eight, and so on, until the end of the loan. Sticking with this example – if in year 6, the SOFR had risen to 1.75%, then in year 6, my interest rate would then be 5.25%. If the SOFR had decreased, so too would my interest rate for that annual period. The ARM terms usually also have 'floors and ceilings' that dictate minimums and maximums that the interest rate could ever be, and maximum increases that could occur in one period. They are used as consumer protection, so, hopefully in year six or after that, you don't end up with a crazy high interest rate. In this example, we're using a 5/1 ARM as it is relatively standard, but they can be of varying lengths. We'll do an example comparing a fixed rate and ARM later.

Discount Points - Discount points are, in essence, prepaid interest to the lender at the time of closing in exchange for a lower interest rate on the loan. Like an ARM, this is all about the *time you'll be holding the loan*. The most basic understanding is that one point = 1% of the loan (not purchase price). If I buy a $350,000 home, but only get a loan for $280,000 and the lender mentions one point, they are referencing $2,800, not $3,500. Discount points also don't have to be whole numbers. They can be fractions, such as 1.375 points or 1.75 points, etc., however, the math related to the loan amount is still the same.

What does a discount point do? A discount point is pre-paying our interest on the loan upfront to save on interest in the long run. Let's look at some real numbers:

Purchase Price: $350,000

Loan Amount: $280,000

The interest rate with no discount points: 4.0%

The interest rate with one discount point: 3.75%

Cost of the one discount point: $2,800

What would our payments be in the two options?

$280,000 loan @ 4.0% = $1,337 Principal + Interest payment (P&I)

$280,000 loan @ 3.75% = $1,297 Principal + Interest payment (P&I)

Here is a breakdown of the interest we would pay to the bank on each of the 2 loans to see where our break-even point would be on the $2,800 to purchase the lower rate. I used an amortization schedule to get these figures:

Month #	Interest @ 4.0%	Interest @ 3.75%	Difference in Interest
0-12	$11,110	$10,412	$698 saved with lower rate
13-24	$10,909	$10,216	$693 saved
25-36	$10,700	$10,012	$688 saved
37-48	$10,483	$9,800	$683 saved
			$2,762 total saved

As you can see, the total at the end of year 4 of the amount of interest saved with the lower rate of 3.75% on this loan was $2,762, which is excellent. However, remember to get that lower rate, we had to pay the lender $2,800. Just after 48 months of having the loan, the monthly savings in interest on the lower rate loan will surpass the $2,800 it costs us to get that lower rate. If you were planning on holding this loan longer than our break-even time of about 48 months, then it may be worth it to consider doing this discount point option, as every month you hold this loan after 48 months, you realize a real interest savings.

Since this loan option is also based on time, this is where having your investment goals per home laid out can really be helpful. This is just one example. In various market and lending conditions, that same $2,800 may save you ⅛, ⅜ or ½ percent on different loans and thus your break-even point will vary. Some investors will say that if you spend $2,800 today to get a lower rate then you have $2,800 less saved for your next home (opportunity cost). That statement is true, however I'm always a fan of paying less interest and increasing your cash flow with a lower payment when possible and reasonable to do so. And when it makes sense for my portfolio, I give this loan tool serious consideration.

As a point of reference, the opposite of a discount point is a lender credit. This is where the interest rate is increased and at closing, the lender gives you a credit to help pay some of the closing costs associated with the loan. While you have a larger monthly payment due to the increased interest rate, you had less cash out of pocket.

Debt to Income Ratio (DTI) - This ratio is commonly used by most mortgage lenders and is usually analyzed in two different ways. The purpose of this ratio is to compare your *debts* to what your *gross income* is. The first way the DTI Ratio is calculated is by using the estimated payment of your new mortgage as related to your monthly gross income. For example, if I'm applying for a mortgage and my estimated monthly mortgage payment, including taxes, insurance and any applicable HOA dues is going to be $1,850, and I make $65,000 per year (or $5,416 per month), then my DTI for my new mortgage would be 34% ($1,850 / $5,416). Most lenders like to keep this DTI around the 30% mark and not too much higher. The second type of DTI also includes the new mortgage, as well as adds in your other debt payments, such as car loans, student loans, credit cards, other mortgages, etc.

Using the same example above, let's also say you have $1,200 in monthly payments that are outgoing for those items therefore your total monthly debt would be seen as $1,850 + $1,200 for a total of $3,050. If we divide that by your gross monthly income of $5,416, that debt ratio would be 56%. Many lenders like to have this secondary ratio closer to 45% and not too much higher.

These DTI's have flexibility based on other factors, such as how much money you are putting down, if you have extra cash in the bank, your credit score, and other variables that may speak to your overall qualification. Your 'income' in this ratio can also be adjusted if you're currently receiving tenant paid rents for other properties you may already own. These ratios aren't always set in stone at 30% and 45% respectively, but rather they are industry guidelines and can adjust based on the individual applicant, the overall economy and risk factors involved.

When it comes to having tenants, paid rents count towards income, and can range based on how long you have owned the property with tenants in them, what your tax returns look like for that rental property, and what your other qualifications are. A lender may count anywhere from 60-100% of your monthly collected tenant rents towards your income calculation. Just as those mortgages you have would count as debt, you would want some of the rents you collect to count as income to help offset that ratio.

Now that we have a few terms down, let's dive deeper into the actual nuts and bolts of some of these things. We're going to run examples of the following:

1. What is a HELOC, and how can we use it to finance an investment property?

2. How can we use an ARM to our benefit?

3. When should we use a Discount Point option?

4. What exactly is a cash-out refinance, and how should we structure it?

Before we get too deep into those items, I want to go back and reference our goal-setting tasks. Now, we can no longer talk in generalities or 'what ifs.' **Time** becomes a significant factor when it comes to making financial decisions on what type of loan to get and how to structure it. Frankly, if you don't have any sort of goal setting for your overall portfolio, and the individual homes within the portfolio, making wise financial decisions is difficult and risky. When that happens, many investors always run to the most stable financial products available, and many times end up overpaying in interest or fees.

I cannot stress enough how important goal setting is related to these financial decisions. If you only retain one thing from this book that resonates with you, please make it the importance of educated goal setting and mapping out a plan. Real money can be made and lost by how you plan and set goals.

Home Equity Lines of Credit

HELOC's, otherwise known as H̲ome E̲quity L̲ines o̲f C̲redit, are typically lines of credit only taken against your *primary* residence. If you have a good bit of equity in your primary home and want to take some of that equity to put into an investment property, a HELOC may be one of the easiest and least expensive tools to utilize. This type of loan is meant to tap into your home's equity. To figure out the payment of a HELOC, you need to have the amount you borrow, the interest rate, and the time the bank amortizes the loan over.

There are three things to know from your bank regarding your HELOC: (1) length of time of amortization for payment purposes, (2) how many years you can draw more money on that line of credit and, (3) is there a balloon payment, which is the time that all the borrowed money is due back.

Typically, most banks amortize the loan over 30 years to keep the payment reasonable and only allow you to borrow money (*called a draw*) on the loan for the first ten years. Banks typically require a balloon payment in 10-20 years to pay back all the money. A balloon payment is the requirement to pay the loan off by the expiration of that time, so while the bank may calculate the payment over 30 years, it may need to be paid back in full sooner. This can be done by you selling the home, paying it off with available funds you may have or a loan refinance.

Scenario:

Primary home is worth: $450,000
Mortgage balance: $218,000
Estimated Equity: $232,000 ($450k value - $218k owed)

The sweet spot to get a HELOC is at 80% LTV, although some will go higher. If our value is $450,000 then 80% of that is $360,000. That is the max value the bank will use in its lending determination. The bank will lend a line of credit on the difference between what I owe at $218k and the max amount of their lending at $360k. That is $142,000 that I can leverage against my primary house to put towards another home.

What are some of the benefits of doing a HELOC?

❖ Many times, the interest incurred on this loan is a taxable deduction.

❖ The cost of setting up a HELOC is relatively low in comparison to alternatives.

❖ Typically, you pay only interest on the money you borrow, i.e., you may have a line of credit open for up to $128k, but if you only draw/borrow $80k, you'll only pay interest on the $80k.

❖ They are relatively quick and easy to set up.

❖ The bank does not dictate what you do with the money.

❖ You don't have to save the full amount required to purchase another property; you can use the money you borrow from your HELOC.

What are some of the pitfalls to consider?

❖ You are borrowing money against your personal house to buy an investment property, which some people find above their risk tolerance.

❖ Most HELOC rates are adjustable and do so more rapidly than most mortgages. While the rates today may look appealing, read the fine print on how often they can change and as to what index the bank bases their adjustments on your HELOC.

❖ If you sell your primary residence, that HELOC will have to be paid off out of the proceeds since it is a lien against that home. That means you'll have less 'take home' money at closing for your primary house sale.

❖ The payment you owe on the HELOC will be factored into your Debt-to-Income ratio moving forward. If you're using this HELOC for a down payment on an investment property, it may accomplish that however, the increased debt payments from the HELOC itself may skew the ratios that the lender uses to qualify you.

❖ The bank may set up payments with varying options, such as interest-only payments where no principal is being paid. They can also be amortized over different lengths of time, which could impact your payment size on these loans. All aren't done so over 30 years.

HELOCs are a great option for people with equity in their primary homes that are looking to use some of it to purchase an investment property. They may want to use it to pay cash for that property if they have enough equity to do so or reduce the down payment portion they have to save for. They could also use it for repairs and upgrades. There are a ton of options if you have that equity. If you consider getting a HELOC, shop around to big banks, as well as smaller, local banks. These types of loans can be like credit cards in the fact that many times banks are running promotions on these types of loans because they are quick, easy, and can be a win/win for the bank and consumer.

Adjustable-Rate Mortgages

Earlier I explained what an Adjustable-Rate Mortgage (ARM) was but noted that we would look at actual numbers later. We have arrived at that point to dive deeper into the subject of ARMs. These mortgages have rates that adjust, and for the most part, we all think that the rate will adjust up, although technically they can adjust down, too. However, the banks make these types of loans because they do hope they go up! The main thing with an ARM to understand is the length of time you're going to hold that mortgage; again, I said to *hold that mortgage*, I did not say *keep that house*.

Let's look at a real-life example of an ARM.

Scenario: I had a property that I was purchasing as a rental home, but I only planned on renting it for a few years before selling because the HOA dues in the neighborhood were higher than average and it had a track record of continual increases. My long-term forecasting had me concerned that the HOA dues may reach a point where the next buyer of that home may feel the dues were too expensive, and thus, it could be a tougher home to sell. However, I still wanted to buy the house because I thought I could make a good profit over the next 1-3 years. Also, based on the home's location, I knew it would rent very quickly and for top dollar, even though HOA dues were eating up some of my cash flow.

Plan: On day one of buying that property, I knew that it would take some sort of massive shift in the market conditions or HOA restructuring for me to hold the property much longer than a few years. I considered renovating it and just selling quickly (as a 'flip'), but I would have gotten crushed on taxes. The market was strong and showed no signs of stopping in the next one to two years, so I felt I could really maximize the profit if I just held it for a few more years.

At this point, I have determined my timeline, long-term forecast and overall goal for the home.

Financing Options: At that time, a 5/1 ARM was at 3.75%, and a 30-year fixed rate was 4.25%. I was borrowing $180,000. Since I knew I would not hold this mortgage for longer than five years, I felt compelled to take the ARM with the initial lower rate for the first five years, but let's look at the numbers.

Typically, with a lower interest rate, you pay less interest overall, have a lower overall monthly payment and apply more towards the principal earlier. It may seem like three benefits: (1) pay less interest, (2) have a lower payment, and (3) pay more towards the principal, but the interest you save = reduction in payment + more principal.

Loan Options

Loan Amount: $180,000

❖ 30-year Fixed Interest Rate option: 4.25%

 ➤ Principal & Interest payment of $885.49

❖ 5/1 ARM Interest Rate option: 3.75%

 ➤ Principal & Interest payment of $833.61

There is an obvious difference in payment with the difference in interest rates to the tune of $52/month. The lower interest rate option would put an extra $624 per year in my pocket. Let's see how much interest I would save over the first 3 years by choosing the ARM:

End of Yr.	Interest Paid on ARM	Interest Paid on 30-yr
1	$6,693	$7,591
2	$6,567	$7,460
3	$6,436	$7,323
	$19,696	$22,374

Both scenarios started with an initial loan balance of $180,000. As you can see in this table, the ARM option pays much less interest over the first three years. Since my planned goal was to own this home for only about three years, and certainly less than five years before the loan first adjusted with the ARM, it would be financially wise to choose the ARM over the 30-year fixed option. No need to give the banks more interest when you could keep it yourself! By simply knowing my goal and plan for that home, I chose a different loan option that saved me almost $2,700 in three years.

I've shared a real-life example of where the ARM has its place in investing. But, what if at the end of those first three years, I decided to hold the property long- term? The market during those three years took a downturn, and I was wrong in my forecasting the future growth. If I decide to hold it until the end of year seven, an additional four years, here is how that ARM could affect me. We already know years one to three from above, but now let's look at years four through seven, with the presumption that at the end of year five, when the teaser ARM rate ends, the new rate increases by 2% in year six and .5% in year seven.

Here is how our interest paid would look:

End of Yr.	Interest Paid on ARM	Interest Paid on 30-yr
1	$6,693	$7,591
2	$6,567	$7,460
3	$6,436	$7,323
4	$6,300	$7,179
5	$6,159	$7,030
6	$9,245*	$6,874
7	$9,862**	$6,712
	$51,262	$50,169

* Rate increases 2% from 3.75% to 5.75% because the ARM adjusts to the current market rate of that time. The P&I payment also increases from $833.61 to $1,020.03 based on the remaining loan balance and time remaining (25 yrs).

** Rate increases ½% from 5.75% to 6.25% because the ARM adjusted again to that current market value. The P&I payment also increases from $1,020.03 to $1,068.14 (24 yrs remaining).

As you can see, when I held the loan beyond the initial five-year teaser rate of the ARM and the rate increased, in this example, 2% in year six then .5% in year seven, not only did our payment increase, but so did our interest we were paying. Our increased payment reduces the cash flow we retain from the tenants' rent and we start to pay a lot more in interest. The interest we saved in years 1-5 with the ARM got completely eradicated sometime between years six and seven of this mortgage scenario. We ended up paying an extra $1,093 with the ARM after seven years, even though we were several thousand ahead after the first five years.

We only looked at the interest paid and not the comparison of payments or principal paydown. Still, we know the formula *interest saved = savings of payment + extra principal paid down*. To check our math, if we added up all the payments we made with the ARM payments ($75,074) together with all the payments we would have made with a 30-year fixed ($74,381), we'd have a difference between the two of $693 after seven years. Then, if we look at the difference in loan balances after seven years with the ARM, having a loan balance of $156,188 and the 30-year fixed having $155,788, that difference would be $400.

Interest saved ($1,093) = savings of payment ($693) + extra principal paid down ($400). Our math checks out!

Does this mean I shouldn't do the ARM because I risk holding it over the initial teaser rate phase? Does it mean you listen to all the people who tell you to always go with a 30-year fixed rate? Do you not even bother to run the numbers and forecast? No. If my *goal* for this property were to hold this *loan* for less than five years, I would be foolish not to explore the ARM option and possibly save thousands of dollars!

If I stuck to my **goal** and my forecasting was on track, but I had chosen the 30-year fixed, I would have given thousands to the bank in extra interest versus my own pocket for the simple lack of education or faith in my plan. As you can see from the numbers, there is a risk involved with holding the property or loan longer than you initially planned. Even in that situation, there are ways to work around that, such as a refinance or other financial tools we'll talk about shortly.

If my goal was to hold this property longer than five years, then doing the ARM may be foolish or unnecessarily risky, but I implemented the financial tool best suited for my goal and, by doing so, may have saved thousands.

If you don't have well-defined and measurable goals for the houses that build your portfolio, you cannot make educated financial decisions. The lack of those educated financial decisions will simply cost you money. It happens all the time. Ignore what people may tell you and follow the math. Numbers don't lie.

Discount Points

I explained earlier what a discount point was; in essence you're paying the lender a fee today, as prepaid interest, for a lower interest rate for the life of the loan - typically done with a fixed rate loan option, such as a 30-year fixed. We ran an example earlier of where our breakeven point was and if it was worthwhile to pay a discount point. Here I'd like to take that analysis one step further and factor in some negotiating with a potential seller.

Let's examine buying a $350,000 home with 20% down, so our mortgage is $280,000 at 4.5%. If this seller is willing to negotiate 1% ($3,500), should I take that off the home's price or use it towards closing costs for a discount point? Here are our two options:

1. Reduce the price by $3,500, so instead of purchasing for $350,000, we would buy for $346,500. This interest rate will be

4.5%, and our loan at $280,000. No discount point.

2. Maintain the price at $350,000, but use that $3,500 towards closing costs to buy down the interest rate via a discount point. For this option, our lender has told us the discount point will cost us $2,800 (1% of the loan), and we'll have a new interest rate of 4.25%. Since the seller is giving us $3,500 to use however we'd like, we'll use $2,800 for the discount point, and we'll reduce the price with the remaining $700 for a sales price of $349,300.

We would be putting down 20% on the purchase with both options, and the rates would be as noted previously - 4.5% if we do option one and take the lower price (not the closing costs credit) and option two would have a 4.25% rate, but a slightly higher sales price/loan amount.

Loan option #1: **No Buy Down Rate, Take Lower Price**

Purchase Price: $346,500
Interest Rate: 4.5%
Loan Amount: $277,200 (80% LTV)
Down Payment: $69,300
P&I payment: $1,404

Loan option #2: **Purchase the Buy Down Rate**

Purchase Price: $349,300
Interest Rate: 4.25%
Loan Amount: $279,440 (80% LTV)
Down Payment: $69,860
P&I payment: $1,374

What are the differences between the two options so far?

❖ The purchase prices are different based on what we're doing with the seller's $3,500 they are offering.

❖ The interest rates are different utilizing the Discount Point option in one scenario.

❖ Due to having two different sales prices, our down payment and loan amounts are different. There is a $560 larger down payment needed with the option that has the higher price.

❖ The payments are different based on the different loan amounts and interest rates.

We analyze this in the same way we did our initial discount point scenario where we were searching for our break-even point. The only difference being that because we now have the option to reduce the sales price and thus, reduce the amount we borrow, *the principal balances start at different amounts* when in the previous example, they began at the same amount.

So, how do we compare these two options? We need to explore the savings as they relate to each other. We need to see where the interest savings on the buy-down option hits our difference in the purchase price. The difference between the two purchase prices is $2,800, so at what point have we saved $2,800 in interest with the 4.25% loan?

We use our amortization schedule for each loan to compare total interest paid over time. Here is a snippet of the amortization schedule as the loans compare to each other.

End of Yr.	Interest Paid 4.5%	Interest Paid on 4.25%	Difference
1	$12,382	$11,785	$597
2	$12,177	$11,581	$596
3	$11,962	$11,368	$594
4	$11,737	$11,146	$591
5	$11,502	$10,914	$588

Total Interest saved with 4.25% loan at the end of five years: $2,966

As you can see, sometime during year five you surpass the $2,800 mark saved in interest by going with the lower interest rate of 4.25%. That savings offsets the higher initial purchase price you took to get the sellers' money to buy down that rate. Everything beyond those five years is going to be more beneficial with the person that took the lower interest rate and higher price upfront. We already know that *interest saved = difference in payment + extra principal paid*, so while there is a difference in P&I payments and principal paydown, we only must run calculations on the interest saved to see where our break-even is.

The ultimate question is - are you holding this loan for longer than 60 months? If the answer is a clear YES and you will hold that loan for a considerable amount of time longer, then choosing the higher price, but lower rate, may prove beneficial for you. This is a great option to ponder for our longer-term property holders that typically buy a home, get a 30-year fixed rate and rarely sell or refinance out of the loan. On the other hand, since you don't start to see the actual benefits of this until almost year six, you must be very confident about the time you plan on keeping this initial loan.

Understanding this type of seller negotiations is important. While our break-even is about 5 years in this example, there are other negotiation opportunities that you may come across where you can save much more money sooner. Many investors are quick to take the lower price all the time, and I'd caution you to learn to be more calculated.

In this example, we did incur what we call an *Opportunity Cost*. Opportunity costs are the potential loss from a future investment because you chose an alternative today. In this example, to get the lower interest rate, we had to take the higher sales price. In doing so, we had an extra down payment amount of $560 in comparison to the alternative option. Since we used an additional $560 to purchase the home, we now have that much less to invest in the future. That extra money is our *opportunity cost* because we don't have it to use in the future easily. In this scenario, the $560 is probably not a big deal when our overall down payment is almost $70k. However, do pay attention when making these decisions between option A and option B because in some circumstances, the opportunity cost can be much larger.

Cash-Out Refinance

The last example we will run in this chapter is how a Cash-out Refinance (COR) operates. CORs are extremely popular in the investment world and can be very effective in growing your portfolio. The main benefit to a COR is that, if done correctly, you don't have to save up a new down payment for every home you buy; you can leverage a current home to help with the money needed. We go over this after talking about ARMs and Discount Points for a purpose, and that is, within a COR, you may have the option to do an ARM and/or a Discount Point, so that base knowledge is helpful.

Before diving into an actual example, let's quickly explain just what a refinance is in general. A refinance at its core is simply replacing one mortgage with a new mortgage while retaining the property. These are called *rate-and-term refinances*, and as they imply, you are just refinancing the interest rate and length of loan (term) but not receiving any cash back. If I purchased my first investment house at $300k and put down 20% with a 30-year fixed rate, that would have me getting a mortgage on that house for $240,000. We'll presume that the interest rate was 4.5% when I got my mortgage, but after three years, maybe interest rates dropped to 4.0%. I would like to take advantage of the market having lower rates. Using an amortization schedule, I know my loan balance at the end of 3 years would be $228k with 27 years remaining on that mortgage.

A refinance allows me to pay off that $228k balance that I have 27 years remaining on and replace it with a new mortgage at the current interest rate of 4.0%. When I get the new mortgage, I can replace it with whatever terms for which I am approved. It could be another 30-year fixed-rate, or even a 15-year mortgage, and I could do a fixed rate or ARM. For this example, we'll assume I'm replacing the first 30-year fixed-rate mortgage with another 30-year fixed-rate mortgage, this time at 4.0%. The refinance may be done through my current mortgage company or a new one. When I get that new mortgage, my remaining 27 years is replaced with a new 30 year amortization and an interest rate that is ½% lower than what I had prior to the refinance.

Owners typically refinance to capitalize on interest rates that have gone down or to pull cash out of their property's equity. In addition, because you're getting a new mortgage, the 30-year amortization has started over. Between the new lower rate and the 30-year amortization starting over, your mortgage payment will probably go down, too. That is your basic refinance in a nutshell, but as you can see, we didn't add in the *"Cash-Out"* part yet. That extra step, which is critical to investors, is explained next.

The Cash-Out part of this process has the same steps as a regular rate-and-term refinance. However, instead of just replacing one mortgage with another, you're also actually receiving cash back. There are additional requirements to complete this, so let's look at those. The main need is that the home has appreciated a decent amount in value, or there is a lot of equity in the house. That equity could be created from market appreciation, originally paying cash for the home, paying down the mortgage and/or value increases from improvements made to the home. Here is a breakdown of how a COR may work.

❖ Purchase an investment property for $300,000 and put down $60,000 (loan balance $240,000). We have a 30-year fixed rate at 4.5% with a P&I payment of $1,216/mo. We'll also presume we had $5,000 in loan closing costs when we purchased the home, and had to put $10,000 in repairs into the home to get it up to par. Our total cash is $75,000.

❖ Let's presume that after 24 months, the home appreciates a good bit and we do work on the house to increase its value. Presume the home is now worth $360,000, through both market appreciation and work that you had done to the home since you purchased it.

❖ After 24 months, your mortgage has been paid down from the original $240,000 to $232,000.

❖ From a technical standpoint, we have $128,000 in equity ($360,000 value - $232,000 loan balance), and of that, $60,000 was our money in down payment, as well as our additional $15k in closing costs and upfit repairs.

Now that we know the basic stats of this home, let's look at the requirements that the lender may have for us to complete a Cash-Out Refinance.

❖ If the refinancing lender allows us to refinance up to 80% LTV *(loan to value)*, then 80% of the $360,000 value is $288,000. That will be the max we can borrow. We know we owe $232,000. **That difference between what we owe and what the lender will let us borrow up to is the "Cash- Out" part of $56,000.**

There are specific lenders and certain market conditions that may change that allowable finance percentage from time to time. In this example, the lender allows financing up to 80% of the value. You may find a lender that will max out at 75%, while others may go over 80%. Since lending requirements change from time to time, do not assume that the last allowable LTV will still be the same allowable percentage on the next one.

If we put in $75,000, all we're doing with this COR is getting $56k back of our money. It's a way to use our money twice. If we don't do this COR, we'd have to save up another total down payment amount before we can buy another home. That could take years and years. As with any new mortgage, there are closing costs associated, so the actual net money back to you may be a little less than $56k after those are paid.

This seems relatively simple, but there are some pitfalls. It's important to note that you don't have to have your next property lined up or even identified when you do the COR. This is a strategy that investors use to grow the number of homes they buy leveraged off of the homes they already own.

What are some of the perks of completing a Cash-Out Refinance?

❖ The most obvious is you don't have to save up as much money to buy another home because you're getting some of your original cash out of the home you're refinancing.

❖ If you qualify and the numbers work, there is no limit on the number of times you can do a COR, which means you can repeatedly do the same house, although lenders may have a time restriction between CORs on the same property. As you grow, you can pick and choose which homes in your portfolio are best suited for this strategy.

❖ Even though you will have closing costs with this refinance, you're able to get another home much more quickly. That next home will hopefully add cash flow to your portfolio, as well as another home to appreciate and another tenant paying down a mortgage on your behalf. And of course, by adding another rental home via this strategy, *you're adding another hose to your barrel without creating a massive hole.*

What are some of the pitfalls?

❖ The interest rates may have increased since you got the original mortgage and you may end up with a higher rate due to that timing. Also, COR's can have slightly higher interest rates in general compared to refinances where you aren't taking any money out. In a rate-and-term refinance, where you're getting no cash back, you're typically doing that for a lower interest rate opportunity and not more leverage. With a cash-out refinance, you're doing this to grow your portfolio and not necessarily chase a lower interest rate; that is just icing on the cake if you can accomplish that.

❖ Since you're getting a new mortgage and the length of the loan is starting over, there are some consequences to that. We already know that you pay more principal towards the loan as it progresses through time. When you refinance, you're exchanging one mortgage where you're spending one amount towards principal per month for another mortgage where you may go back to paying less at first.

❖ Your overall debt may go up. You're borrowing more than you initially did. In our example, when we purchased the home, we had a $240k mortgage, and after the COR, we had a $288,000 mortgage.

❖ As with any new mortgage process, there are closing costs. You may choose to *roll them into your new mortgage* or pay them out of the "Cash Out" part, but there are fees, nonetheless. Some of those costs associated are fixed whether you're pulling out $10k or $100k, so you want to make sure that the money you're getting from the cash-out refinance is worth the costs incurred to get that money. There is no easy way to measure this tradeoff but ensuring that you put that money to work in another investment in a timely fashion can help.

❖ Since most investors are doing a COR on an investment property, the new mortgage payment, in this case on a $288k mortgage, will count as a debt in their Debt-to-Income ratio. The original $240k mortgage debt goes away, but the new one is added in. The partial or full offset to that debt is the allowable usage of the tenants' rents as counted income for your ratios. Remember, in this example, we owned the home for 2 years, so we should have tenants in there paying rent. It's going to be important that whatever rental amount your tenants are paying covers the new mortgage payment that comes with the refinance. *Rules for how much of the rents can be included towards offsetting this debt can vary from lender to lender, and through various market conditions. A lender may use the full or partial amount of a tenant's rents paid to you, or they may use the rent schedule (Schedule E IRS form) from your tax returns for that property. If the lender uses the tax returns, and you have written off a lot regarding expenses or renovations, please be aware that it may hurt the profitability of your rental on paper. That could then provide less of an offset against the new mortgage debt if the lender does not use the rental amount the tenant is paying, but rather what you show on your taxes. Consulting with your mortgage lender for your specific deal is critical before starting this process so you can strategically plan.*

❖ There can be time constraints in doing a Cash-Out Refinance too quickly after purchasing the home. In our example, we owned the property for two years, which is plenty of time. However, some investors may have the equity built into their homes much sooner. Those investors may want to refinance within a matter of months of owning the house, and not all lenders are on board with that timeline. The issue is that lenders want that original loan or the tenants' payments to be *seasoned*. In essence, they want to see that the tenants have been paying rent for a certain amount of time, typically at least six months (but not always). They may also want to make sure you've had that original mortgage, if applicable, for a certain amount of time, again, typically, six months. Make sure you know the rules for your lender regarding this because you could be ready to do the COR quickly after the initial purchase but be prevented due to lending regulations.

The correct timing and protocol of doing a COR successfully can be tricky as the lending market is ever-changing. Just like paying attention to the max loan to value you can do, you'll also need to pay attention to your rents. If you're doing a cash-out refinance because you improved the property and want to pull out equity, and you plan on raising the rental amount due to the condition of the property, ensure you do so before initiating the COR process. A lender will use the rents they have seen in the past, not what you're going to charge in the future. Some investors don't have enough months of the new, increased rental amount before initiating the COR, and it can hurt their chances of getting the best rates or even loan approval. The timing of these steps is critical and once a mistake is made, it's tough to get a do-over with a lender.

I think it's also important to note that in a perfect world, when you do a cash-out refinance, you find the path to pull out all, or at least the majority, of your initial down payment to put into your next home. That way, you don't have to put any *new* money into the next house because you're reusing everything from the home you're refinancing. Not only does that reduce how much of your personal money you have in the deals, but reduces your risk because now your money isn't all leveraged against one property, but rather two now. There are certain circumstances that a savvy investor would do a COR even if they can only get out part of their original cash input. As you sit on the sidelines, waiting to get enough equity to pull out all of your money, you may be incurring a significant opportunity cost versus if you just pulled out some of your money and made another purchase. These situations can vary from investor to investor and property to property. While pulling all of your money out is ideal, don't write that rule in stone.

Some novice investors have difficulty visualizing the actual gains of doing a cash-out refinance, so let's look at a quick example.

We already have our original home that we looked at with these stats:

Purchase Price:	$300,000	Value in 2 years:	$360,000
Down payment:	$60,000	Interest rate before COR:	4.5%
Purchase Costs:	$5,000	Upfit Costs:	$10,000
P&I Payment:	$1,216		

Let's presume it takes us *another* five years to save $50,000 to put towards another home if we don't do the cash-out refinance. This is beyond the original two years we owned the home as a rental. In that case, we would have owned this house for a total of seven years. If we held this property for five more years while saving that down payment, here are some updated stats on the house. We'll need to make some presumptions as well to forecast.

❖ Modest 3% appreciation rate for years 3-7.

❖ Full mortgage payment with taxes & insurance, called our PITI (*principal, interest, taxes, insurance*), is $1,747. P&I was $1,216 as noted above.

❖ Rent the home for $2,400, so a gross cash flow of $653 per month ($7,836 per year).

❖ Misc. repairs/expenses of $3,000, taking that annual cash flow down to $4,836.

Value at end of year 7: $417,000

Mortgage balance at end of year 7: $208,863

At the end of year 7, what would our benefits be?

Appreciation Factor:

Value:	$417,000
Original Closing & Upfit Costs:	-$15,000
Purchase Price:	$300,000
Gain:	**102,000***

* *This section does not change regardless of if we refinance or not; the appreciation will still occur*

Principal Paydown Factor:

Original Mortgage:	$240,000
Mortgage at end of year 7:	$208,863
Gain:	**$31,137**

Rental Cash Flow Factor:

Cash Flow Years 1-7 of $4,836/yr:	$33,852
Gain:	$33,852
Gain:	**$166,989**

When adding those three main factors together, we get a **gross gain of $166,989** if we did not do the cash-out refinance and just saved our money to buy a second investment property.

Now, let's examine what would happen if we did our cash-out refinance at the end of year two and added that second home in our portfolio to give us extra gains for those five years that we would have been saving for a new down payment instead of the COR. Before we look at the actual numbers, let's determine why we may want to do a cash-out refinance and buy another property. By purchasing another property, we're trying to get appreciation on another property, principal pay down on another property, and rental cash flow from another property. This is one of those "two is better than one" situations.

We know from earlier we can get $56,000 from our cash-out refinance, and let's presume the closing costs from that cash-out refinance cost us $6,000. Therefore, we have $50,000 to use. Let's also assume that if we were to save money to the side to purchase another rental property, and that we could do so at a rate of $10-15k per year. During the first two years of owning the first property, we were able to save $25,000 for our next property, and as noted, it would take another five years to save the remaining $50,000 we're getting via our COR. By doing this type of leverage strategy, we'll be able to purchase our next investment property five years sooner. With this example, we'll also presume rates increased instead of decreasing, and if we do the COR, our rate will be 5.0%, not the 4.5% we had with the original mortgage. If our new mortgage is for $288,000 at 5.0% for 30 years, it will put our full monthly payment at $2,077, with taxes and insurance, while rents will remain at $2,400 and our annual expenses at $3,000.

First, what will happen to the first property if we do the cash-out refinance?

Appreciation Factor:

Value after an additional 5 years:	$417,000
Closing & Upfit Costs:	-$15,000
Cash-out refinance Costs:	-$6,000
Purchase Price:	$300,000
Gain:	**$96,000***

* *The appreciation does not change whether we refinance or not, however we will have additional expenses with the refinance.*

Principal Paydown Factor:

New mortgage taken for Cash-out refinance:	$288,000
Mortgage balance after an additional 5 years:	$266,749
Gain:	**$21,251**

Rental Cash Flow Factor:

Cash Flow Years 1 + 2:	$9,672
Cash Flow for an additional 5 years*:	$4,377
Gain:	**$14,049**

* *Due to having an increased mortgage payment after the cash-out refinance, our cash flow decreases, but our rents & expenses remain the same.*

Total Gain: $131,300

As you can see, we make less money in cash flow and principal paydown because we did the cash-out refinance on this first property. The objective is to surpass that decrease when we buy our next property using the money we took during our refinance. If we have $50,000 to use after costs from our cash-out refinance, plus the $25,000 we saved over the first two years of owning this first property, we have

$75,000 to apply to our next property. Of that, $50,000 is money we had already put into the first property that we're using again.

Now, let's look at the next property we will buy with that money and see what that home looks like after five years.

Purchase Price: $325,000   Value in 5 years (3% appreciation/yr): $376,764

Down payment: $65,000   Mortgage Amount: $260,000

Purchase Costs: $5,000   Interest rate: 5.0%

P&I Payment: $1,396   Upfit Costs: $5,000

Rents: $2,500   Payment w/ Tax & Insurance: $2,096

Rental Expenses: $3,000   Gross Cash Flow after expenses/yr: $1,851

What are our gains on this property?

Appreciation Factor:

Value after 5 years of ownership:	$376,764
Purchase & Upfit costs:	-$10,000
Purchase Price:	$325,000
Gain:	**$41,764**

Principal Paydown Factor:

Original Mortgage Amount:	$260,000
Mortgage balance after 5 years:	$238,754
Gain:	**$21,246**

Rental Cash Flow Factor:

Cash Flow for 5 years:	$9,256
Gain:	$9,256
Total Gain:	**$72,266**

Now that we have our scenarios laid out, let's examine them in terms of total gains.

Had we only owned one property and not done any cash-out refinance, our total gain would be $166,989 on property #1 at the end of year 7.

Had we done the cash-out refinance on our first property at the end of year two, our new total gain would be reduced to $131,300 at the end of year 7. At that point, doing the cash-out refinance would have cost us an estimated $35,689 in gains.

However, because we did the cash-out refinance, we could buy property #2 five years earlier than if we had just tried to save the money we got from the refinance. On our second property, over the first five years, we would have had an estimated gain of $72,266. Plus, our property #1 gains of $131,300 for a total of $203,566.

In essence, we gave up $35,689 in gains on property #1 to receive $72,266 in gains on property #2, for an overall extra gain of $36,577. By doing the cash-out refinance and purchasing a second rental property five years earlier than by just saving the money for the down payment, we made an extra $36,577. You can see how powerful this can be by doing it just a few times. This is a conservative view, as we used modest appreciation gains of only 3% and had our interest rate actually increase when we did the cash-out refinance. We would have made even more if appreciation was higher and/or interest rates lower.

If we want to look at it as a percentage of return on the money we put up over the seven years, this is how that would have looked:

If we only purchased property #1, we would have put in $75k of our own money and received back $166,989. That is a return on our cash, over the seven years, of 44.9%.

Had we done the cash-out refinance and added $25k of personal money to assist in the purchasing of property #2, our total gains would be $203,566 with an investment of $100k total. That gives us a return of 49%. Our overall cash returns, and our return on our investment returns were higher by doing the cash-out refinance. If we were able to pull out more than the original $56k via the cash-out refinance, the return on our investment would be even higher because we would have needed less of the extra $25k to complete the purchase of property #2 and thus, our total cash in would be less, but our gains would remain the same.

Some may be wondering why I didn't show the down payments we put into the properties as gains when we sell, and that's because getting our down payment back is not a *gain*. You're just moving it from your bank account into a house and then from one house to another via the COR. Also, during the cash-out refinance, we'll get less of our down payment back from property #1 because it was rolled over into property #2. In our example, we took $56k out of property one, and after closing costs of $6k, we put $50k into property two. We accounted for that $6k as a cost, but otherwise, we just moved money from one asset to another; there was no gain or loss on that money, thus not noted.

Other financial and leverage options, such as paying cash for the entire property, using the tax code 1031 like-kind exchange method, or the BRRRR strategy are all options to consider. We'll talk more about these later when we discuss long-term strategies, but they are sometimes less common for the first-time investor.

I want to make it abundantly clear that I understand learning some of these financial tools to purchase and leverage real estate may seem overwhelming at first, but if you feel that way, please go back and read this chapter a few more times before moving on. The best investors know when to press pause and try to learn more about a particular concept before jamming more information into their heads. In the examples we did in this chapter, we were fine-tuning them down to the dollar, and while that's important, I would encourage you to worry less about where each dollar came from and more so focus on the concepts of these financial tools and when they may be applicable to implement.

It's usually the lack of education and fear of a mistake that nudges investors into those comfort zones of financial options that are more commonly understood. It is not uncommon for novice investors to focus more on the real estate asset itself and less on the financial tools used to obtain that asset. Throughout my years of teaching, it has always amazed me how many investors just automatically assume a 30-year fixed mortgage is always the best loan option and that saving another 20% down payment is the only growth strategy. These loan options, leverage strategies, and even tax code opportunities exist to be utilized.

Lastly, and possibly just as important as anything else in this chapter, don't presume your mortgage lender knows how all these various options work either. Money is notoriously one of those subjects often spoken about by people who don't truly understand how it works. Don't take advice from people on subjects about which they know nothing. Learn these tools for yourself and make your own decisions, as it's the only way to feel confident in your portfolio. You may not always be right, but I'd rather be wrong while trusting myself than leave these big decisions up to someone else with no skin in the game!

At the end of the day, you cannot make these final decisions confidently without a clear goal for the actual property and a long-term vision for your overall portfolio with a timeline that ties it all together. This goes back to having *measureable goals*. The most significant factor in these financial decisions revolves around the *element of time* and if you don't have some sort of idea about time as it relates to your goals and portfolio, making educated financial decisions is next to impossible.

Chapter 6 - *How to run a complete cash flow*

Properly forecasting cash flow is one of the most important parts of owning rental properties. Without cash flow, it's like owning a business where you sell something but don't make money on the sale. At their core, rental properties are pretty simple - you're selling temporary housing. The 'temporary' here is subjective – it could be as short-term as a weekend stay or as long-term as a ten-year tenancy contract, but at the end of the day, it's always temporary because the tenants don't own the property. On the surface, cash flow is a very simple calculation:

Tenants' paid rent - owners financial obligations = cash flow.

It's the part of the received rent that the owner keeps after paying off other expenses.

This is probably, single-handedly, the most written-about or talked-about part of rental properties - and rightfully so - as it can have the most immediate impact. Despite being the main focus in various books, blogs, podcasts, and social media posts, cash flow is not the end-all, be-all for real estate investing. As I explained earlier in chapter 2, there are a few great benefits to owning residential rental properties, but cash flow is the most immediate, most consistent, and least impacted by outside market conditions. For instance, while the value of my rental property may go up and down based on supply and demand, economic conditions, and various other factors, it does not immediately impact me unless I'm selling it or using it as immediate leverage, nor is it always consistent. We also looked at the benefit of principal paydown of the mortgage and equity in the home. Both of those are great items and are typically subject to less of an impact by outside market conditions. However, they're usually not an immediate benefit to me, either. Those benefits show up at the time of sale or time of pursuing a leverage strategy, such as a cash-out refinance. In contrast, cash flow should be realized immediately, every single month. It also should be relatively consistent month after month after month. Yes, you will have vacancies from time to time, and yes, you may encounter a bad tenant every once in a while, but more often than not, your cash flow will remain consistent.

Every investor has different thoughts as to what they'll do with their monthly cash flow. Similarly, what you do depends on your long-term goals and timeframe. I reiterated in previous chapters about being able to make financial decisions based on your goals and time frames, and the same thing applies to your monthly cash flow. Here are just a few examples of how investors use their cash flow:

1. Pay down their mortgage/debts faster by applying cash flow to those balances

2. Set money aside to assist in making a down payment and the money needed to buy their next property

3. Live off of it as they would income from a normal job, i.e., they use it to pay their day-to-day bills. Typically, this is when you have enough properties or cash flow to almost completely rely on real estate investing as your main source of income.

4. Waste it. Give it to a fancy restaurant, hand it over to an airline for a 1st class seat, or pay for a much nicer car than they need – you get the idea. As you can imagine, the list in this category goes on.

The point is the best investors *find a way for their money to make them money*. They don't just fill their barrel but search for ways to add another hose to that barrel.

Based on your goals and timelines, you should be assigning your cash flow to a particular place every month. Just as if you owned a store and sold a product, you'd use that money to go buy more products for you to sell; it's the same idea. If this isn't on your agenda, it's a quick way to slow down your business's growth.

Now, let's look at how to run a complete *forecast* for cash flow, starting with the simplest and going down the line. One of the most important things to remember when running cash flows is that there are expenses that may show up annually, or even every few years, that don't show up on a monthly basis. So if you run a singular monthly cash flow, you won't get the annual cash flow by simply multiplying that value by 12. On an annual basis, I may encounter things like a vacancy in between tenants, repainting of a room or two, possibly some deep cleaning, or even HVAC servicing. Every few years, I may encounter a larger expense, such as a new HVAC, water heater or roof, a paint job for the entire property, or all-new flooring. When we run cash flows, we need to understand the entire picture. This way, we're also setting aside some of that money to use later for expenses that pop up every few years.

Luckily, running cash flows is typically much easier than using some of the previous financial tools we looked at. Nevertheless, it's important that you understand those concepts because one of the biggest expenses within the cash flow equation is typically your complete mortgage payment. It's hard to run an efficient business if your largest debt is structured inefficiently.

Let's run a full cash flow analysis. Once again, don't get lost in the price point or rental amount of the home. The price and other expenses of the home are interchangeable. This is all about learning and understanding the concept and formulas. Also, in our example, we have some early appreciation factored in, but by no means is it mandatory. If your rental home comes with some early appreciation opportunities, great, but if not, that doesn't mean it's a poor investment at all.

Here is our sample house breakdown:

Purchase Price:	$375,000	Down payment:	$75,000
Mortgage Amount:	$300,000	Down payment %:	20%
Purchase Costs:	$5,000	Interest rate:	4.75%
P&I Payment:	$1,565	Upfit Costs:	$15,000
PITI Payment:	$2,096	Property Taxes & Insurance:	$531
Rents for:	$2,800		

If we rent it for $2,800 and our PITI (principal, interest, taxes, insurance) is $2,096, then it looks like we'll be making $704 per month.

For this example, we really just need the loan & rent numbers. We'll also presume that the $531 per month in taxes and insurance were made up of an annual tax bill of $4,887 and a homeowners insurance annual bill of $1,485. This is where I get pushback from investors in different markets who say their property taxes are much higher, or some that say they are lower, etc. To them, I say: learn the concepts of cash flow, then plug and play your market numbers.

I did not utilize a property management fee for the sole reason that many novice investors I work with, who start out only owning 1-3 properties, typically manage the homes themselves. We'll talk about property management later in the book, but that monthly fee typically ranges from 8-10% of rent collected per month. In this example, you have to pay a fee of $224-$280 per month, which is taken from the $704 on a monthly basis.

I don't know many people who would gripe about an extra $704 per month in their pockets. And, if you remember, between the down payment, initial closing costs, and upfit money, the 'all in' amount to buy this home was $95k, so getting $704 per month on an invest-ment of $95k would equal out to almost a 9% return on just your cash invested. Again, pretty stellar returns. On the surface. That 9% is cal-culated like this:

Gross monthly cash flow: $704

Annual gross cash flow: $8,448 ($704 x 12)

Money all in to purchase: $95,000 ($75k down payment, $20k in costs/upfit)

Return on our money: 8.89% ($8,448 / $95,000)

Anyone who has ever owned a rental property knows that there is so much more to the picture than this very quick monthly gross cash flow.

One of the ways that investors screw up their forecasted cash flow when starting out is improperly assessing the following items:

❖ What will my vacancy look like?

➢ The property will not be rented 365 days a year from the day I buy it until the day I sell it; therefore, there will be times the home is vacant. During those times, I'll have the following items to address:

145

- No rental income during that time

- Be responsible for paying the PITI payment

- Be responsible for maintaining utilities

- Be responsible for any yard maintenance that a tenant may normally address

❖ What expenses will I see on an annual basis that doesn't show up on just one monthly cash flow statement?

➢ When repairs happen, they typically don't happen every month. They occur randomly, so repair expenses will be higher during some months

➢ Annual maintenance items, such as cleaning the gutters, having the HVAC serviced, or any other one-time per year expenses

➢ Any marketing costs to find the next tenant or expenses I incur when one tenant leaves and I'm preparing the property for the next tenant

❖ What amount should I set aside to start saving for bigger, long-term expenses?

➢ Installation of big-ticket items, such as a new HVAC system, new roof, new hot water heater, appliances, etc. can take place, and we need to be saving for those future expenses all the time

> ➢ What about larger expenses like all-new interior home paint or all-new carpet every few years

> ➢ General home maintenance that can cost money but not necessarily add value, such as large tree pruning or asphalt driveway resealing every few years

> ➢ Large ticket items don't discriminate, so it doesn't matter if you own one home or a hundred; things break for everyone

Let's look at each one of these individually to better understand how our monthly cash flow statement will differ from our annual one.

Vacancy Estimates

Early on in your real estate investing career, you may believe that vacancy is out of your control and is just a pure cost of the rental property-owning business. I don't disagree with that completely, but there are factors that the landlord controls that may impact vacancy. Generally, two factors impact your vacancy rates. The first involves what you are doing within your control that *makes your home more or less desirable*. The second factor involves what the economic *rental market is like in your housing market*. At the time of writing this book, the national average vacancy rate is less than 9% and can be much lower in specific regions of the country. During the economic recession of 2008-2011, some parts of the country were pushing almost 13-14% rental vacancy, while other parts of the country were hovering closer to 6-8%. Those ranges can vary based on your particular market. As we move forward, I would encourage you not to use national statistics for your estimations but to really try to learn your local market. The more accurate and educated you are when it comes to your market, the better financial decisions you can make. You'll practice more accurate portfolio management, too.

Obviously, we cannot control the rental market in regards to vacancy averages, etc., but what can you control in regards to vacancy rates? There are several actions directly within your control that can impact vacancy. Here are a few:

1. The rental amount you're charging is an obvious factor in how long you may have a vacancy. What's interesting to me is that when an owner of a property goes on to sell their home, they seem to do quite a bit of research on what the best price would be. Most understand there is a fine line between maximizing their sales price but not pricing so high that their homes sit on the market for too long and become 'stale' to the general masses of buyers out there. However, when it comes to pricing rental homes, the process is less methodical or researched among many investors. Instead, they rely on online algorithms. These are by companies that don't know the nuances of the market, and they never see the property either. Just because a renter may only plan to live in your rental home for a year or two does not mean they are not price-sensitive or not out there looking at other options. Those other options are your competition. While renters may be quicker to make a decision than someone who is buying a home, don't be fooled, they have typically looked at everything similar that is up for rent as well. Also, since tenants typically aren't planning on staying in the home long-term, they have a tendency to expand the range of areas they look for homes in. When potential tenants increase

their search area, it can actually create more competition for you since they're looking at other homes as well. If I was going to buy a home, I'd probably want to be close to my job, so my area to search may be narrowed down based on that factor, or possibly proximity to certain school districts. However, if I'm a renter and planning on renting for a year or maybe two, I'm more likely to be flexible on some of those factors and thus widen my search area.

Do your research on pricing, and I would suggest that you expand your search to cover a wider area than you initially considered. Also, when possible, actually go look at some of the competition in person. If you can't get inside the competitive properties, drive by some of them at the very least. We're so inclined to lean on the internet and what is shown to us that we just make quick decisions on what is nice and what is not as nice. Remember, those pictures and descriptions of houses are done by who? They are either done by an agent who is getting paid to make that property look as pretty and appealing as possible or by the actual owner who is trying to do the same thing. As you own more rental homes, you'll become more experienced in the finer nuances of pricing your properties, but in the beginning, nothing replaces doing the legwork. I advise clients to put on their "renter hat" and imagine 'if you're a renter, looking for a home, and there are ten homes for rent on the market, all within $100-200 of each other and all within a few miles of each other, what would make you want to pick your rental home?' Price will be a major factor in that as it relates to condition, which brings me to my next point.

2. Investors tend to underestimate how big of a role the condition of a property plays in a tenant's decision and, consequently, the chances of ending up with vacant property. I know many landlords who keep their properties in minimally decent condition – just good enough to live in. That strategy is typically for one of two reasons. The first is that they are just cheap. Plain and simple - cheap. In my opinion, they are missing the bigger picture, the impact that the quality of their home may have on tenants and thus lower vacancy rates, but also long-term effects on the property. Personally, I like to keep all my properties in relatively great condition because I never know when an opportunity of an unexpected sale may present itself. The better the condition you keep the home in, the easier it will be to sell at any time, and you'll need less cash put back into the property before making a sale. That is the selfish part of me as to why I keep the properties in great condition. The other reason that many landlords keep the properties in mediocre condition is simply that they *undervalue their tenants*. It's been my unfortunate experience that when talking with investors about tenants, I sense the presence of an unseen hierarchy of class in which the owner is better than the renter. Obviously, that couldn't be further from the truth. There are many times investors have this misconception that the renter must be *forced* into being a renter as opposed to *choosing* to be one. The old mindset of, 'if you're renting, you must have bad credit, or can't afford to buy,' or whatever other misinformation that has been spread around. The reality is many renters are *choosing* to be renters. In many circumstances, I know renters who make more money than their landlords and have a higher credit

score. If you apply the 'employer versus employee' mindset to the owner-tenant situation, I would strongly encourage you to change it. If we think back to our previous analogy of running your rental properties as individual businesses and looking at them through different lenses, we'd see that the business owner is nothing unless they have customers who buy the products. They NEED the customers. And, if the store wouldn't be there, the customers wouldn't have a place to get their goods. Therefore, the customers NEED the store. Both are interdependent on each other, and there is a fine line between how they interact. Many landlords don't view their tenants that way and feel they are better than them. It's sad but true. I do see that mindset changing some, but not completely yet. That's another reason why some landlords don't properly invest in the condition of their rental homes. If they did, they could probably charge more in rent and reduce vacancy rates, as well as the added bonus of always having more options on hand for a quick sale while requiring less cash to do so when ready to sell. Some landlords will say that they don't want to make the property nice because a tenant will destroy it, and if that's their experience, they are doing a poor job of qualifying their tenants. Over 95% of my tenants treat the home like their own. People want to live in nice places. They want to invite their friends and family over to a nice home. One final comment as it relates to the mentality of how tenants may treat the property: please look around your own home. Do you have some scuffs on your walls? Maybe the occasional carpet stain? Maybe your stove is a tad dirty? Maybe some grout and tile that could be cleaner, or maybe the tub could use a deep clean? The point is, sometimes we get so quick to judge a tenant because they're a tenant, yet they're not too different from us and our own homes. To conclude, the home's condition will directly impact pricing and vacancy, but is often overlooked or undervalued.

3. Another important factor within your vacancy analysis is how you structure your leases. Different investors have different thoughts on lease structures as they relate to the length of time. Some are fine with initially signing longer-term leases, even though that could mean not increasing rents over the course of that time. Meanwhile, others prefer more traditional leases on a yearly basis so that they have the option to increase rents annually. The longer your lease, the less vacancy you incur. It's a fine balance of having a long enough lease to reduce vacancy but also keep rents up with market values. The best investors will aim to sign longer-term leases with automatic increases built in them. You'll want some increases to keep up with increases in property taxes, insurance, and HOA dues. Of course, if you have any sort of adjustable loan like we've previously mentioned, watching that clock is imperative as well. When you sign leases with very long terms, such as several years, you are doing so with a tenant you don't know. Obviously, you're qualifying them and going through that process, but at the end of the day, you don't know for sure how they will turn out. It's like signing up for a long-term relationship on a first date!

There is a happy medium between short and long-term leases if your main concern is that you'll miss out on increases in market rent value by signing long-term leases. You can add an automatic increase built into your lease. Let's say you have a tenant who wants to sign a 3-year lease. Some reasons why someone may want to sign an initial long-term lease is they are going to be there with a job for a few years, or they have a child starting high school, and they want to ensure that they finish school in the same neighborhood. There are many reasons why someone would want to stay put for a while. In this case, we can structure a 3-year lease with various prices. So, from months 1-12, rent would be $2,200, then from months 13-24, rent increases to $2,250, and finally, from months 25-36, rent would be $2,300. The best thing about this type of structure is that the tenant is aware of these increases up front; there are no surprises, and you've hedged yourself against increases in your taxes, insurance, and possibly HOA dues to the tune of an extra $600 each year. Had you signed a 3-year lease at $2,200, you would have had total rents collected of $79,200 over the three years, but with the built-in increases, you'd end up collecting $81,000 over those three years with that simple tweak. When I use this strategy, I like to be reasonable with the rental increases I require. If you get too aggressive, you may scare a good, long-term tenant away from wanting to sign a longer lease. So you're opting for a fine blend of rental increases and lowered vacancy.

4. You also have some control over your relationship with your tenants. Most of us have been renters in our lives at some point, and maybe, in our younger years, we weren't the best of tenants, but we've also experienced different types of landlords and property managers. Maybe you're one of the lucky ones who always had great landlords, but the reality is that most of us have come across a not-so-great landlord before, too. So,

how does my relationship with a tenant as a landlord affect vacancy? The way you handle repairs is a huge factor. The way you communicate with your tenants is very important. If you can make a tenant feel like the home is theirs and not just a rental, they have a tendency to stay longer simply because they become more comfortable. The reality is people are less likely to seek out change if they are comfortable with their current situation. Here are some things that I personally do:

a. I always fix any requested repair items on time. Even if the repair request may seem minor to me or even annoying that it was requested in the first place, I always address it quickly. This not only makes them happy, but it also shows that I'm serious about what I do. Being serious about repairs shows them I care about my asset because if I don't fix the items, the tenant may think, "if the owner doesn't care, why should I?" It also lets them know that I'm not an absentee type of owner, i.e., I'm going to be involved because I'm serious. I am going to be equally serious about collecting rents on time and how you maintain the property.

b. When tenants move in, especially if they are from out of town, I usually get a small gift card to a local restaurant with a little note of gratitude for them choosing my property to rent. If they have a pet, I usually get a small bag of pet treats too. It gives them the 'warm and fuzzies' right away on day 1 and welcomes them to a new home, new neighborhood, and new landlord. They usually start out with a positive attitude towards their landlord, and when you like someone, you're less likely to destroy their stuff. If you dislike your landlord, you probably won't care as much about the property itself.

c. I remember their birthdays too. A simple text message or email to them on their birthday, just acknowledging their special day, goes a long way. Again, I'm trying to continually form a positive relationship. Too many landlords feel that there needs to be animosity between them and the tenant, and I wholeheartedly disagree. You can be firm and still nice in business. With that said, I'm not a pushover, and you shouldn't be either.

d. I have the HVAC serviced, gutters cleaned, and large trees trimmed back on a regular basis. This is a benefit to me as the owner, of course, but it also, once again, shows them I care about the asset. I'm not going to let my gutters look like crap in the fall and overflow with wet leaves. I'm not going to run the HVAC into the ground and not maintain it. And I'm certainly not going to have large tree limbs hang over the house or tenants' cars. These little acts of routine maintenance help tenants enjoy the home even more and have pride in where they live. Many tenants don't want to have friends and family over if they are embarrassed about the way their home looks. HVAC servicing can also help them keep utility costs low. Plus, I offer to connect them to someone to manage the yard or blow the leaves. I rarely pay for those services myself, but I will help coordinate them.

These items I just mentioned are relatively minor expenses and take up little time but can go a long way in making the tenant feel comfortable and building a positive relationship with you. And when you have someone who thinks fondly of you and is comfortable in the home, they are less likely to want to move, plain and simple. This directly relates to my vacancy rates.

As far as the things I can't control that affect my vacancy rate; those fall into several categories. The first is what the competition is like. Are there 5 other homes for rent in a similar price range/location, or are there 25? Obviously, the more there are, the harder it may be to find a tenant. I can't really control the number of other homes up for rent at the same time, but I can adjust my property to be more competitive.

Besides impacting my vacancy rate, the amount of competition also affects how much rent I can charge. If there is more competition, it may impact what I can charge. Of course, it goes in the opposite direction when there is very little supply of available homes on the market. Things like the local unemployment rate and how the economy is doing can impact my vacancy as well. If people aren't moving as often due to the economy or fear of job security, I may end up with a vacant home for a longer period of time. Even though these are all things outside of my control, they shouldn't be ignored.

How should we forecast vacancies? If rents are $2,800 per month and we had a full month of vacancy between tenants, our vacancy rate would be as follows:

$$\$2,800 \: / \: (\$2,800 \times 12 \text{ months}) = 8.3\%$$

That rate itself is currently at the higher end of our particular market average, but when you think about it, having one month of vacancy between tenants is not absurd by any stretch. I typically forecast about 1-month vacancy between tenants and adjust accordingly if the market is hotter/colder during that time. If I have a 2-year lease signed, I will skip that month of vacancy when the lease moves past year 1 into year 2, so my forecasting *before* I find a tenant may change *after* I have the tenant in place with a confirmed lease length.

Our numbers on an Annual Cash Flow Statement will start to come together and look like this over a single 12 month period:

Rents collected per month: 11 of 12 months of collecting $2,800 = $30,800

Utilities I carry during that month of vacancy = $250

PITI paid for the 12 months of that year: $2,096 x 12 months = $25,152

You can already see how our preliminary monthly cash flow statement of $704 has been adjusted. *With just estimated vacancy factored in, our estimated annual cash flow of $8,448 ($704 x 12) had been adjusted down to $5,398 ($30,800 - $250 - $25,152)*

Now, let's move on to another item to analyze within our annual cash flow statement - repairs, maintenance & capital expenditures.

Repairs, Maintenance & Capital Expenditures

Just like you'll need to forecast for an estimated vacancy, you'll also need to do the same for repairs, maintenance, and future capital expenditures. I break our repair expenses down into three categories. The first is your run of the mill, unexpected repairs, such as the toilet won't stop running, the microwave broke, or a towel bar falling off the wall. The second category is what we call Capital Expenditures. Those are larger expenses that you should constantly be saving for. You'll need it when your HVAC system dies or the home needs a hot water heater replacement. Or things like a new roof or replacing really old appliances. In this category, I also add big changes like repainting the entire inside of the home or replacing all the carpets, things that I don't typically do every year, but rather every few years. These are typically larger expenses, some of which can add value and should only occur every few years at most. The life span of these items should be relatively lengthy. As for maintenance, our third category leads back into some of the things I've previously mentioned, such as having the HVAC serviced, gutters cleaned, etc.

Let's go over your basic repairs and how to forecast. Some property owners have a mindset that pushes them to put as little money into the property as possible, so they just address repairs as they pop up. Personally, I think it's more efficient to be *proactive* versus *reactive* when it comes to these repairs. I'll purposefully go through the entire home between tenants and try to test all the plumbing fixtures and electric outlets and give a gentle tug on things attached to the walls. I run the appliances and really see what items are working properly or may cause an issue in the near future. Those items get addressed right away; I don't wait for a tenant to point them out or complain. If I can address them on my time, it is beneficial in several ways:

1. I don't have to add the extra layer of working around a tenant's schedule to get someone in the home. When the home is vacant, a contractor or handyman can just go any time

2. I have the ability to get multiple estimates or try to find ade-

quate pricing for the job at hand, or possibly even fix it myself if I'm so inclined

3. If I have to buy materials, it gives me the opportunity to look around for the best pricing on those

4. The tenant isn't upset, inconvenienced, or aggravated with the headache of repairs and access to the home

As you own more properties, you will appreciate the ability to bundle multiple repair items into a single day or two. If you can do that, it will save you from having 5-6 calls over the course of the year and losing some of the benefits I just mentioned to having them done up front. One of the items we talk about later in the book is about creating efficiencies within your portfolio. That means, how can we take care of things quicker, more affordably, and *on my time and schedule versus the time and schedule of the tenant?* Being proactive on these repair items helps become more efficient.

Some investors, especially ones that own many, many homes, have a tendency to apply a blanket percentage to their annual forecast budgets for general repairs. I've seen them range wildly from a guesstimate lump sum for repairs down to a percentage of rents or home value for repairs. If you ask 5 different investors how they forecast repair costs, you will probably get 5 different answers. Here are just a few I've heard investors say they use:

❖ Set aside 50% of your monthly rents for operating costs. Repairs are a part of operating costs, but it also includes other expenses like property taxes and insurance.

❖ Set aside 1% of the cost of the home for annual repairs. If the home is worth $300,000, then save $3,000 for general repairs annually.

❖ Set aside 10% of your monthly rent per month for repairs. If you rent the home for $2,800, then save $280 for repairs.

Honestly, I think most of them are just an 'easy out' instead of trying to really dial in some firm numbers. Admittedly, these are *variable costs, not fixed costs,* so no one knows for sure until the repairs actually happen. When you're working with variable costs, they are just that - variable. To be clear, for right now, I'm talking about just general repairs, not maintenance or saving for future capital expenditures. Once again, these are variable costs and not fixed, so we do have to talk in generalities because there is no way to be 100% accurate when forecasting for something that can vary.

The one I dislike most is saving 50% per month of your rental income for all operating expenses (variable & fixed costs). Maybe your operating expenses do end up being close to 50%, but the reason I dislike it is simply because of its large generality. If you don't have each category broken out, how can you ever become more efficient? How can you save money and increase cash flow? How can you improve your forecasting in the future as you grow if you're always just using 50%? Think about when you pay federal income taxes out of your paycheck; maybe you use an overall figure such as 30% for taxes. There are several items that make up the overall 30% and understanding what they are and how your situation or income affects those percentages is the only way you can try to structure your taxes in a way that saves you money. Part of that 30% for income taxes is made up of estimated taxes owed to the IRS, plus some for social security, some for medicare, etc. Your accountant may say, "just save 30%," and that may be fine for day 1, but if you're not diving deeper and saying, "what makes up that 30%?" and "what can I do to maybe bring that 30% to 25%" then you're doing yourself, and your wallet, a disservice. So, my main gripe about this 50% 'rule' is the overall generality and total lack of detailed information. Too many forecast models aren't detailed enough because landlords don't take time to do it. Force yourself to really think about the operation of these homes as a business and look at all the costs.

The more commonly used 'rule' I'll talk about is applying a percentage for repairs, as it relates to the sales price or value of the home or even as it relates to the gross rents. A typical example would be to save 1% of the home's value or 10% of gross rents. So, if the home is worth $300,000, I would want to set aside $3,000 per year for repairs. If the home was rented for $2,800, I'd want to save $280 per month or $3,360 for annual repairs. By the way, when saving based on price, some will say to save based on the purchase price, and some will say to save based on the value of the home. The purchase price will always remain the same, while the value will fluctuate, so if you choose to use this model, distinguish between the two as time goes on. My main issue with these methods is that in no way is price or value related to repairs. The thought process behind this is usually that the price relates to the size of the home, and the size of the home may be closely related to the number of repairs (larger house = more repairs). In reality, that very well may not be true. Think about where you live: is it more expensive to live near the part of town that's close to more restaurants, shopping, highways and good schools? Does that 2,000 sq. ft house cost the same as a 2,000sq.ft house out in the country, away from all those things? The answer is probably no. But aren't they both still 2,000sq.ft. homes made with the same 2x4 walls, same siding, and same roof? The difference impacting your price isn't the structure – it's the location. You're paying more within that purchase price for the land, not the structure. Yet, with this *rule* focused on price, you're losing sight of the actual structure. That 2,000sq.ft house in the country may cost me $250,000, and the 2,000sq.ft. house closer to those more desirable amenities may cost $400,000, but they're both still 2,000sq. ft. In one example, I'd be saving $2,500 per year for repairs, and in the other, I'd be saving $4,000, yet the actual structure that would impact repairs is relatively identical. The same goes with rental amounts; the one closer to the amenities will probably rent for much more, with no relation to the physical structure, yet if I used the '10% of gross rents,' I'd be saving two different amounts for the same structure. Another thing I'm not a fan of with these general calculations is that there is no breakdown of the number of bathrooms, the age of appliances, or any of those items that will be more likely to incur repair expenses. A home with multiple bathrooms or extra appliances (if the home has a dishwasher, microwave, washer, and dryer) will incur more expenses typically than homes without them. These general price/rent rules typically don't account for those items.

Each one of these *rules* can be picked apart for its own deficiencies, and again, for investors who own a lot of properties, applying a general rule works great because the time invested in analyzing each property each year would be pretty time-consuming. The issue comes in when beginner investors, who own maybe 1-5 homes, start to apply these general rules that were created by investors who own 10-50 homes. There is a disconnect that is created, but rarely spoken about.

Now that I've dismantled some of the more common forecast models, you may be asking yourself how I suggest you do it. I like to break my forecasts down into two models. The first is the one I do when I'm buying the home and have no past experience with the home. This is a forecast because I really don't know how the home will perform quite yet. Then, the second is for year two and beyond. That is when I do have some knowledge of the home under my belt and know where the home seems to have deficiencies. Keep in mind that we're looking at this from the perspective of the beginner to intermediate investor who doesn't own a bunch of homes yet. These methods can be a tad more time-consuming, but I think it's more accurate and worth the learning curve it entails.

Let's examine a better way to forecast repairs for year 1 prior to you owning the home for any real length of time. As we progress through this, it is important to remember a few things. As previously mentioned, this is a variable forecast with some unknowns. Also, and a possibly more important item to keep in mind, is that with any forecasting model, where you are starting from is critically important. For instance, when you bought the home, did you have a home inspection done and address the majority of the items already, or have you done very little research into the structure and fixtures and don't know what could be wrong with the house. If you fall into the latter category, then I hate to say it, but it almost doesn't matter what forecast model you use. That's because, honestly, you have no real idea of where you're starting from. Since I address as many items within the house as I can prior to anyone moving in, it means I'm doing that due diligence & research on the property. My forecasting models all start with the home having its fixtures and systems in *good working order*. No house is perfect, but when starting with my forecasting, I typically don't have obvious repairs on my to-do list.

From there, for year 1, I prefer to use a method that is still a 'percentage of value,' but I think it will be more accurate than some of the previously mentioned methods.

3) Use a percentage of the <u>building value</u> (remove the estimated value of the land). Don't worry about having to be extremely accurate on the land value, but do assign it some sort of value, which helps reduce some of that location issue I spoke about. You may use a purchase appraisal, tax assessment, or another source to guesstimate the value of the land. Previously, I showed an example of where two houses of the same size, bath & bed count, etc. were priced dramatically different based on location, so if I applied a universal repair percentage off of just the price, one would be way higher than the other, yet the homes themselves were the same. If we used that same example, but this time had removed the value of the land from the equation, now we'd be looking at just the homes themselves, and thus, they would be equal, irrelevant of location and its value. When you remove the land aspect, you may have to increase the overall percentage applied.

The example we looked at had one home at $400k close to town/amenities and one that was $250k but was further out, both with the relatively same 2,000sq.ft home on them. If the lot value on the home near town was worth $215k, then the building structure would actually be worth $185k. If we're using a percentage applied to value, I think it's more accurate to apply it to the $185k. If we look at the $250k home out in the country, where the lot value was maybe only worth $75k, then that home structure value would be $175k, and the percentage of repairs should be applied towards that amount. What we've done is more effectively focused on the home structure itself, which is where the repairs are most likely to happen. If we used one of the more common methods, such as the 1% of value, we would have had either a $4,000 repair budget or $2,500 for the same home. Now, with this revision, if we use these numbers and use 1%, the numbers would be $1,850 or $1,750 – you see, we've gotten much tighter within our range and tightened up our forecasting. The next step is to now decide on what percentage of that revised structure value we should apply for repairs for year 1. Should we only do 1% of that new value, or 2% or 3%, etc.? Again, presuming the home is in good condition, I think our multiplier factors should be based on square footages. For instance, you may use a range like this:

Home Size	Multiplier
1,000 - 1,500 sq.ft.	1%
1,501 - 2,000 sq.ft.	1.25%
2,001 - 2,500 sq.ft.	1.5%

So, if we used the example of the home we just adjusted, which was 2,000sq.ft, and the value of the structures were $175-185k, then I would use the 1.25% multiplier for a forecast repair range of $2,185-$2,300 for this home. By making these tweaks, I've accounted for the size of the home, as well as have removed the value of the land, which can severely affect the end price of the home.

In my opinion, those two tweaks (remove the land value and adjust based on square footage) take less than 10 minutes to do and make your forecasting much more accurate.

If you're like me and really want to get nerdy about it, you can make adjustments for some of the following items (and these are just examples):

Property Factor	+/- to Multiplier
The HOA takes care of the exterior of the home	-.15%
Bathrooms or Kitchen renovated within past 2-3 years	-.10%
Plumbing fixtures work, but are very old	+.15%

These are just some of the examples for tweaks you can make, and your 'multiplier' would be adjusted accordingly to your market prices and the home. Again, they are just examples here. If I used the 2,000sq.ft home above, which was at a 1.25% multiplier, but the plumbing fixtures were really old, I may increase that first year's multiplier from 1.25% to 1.40%, and now I'd want to forecast saving for repairs in the $2,450-$2,600 range. If you're really well versed in the working parts of a home, you can take these ranges and actually allocate estimates of how much will go to various parts of the home so that you can compare at year-end what happened in reality. You may assign $300 of your estimate to plumbing, $250 to general handyman stuff (doors not closing, broken locks, towel bar falling, etc.), and so forth and so on. At the end of the year, you'd see how much of your overall repair budget was used, but also directly to what categories. The more specific you can forecast, the more accurately you can improve those forecasts in the future. Most of our goals won't be to own 10 homes, so having the mindset of making our few rentals run very efficiently becomes even more important because it reduces our margin of overall error.

For the example we're using here, I'm going to use the average of my previously mentioned range and will apply a $2,240 repair forecast for our cash flow.

For year 2 and beyond, I think the best investors start to use the numbers from year 1 to adjust their forecasts. You could still apply the same type of percentage of the value, but I think it would be wise to start adjusting your multiplier up or down based on the home's performance. Did you have more repairs than you thought in year 1? Did you discover that maybe the plumbing is causing more issues than you thought? Maybe your windows aren't working as great as hoped? You will now have a full year of someone living in that home and using it, so you should be able to adjust your forecast to become more accurate. Again, these are general repairs we're talking about, not basic home maintenance or saving for capital expenditures. You may choose to switch forecast methods after year 1 or 2 and scrap the 'percentage of' method and really dial in some actual category numbers for specific parts of the home. Whichever method you choose, at whatever time, I would encourage you to take the time to not just apply some percentage you heard on a podcast, read on the internet, or had your neighbor tell you, but rather actually sit down and think about the particular property. Just adding universal percentages implies that each home is the same or will operate the same, and that's just not true.

Let's see how possible repairs affect our cash flow. Here is what our numbers look like so far:

Rents collected per month: 11 of 12 months of collecting $2,800 = $30,800

- **Utilities I carry during that month of vacancy = $250**

- **PITI paid for the 12 months of that year: $2,096 x 12 months = $25,152**

- **Repairs throughout the year = $2,240**

Next, we'll look at general maintenance expenses. These are usually easier to forecast because they are items you are choosing to do proactively versus repair items which usually are items you have to do and don't get much notice of. There are a few general maintenance items I do on an annual basis. Here is that list and average cost:

Gutter cleaning & roof inspection	$125
HVAC servicing & inspection	$135
Termite inspection	$85
Yard maintenance	$150
Total	$485

Those 4 items usually run about $500 per year and are pretty consistent. These have nothing to do with a tenant moving in or out, even though I do these annually. These are irrelevant to the tenant.

Gutter Cleaning & Roof Inspection - In my market, we have huge oak trees, so leaves fall from October till early January, and when they are wet, they constantly clog up gutters. I have the gutters cleaned for appearance purposes but also to prevent overflow onto my foundation, backflow into the eaves, and any other issues that clogged gutters cause. I have a 'roof inspection' note as part of this too, but really it's just asking the gutter cleaner contractor to quickly check the roof for obvious issues, such as broken shingles or nail pops. I'm not a fan of getting on ladders to check, and there's no need to pay someone separately when they are working on the roof anyways. Several times, I've had a gutter cleaner point out an issue that I was able to address before the snow started sitting on the roof for long periods of time or any other issues occurred. Being proactive like this can save you a ton of money and time.

HVAC servicing - This one is actually one of the favorite multi-layered items I get done. It's multi-layered because I get a few things done for the price of 1!

❖ Obviously, HVAC servicing keeps the unit in good condition and can extend the life of one of the largest house expenses we could incur, so extra years of not having to replace an HVAC is money in my pocket.

❖ An 'up to par' HVAC that runs efficiently will typically keep the tenants' energy bills in a more expected range. I've had tenants move in and complain about energy bills, especially in older homes, so having an efficiently running HVAC can help with that. It gives me another reason to look after the tenant instead of saying, "oh well." If the bills are too high, tenants are bound to start looking for other places sooner, affecting my vacancy rate.

❖ If there is an issue with the HVAC, I'd much rather know in advance instead of needing to get an HVAC replaced in the dead of the winter or peak of the summer when HVAC techs are in high demand and price shopping becomes much more difficult. If I know I have an HVAC that won't be running for long, I can shop prices and vendors for a few weeks and save money as opposed to the HVAC dying on me during the July 4th weekend and putting me in quite a pinch! In that situation, I'd shop prices while I pay for my tenants to stay in a hotel while the HVAC is replaced, or I'd pay whatever price I get quoted from whoever can do the work that day. Being proactive here pays dividends!

❖ Another great perk to having the HVAC tech in the house is that it gives me another opportunity to have eyes & ears on the tenant. I always ask the HVAC tech to look around and report back to me on the condition of the home, etc. Just like the gutter guy checking on the roof saves me time; an HVAC tech checking up on the condition of the home does the same.

Termite Inspection - This one is pretty simple. In my particular market, we have bad termites, so instead of carrying an expensive annual warranty and servicing on the home, I simply get an annual inspection done for a fraction of the cost. If we don't have termites, there is no need to spend more. If there are signs of termites, they are typically new, making them easy to treat.

Yard maintenance - This one typically doesn't have any lingering expenses if I let it go too long, but I like to keep the yard cleaned up, so tenants appreciate the curb appeal of the home they live in. It's also, so the neighbors have less to complain about. Some neighbors just instinctively complain about living next to a rental, even when there's no reason. When I keep the gutters and roof looking nice and keep the flowerbeds and trees trimmed, the home ends up looking nicer than many of the neighboring homes. This typically just includes some fresh mulch and some light tree/shrub trimming. Many times, this is actually done every other year and not annually. Occasionally, we'll also have large tree limbs trimmed back for similar reasons, as well as safety. That is usually every few years, and I combine all my rental homes with one company to do the work at the same time and receive a discount for doing multiple properties at the same time.

Here is our cash flow when general maintenance is added:

Rents collected per month: 11 of 12 months of collecting $2,800 = $30,800

- **Utilities I carry during that month of vacancy = $250**

- **PITI paid for the 12 months of that year: $2,096 x 12 months = $25,152**

- **Repairs throughout the year = $2,240**

- *General maintenance = $485*

The last repair/housing category that we want to ensure we're setting aside for is Capital Expenditures or Improvements, otherwise commonly abbreviated as "Cap Ex." Just as we forecast for common repairs, we do the same for those larger ticket items as well, such as HVAC, roofs, water heaters, etc. And just as there are many inaccurate ways to forecast for common repairs, there are also inaccurate ways to forecast for Cap Ex. It can be estimated using a *percentage of rental revenue* or *percentage of property value,* or even just setting aside a *flat fee per month* that the owner "feels" will be enough. However, just as I said, we should take a few extra minutes when we analyze repair budgets, we should do the same for cap ex, and it's not that complicated. Just like with general repairs, we're making assumptions and, at the end of the day, may have a surprise tossed our way, but overall, we'll be more accurate.

Saving for cap ex can be one of the more challenging parts for new investors, especially investors who don't own a lot of homes yet or are taking their cash flows to reinvest, but it is critical that you do save accurately. Here is a simple example of how to save for cap ex.

Make a list of any items in your home that you think would cost more than a few thousand dollars to replace. The basics would be your

HVAC, hot water heater, roof, flooring, whole house painting, etc. Next, try to identify how old those items are and how long before they stop working. You'll never know for sure how long they will last, so this does require a little bit of guesswork based on how long those systems typically last and what condition they are currently in.

Presume your HVAC is 6 years old in your rental home, and we think we'll get a full life out of the unit of 18 years. If a new unit is $6,500 and we have 12 years left to save for it, then we need to set aside $542 per year, or $45 per month, to pay for that unit when the time comes. Whenever I go over this example, I usually get two questions:

1) What if I don't plan on owning the home in 12 years?

2) Is the cost of the HVAC unit going to be way more in 12 years than the $6,500 I may be estimating today?

I'll take the second question first. Yes, I do think that the cost of big-ticket items will increase over time, just as they do for other things. But hopefully, wherever you sit that cap ex fund to the side, it is earning some sort of return or interest in the meantime to help offset that increase. You don't need to put it into anything risky, but also don't just stuff it under your mattress. Any safe returns you can get on that money being saved is better than zero.

The first question is a little more challenging because it can be situational and unique to you and your market. If your plan is to only hold this home for 3-5 years and not get anywhere near the 12-year mark left for that HVAC, then skipping out on saving a full $45/mo is probably a reasonable thing to consider. There is a line between being too conservative and just hoarding all your cash flow and not reinvesting it. However, if you are going to be holding it longer, such as 8-10 years, keep in mind that your HVAC may still be working but will certainly be near the end of its working life by then. The next buyer purchasing that home, especially if we're in a buyers' market at that time, may want a reduction in the price or compensation for that large expense they are going to incur soon after purchasing the property. You may not be saving the full $45/mo once again under these circumstances, but please be smart about how you forecast your future sales price as they may be impacted by some of the cap ex items that are nearing the end of their life. And remember, if your goal changes in the meantime and you do choose to hold the home for longer than the 12 years, you'll have some catching up to do to pay for that future HVAC if you haven't been saving.

Please keep in mind that you should adjust your replacement costs for the individual house. For instance, the cost of a roof on a 3,000 sq. ft. house will be higher than a roof replacement on a 1,500 sq. ft. house, so make sure you're not using universal flat costs. Personally, I like to add things to my cap ex, such as flooring and complete paint every few years between tenants. I don't typically add that into my 'repairs' or 'general maintenance' account because I usually address these items in between tenants every few years, not every single year. Here is a sample cap ex schedule with a few extra items to give you a good idea of how to set one up:

Item	Estimated Replacement Cost	Years Left	Amount per month
HVAC	$6,500	12	$45
Roof	$8,000	17	$39
Hot Water Heater	$1,200	6	$17
Repaint Interior	$1,600	4	$33
New Carpet	$2,100	5	$35

This is just a *sample* of how you break down your cap ex schedule. In this example, we would want to set aside $169 per month to hit the above target replacements. Each home should have its own cap ex schedule. Keep in mind if you're saving $169 per month each year, you'll have $2,028 set to the side. If you don't need to use any of that money for a few years, you could easily have thousands and thousands of dollars set aside. My suggestion would be to consider investing these funds into relatively safe and liquid accounts but don't have them sit in a .01% basic savings account. I'm a fan of money markets or S&P dividend funds. Your personal financial advice should come from a professional in the field who takes your risk threshold into consideration, but as an investor in general, I would consider all options at hand to try and safely earn a higher rate of return on these savings. Even though you are setting aside that capital expenditure money for future use, your cash flow would be subject to annual taxes in the year you earned it because you haven't actually spent that money for capital expenditures yet. Once you actually incur the expense, such as installing the new roof or HVAC, there will be a tax adjustment for the expenditure or improvement and possible depreciation of that item.

Here is our updated cash flow statement:

Rents collected per month: 11 of 12 months of collecting $2,800 = $30,800

- **Utilities I carry during that month of vacancy = $250**

- **PITI paid for the 12 months of that year: $2,096 x 12 months = $25,152**

- **Repairs throughout the year = $2,240**

- **General maintenance = $485**

- *Capital Expenditure savings: $169.00 x 12 months = $2,028*

Gross cash flow to this point: $645

The only thing left to calculate is the money it costs to *turn* a property. When we say we're going to *turn* the property, we're talking about transitioning from one tenant to the next. Basically, the few odds and ends you may have to take care of between tenants. Typically, this is very minimal, especially if you really qualify and work with the best tenants who maintain the property. I also put in the lease requirements that the tenant will get the home deep cleaned and carpets steam-cleaned when they move out. Even still, there is inevitably some normal wear and tear that I'll have to have taken care of. These aren't items that would come out of a tenant's security deposit simply because they are considered *normal wear and tear*. Typically, I spend between $250-350 per tenant turnover. Remember, things like repainting the inside every few years, or new carpeting, etc., are put into my cap ex fund, so I'm continually saving for those bigger turnover items that occur every few years. If we use the average of the above range of $300, then our final actual cash flow looks like this:

Rents collected per month: 11 of 12 months of collecting $2,800 = $30,800

- **Utilities I carry during that month of vacancy = $250**

- **PITI paid for the 12 months of that year: $2,096 x 12 months = $25,152**

- **Repairs throughout the year = $2,240**

- **General maintenance = $485**

- **Capital Expenditure savings: $169.00 x 12 months = $2,028***

- ***Between tenant upfit = $300***

Gross cash flow to this point: $345

* *While we're setting aside $2,028 for future capital expenditures, if we did not actually spend any of this money on those expenses this year, the IRS will still tax us on that money. This $345 should be considered money that is not assigned to anything for the home.*

I realize that this cash flow, once broken down on an annual basis, along with the savings for the capital expenditure money, does not seem too exciting. Let's look at a better visual to see where the money is going; it can really help us when evaluating a new property and controlling expenses. I did not include the PITI payments in this graph because that expense is so large it would minimize the other expenses that we can control.

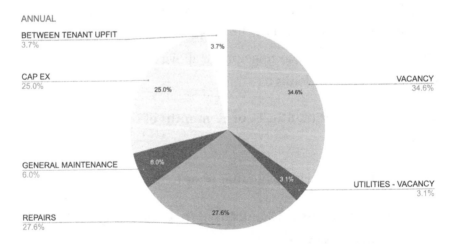

Many investors, writers, and people who sell various seminars and programs have a tendency to cherry-pick the best example of rental homes, so the numbers amaze you. All the while, when you actually go into the market to find those deals, you quickly learn that they are nearly impossible to find. This can include a true *needle in the haystack* or a property that needs so much work or has so much risk that the average beginner investor would not move forward with it. After talking to many novice investors, I came to realize many of them held off from ever really investing in real estate because they couldn't find those *needles in the haystacks* with amazing cash flows that they'd been told are out there in abundance.

Real estate investing requires a mind shift in many respects. Novice investors can be put in a tough spot where they want to learn and gain experience, yet a lot of information out there either does a poor job of being realistic or they focus on growing at an accelerated pace, which is beyond the comfort level of most beginner investors.

When I teach, one of my favorite analogies is a baseball one. I mentioned this earlier in the book, but I think it is worth repeating in this cash flow section. Less than 3% of all baseball games are won with a homerun, yet, those games get the most attention. I understand that when things have low odds of happening, they gain more notoriety. I'm fine with that in sports, but not as much in investing. I doubt that the baseball manager is coaching his players to only focus on walk-off home runs. Instead, they are coaching players on winning the game pitch by pitch, inning by inning. The boring way, if you will. We need to consider real estate investing similarly. While cash flow is important, please don't hang your hat on it as if it's the end-all, be-all. There are countless other benefits of investing that we've spoken about.

As for this cash flow example, please remember the cash flow forecast was just that - a forecast. It was done at the very beginning of the purchase. I mention that because cash flow should increase over time. Here are some variables that can quickly increase cash flow:

- ❖ **Lease terms** - the cash flow statement we just did looked at a 12-month time frame. The first month was vacant, and then we collected 11 months of rent for the remainder of that calendar year. What if we had our tenants sign a 2-year lease up front? If we duplicated that cash flow forecast over 2 years, we'd still only have 1 month of vacancy (the first month) but 23 months of rental income. Our overall cash flow would increase by the rental amount charged because we're not facing that month of vacancy in year 2.

- ❖ **Repair expenses** - repair expenses are a very large part of our cash flow, so being able to reduce them is critical to increasing our returns. To reiterate, I think spending more when you purchase the home for proper 'upfit' of the home and getting it in great shape is the easiest way to reduce expenses for repairs throughout the years. Furthermore, replacing broken fixtures and appliances when they are near the end of their useful life instead of continually pouring repair money into them can help reduce your long-term expenses. You may take an initial cost hit for replacement v. repair, but it very well may save money in the long run. It has been my experience that most tenants find the majority of 'broken' stuff within the first few weeks of living in a home. On my longer leases, my repair expenses typically drop off dramatically as the tenants live in the home for a longer period. Of course, things still break, but it seems as though tenants are looking for items earlier in the lease, and that dissipates as the lease continues.

A longer lease is another way to decrease those repair expenses because it reduces the number of new tenants you have in the property over time.

❖ **Rental increases** - you should definitely increase the rent in between tenants and, as I've mentioned, possibly have periodic increases built into your longer-term leases. These rental increases, at a minimum, should keep up with market rents, all while still staying competitive, of course. At the very least, they should be equal to the increases in your property tax and homeowners insurance amounts and HOA increases, if applicable.

After owning a home for 1-2 years, most investors start to see that this forecast is pretty conservative overall, and their actual cash flow is actually higher. If you don't take the time to accurately forecast your expenses and properly identify the market rental range, your initial cash flow analysis may be useless, and you're at the mercy of reality once you get a tenant in the property. There is possibly no better time than now to reference the title of this book and what it means. *Plug the holes, fill the barrel.* If we visualize the rents we collect as the downspout filling up the barrel, and we consider the expenses we just went over as the holes in the barrel, then the objective to cash flow becomes pretty obvious. Simply put, plug the holes, fill the barrel.

Let's look at what the cash flow could realistically look like a few years into owning the home. Here are some variables that may have changed:

❖ Increased rents

❖ Increased expenses of higher property taxes and insurance

❖ Lower repair expenses

❖ Less vacancy

❖ Less between tenant maintenance

Let us presume that our year 1 forecast turned out to be very similar to the actual cash flow we received, but then in year 2, we had the following happen:

1. Our new tenants want to sign a 2-year lease. We structure the lease with an automatic increase at the end of their year 1 as they go into the beginning of year 2

2. At the beginning of these new tenants' leases, we were advertising a new lease price. We started rents with a 5% increase from $2,800 to $2,950. Within our lease agreement, they agreed to pay $2,950 for year 1, and in year 2, there was a modest increase of less than 3% to $3,025. This small increase gave them the security of them having the home for a full 2 years.

   On a side note, sometimes as landlords, we think that the tenants signing a longer lease is only helping us, when in fact, many times a tenant wants the security of spending some time in one place, so a modest increase (pending market conditions) can be easily accepted.

3. We also will see a 3% increase in our property taxes and insurance in both years, raising our initial PITI from $2,096 to $2,112, and then in the following year (year 3 of ownership), it goes up to $2,175. Remember, this is only an increase on the taxes and insurance portion of my PITI; the principal and interest amounts are fixed.

4. Since we are signing a 2-year lease, we only have our initial first month of vacancy to factor in, so we'll receive $2,950 less in our forecast.

5. We were factoring in $2,240 per year for expenses, but the reality is that over the 2 years of the lease, that amounts to $4,480. In my opinion, that's pretty high, considering you have the same tenant in place. I would lower our repairs down to something near $3,500 for that stretch of time. As we mentioned before, most of our tenant complaints are going to hit us early in the lease and should slow down during the remainder of the lease.

6. We will still incur the $300 between tenant upfit expense, but only once the two-year lease period is over.

7. We will still save the same $2,028 for Capital Expenditures and pay $485 for general maintenance every year.

If we do all of that, here is our cash flow schedule for 2 calendar years:

Month 1: Vacant - No rent collected
Month 2-13: Collecting $2,950 = $35,400
Month 14-24: Collecting $3,025 = $33,275
Gross rents = $68,675*

> **We still have 1 month of rent left to collect in the 2-year lease as the above only shows 23 months of rent collected. However, that last month will roll into the next calendar year, so it doesn't fit into the example of 2 calendar years.*

-   **Utilities I carry during that month of vacancy = $250**

-   **PITI paid for the first 12 months of that lease: $2,112 x 12 months = $25,344**

-   **PITI paid for the second 12 months of that lease: $2,175 x 12 months = $26,100**

-   **Repairs throughout both years = $3,500**

-   **General maintenance for both years = $485 x 2 = $970**

- Capital Expenditure savings: $169 x 24 months = $4,056

- Between tenant upfit = $300

Gross cash flow: $8,155 for the 2 years, or $4,077.50 on average per year.

Now, all of a sudden, with a few easily achievable adjustments to the length of lease, rents charged, and expense management, this same house has gone from a conservative up front cash flow forecast, to a very profitable rental home. This is very realistic to obtain. This extra cash flow also gives you the ability to hire a property manager so you can continue to grow your portfolio instead of personally managing them all. Our rental increases were modest enough not to discourage a tenant from signing, and we were able to reduce repair expenses over the course of 2 years, in addition to factoring in typical increases in tax assessments and insurance premiums.

When purchasing a home, I typically do a conservative forecast as we initially did but then evaluated how the home could perform in real-life situations if I manage it correctly.

Principal Paydown

While we have talked about our cash flow statement, we have not talked about a few other benefits that don't show up on a cash flow analysis but have a direct impact on your annual gains.

Those factors are principal paydown from the tenant and depreciation write-off allowed by the IRS. First, let's talk about the principal paydown because it can be very beneficial and impact your annual taxes.

Principal paydown is often one of the least spoken about benefits of owning real estate rentals, yet it can be one of the most impactful over time. While some owners may not realize the true value of this until they sell the property, other investors would not be able to complete a cash-out refinance without the principal paydown factor. Just like a normal mortgage on a personal home, every time you make a mortgage payment, a portion of it goes to interest and a portion to the principal. While the total payment of principal and interest may not change (based on interest rate/loan), the ratio of how much goes into those two stacks does. And it does so every single month. For instance, on our very first mortgage payment, only about 24% of the payment may actually go towards the principal and the remaining 76% towards interest. After 36 months, that ratio will look more like 28% towards principal and 72% interest. By the time you get to 10 years of that mortgage, the ratio is around 39% principal and 61% interest. Again, your payment never changed, but more and more is going towards paying down what you owe. It may seem like a slow process with small impacts, but they all add up in your favor over time. Even if your cash flow doesn't seem like a lot at first, you're still getting a continually increasing gain because the tenant is paying off what you owe. They are doing so at an increasing rate every month too.

We know from the cash-out refinance example that the more equity we have in the property, the easier it is to leverage that property to buy more properties. One of the factors in equity is the amount of your loan balance as it relates to the value. The quicker you can pay down that loan balance, the sooner you'll have enough equity built into the home to use as leverage.

Even though you pay down that loan balance every month, you don't actually receive that money in your pocket that day. The gain you get from the tenant paying down your mortgage is usually realized in your pocket later down the road when you sell the home or use it for leverage. However, the IRS says that you actually realized that gain when the mortgage payment was made and the principal paid down. Therefore, when the tenant pays you and you pay the mortgage, the part that goes towards principal is a gain to you today and therefore should be taxed this year. The good news is that because you pay tax on that principal paydown in the year it occurred, you don't pay it again when you sell the property.

Here is how that looks. We'll reference a previous example of us renting a home for $2,800 with a PITI of $2096 (this is for the $300k mortgage @ 4.75% interest). For that example, we'll look at the first calendar year when the home was vacant during the first month, so you didn't collect any rent, which also means that the tenant didn't start paying our mortgage principal for us until month 2.

Rents collected per month: 11 months of collecting $2,800 = $30,800

- **PITI paid for the 12 months of that year: $2,096 x 12 months = $25,152**

Of that $2,096, we knew that $1,565 was just principal and interest. However, what we did not break down was the principal and interest ratio individually. The interest part is an 'expense,' and the principal part is a 'gain.' Therefore, you need to break them down accordingly. It may not change the real dollars in your pocket every month, but there is a gain on an annual basis, and that is how the IRS views it, too. Let's break it down for year 1. Utilizing an amortization table, our first year's payment schedule would look like this:

Month	Payment	Principal Portion	Interest Portion	Loan Balance
~~1~~	~~$1,565~~	~~$377~~	~~$1,188~~	~~$299,623~~
2	$1,565	$379	$1,186	$299,244
3	$1,565	$380	$1,185	$298,863
4	$1,565	$382	$1,183	$298,481
⋮				
12	$1,565	$394	$1,171	$295,371
Total Principal Yr. 1		$4,629		
We paid month #1		-$377		
Principal *paid by tenant*		$4,252		

Since the home was vacant in month #1 until the tenant moved in, we only had 11 months of tenant paid principal to report for this calendar year.

You can clearly see that our P&I payment remains the same every month, but more goes towards principal than interest each month, too. Over the 11 months that the tenant was in the home, the total principal paid down was $4,252, and our borrowed amount of $300,000 has been reduced. That is a gain to us, even though we may not have that extra cash in our pocket at that time.

If we go back to our initial cash flow example where we were making $345 for the year, it now jumps to $4,597 by adding in that principal paydown from the tenant. Please note that I did not call that amount the *Taxable* Cash Flow because of our cap ex fund. While we're setting that money aside for future large expenses, if we didn't have any of those large expenses within this year, the IRS will still look at that money set aside as gains and, thus, subject to taxes. Our Taxable Cash Flow would add the savings of $2,028 for capital expenditures back in, and then, before the depreciation expense, would be $6,625 ($4,597 + $2,028).

As an investor, someone else paying your debts is clearly a benefit. I want to share with you a chart of how principal and interest change over time so you can visually see the progress and how it can amp up the returns on your rental property. This image is just the breakdown of principal and interest, irrespective of who paid the mortgage payment (you or the tenant)

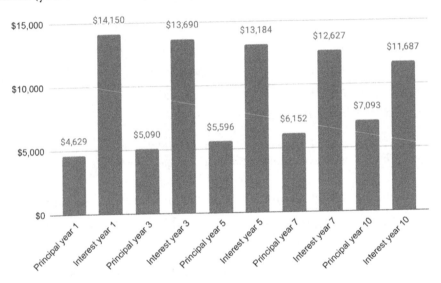

Depreciation

When investors talk about *tax benefits* from owning a rental property, they are typically speaking of things like *expense write-offs, reduced long-term capital gains tax rates, 1031 Exchange options,* and *depreciation.* The most commonly touted benefit is what we call Depreciation. Depreciation is a method in which you take the cost basis of your property and deduct a portion each and every year against the operating income. Depreciation is looked at as an expense. Of course, it's more complicated than one sentence, but the concept itself can be relatively easy to grasp in a few steps.

The IRS depreciation rules basically say that if you own an asset (*a house*) that you plan on putting into service (*using as a rental property for someone*), then you can depreciate parts of the asset that are depreciable (*whatever part of the property that has a determinable useful life*). The tail end of that last sentence is very important because when determining the cost basis for depreciation, you don't depreciate the land. Only the structure is depreciable. The reason is that the land has not been deemed to have a *determinable useful life*. In essence, a bucket of dirt today is the same bucket of dirt in 100 years. However, a home built 100 years ago has probably deteriorated in that time, and the materials have lost value. If you make land improvements that increase the value, then you may be able to depreciate those. Examples of land improvement could be hardscaping, patios, exterior lighting, sprinkler systems, and other similar improvements. Outside of the structure itself, any future capital expenditures/improvements you make, such as when you replace a roof or HVAC, etc., those items are typically considered _improvements_ and not _expenses_. Expenses, which are typically used as a tax write-off in the year it occurred, are not depreciated. New paint, for example, may make the home look nicer and even sell for more, but it is typically considered an expense, not an improvement, and is therefore not depreciated. Improvements to the home are usually depreciated just as the building structure is. Whether it's an expense or improvement classification, it will either be factored into your current year's operating expenses or end of sale gain calculations as a cost incurred and will be accounted for in some manner.

I'd like to be very clear that the categorization of what is an expense v. improvement is not always black and white. One investor or accountant may view it one way, while another may view it a different way. When the actual work occurs can be a factor in the improvement

v. expense decision as well. We can use window replacement as an example of something that may be classified as an improvement or an expense. Did you replace the windows right after you bought the home during the initial upfit renovations, or did you do them a few years after owning the home while it was up and running as a rental? My suggestion is that when you're doing your taxes and identifying expenses, improvements, and depreciation, consult a tax professional. Even though a capital improvement may be depreciated over 27.5 years, they don't all last that long. So, what happens if you pay $10,000 for a new roof and you start to depreciate it over 27.5 years, but then in year 20, you have to replace the roof again? You have not completely finished depreciating the full $10,000 at that time; you still have 7.5 years left. In that case, the remaining depreciable life could be treated as a possible expense on that particular year's tax returns.

There are a few checkbox rules that the IRS says have to be met in order to depreciate an asset:

❖ You own the property

❖ You are using the property in your business or as an income-producing activity (rental houses meet this criteria)

❖ The property has a determinable useful life (we just spoke about that)

❖ The property is expected to last more than one year (this is why you typically would not depreciate a buy-fix-flip property because you own it for less than a year)

Most residential rental properties meet the above criteria, so depreciation typically comes into play. Here are the 3 items that need to be established:

1. How long is the 'useful life?'

2. What method of depreciation to use?

3. What is the cost basis?

The first two questions are pretty easy to answer in most cases. Most investors use the method of straight-line depreciation over the course of 27.5 years. The straight-line method basically is as its name implies. Depreciation follows a straight line or equal amounts of the cost basis deducted each year. The 27.5 years actually comes from the IRS's General Depreciation System that gives the depreciation guidance of 27.5 years for the determinable useful life of the residential property. Depreciation may occur in different ways, and some people may benefit from other IRS-approved methods, but since the majority of real estate investors utilize the 27.5-year straight-line method, we'll speak about that here. Always consult your CPA for the best advice on your situation and property.

The third question that needs to be answered is a tad more challenging. In order to get our cost basis, we need to figure out this formula: *Our Purchase Price = Land Value + Building Value.* Separating the land value from the purchase price is not something that most buyers do when purchasing a home. For instance, if we bought our example home for $375,000, we typically don't offer the seller $125,000 for the land + $250,000 for the building. Instead, we just offer $375,000 for the entire package with no breakdown agreed to. Some loan appraisals may break down their opinion of land v. building costs, but many don't. There are various ways to establish the values for depreciation purposes. Personally, I use my local property tax assessment to help establish the value.

Each state, county & jurisdiction conducts assessments differently, but where I personally invest, our county tax assessor assigns our property a value for annual property taxes. In doing so, they break down their opinion of the land v. building costs to get the total taxable value. I utilize the calculations they provided when I purchased the home as my depreciation ratios. In my county, most times, the total tax assessment *does not equal* the purchase price. We'll assume at the time of purchase of this $375k house that the county had this breakdown:

Land value: $108,884
Building value: $249,993
Total value: $358,877

I'm not overly concerned with the actual value of their assessment, but rather, I want to capture the ratio of what they consider the building structure in the overall value. If they say the building value is $249,993 of a total value of $358,877, then the tax assessment office, which is an independent 3rd party, presents a building to a total value valuation of 70% ($249,993 / $358,877). One optional way to determine our cost basis for depreciation is to use that valuation from the tax assessor's office applied against our purchase price. Now that we have the 70%, we can apply it to our sample property.

$375,000 x 70% = $262,500 Depreciable Cost Basis

We noted that for residential rental property, using straight-line depreciation, depreciation would be spread out over 27.5 years. $262,500 / 27.5 years = $9,545 per year depreciation against our Taxable Cash Flow

If we said in our forecasted year 1, that including principal pay-down and cap ex savings, we would have a Taxable Cash Flow of $6,625 and can now write off the depreciation expense of $9,545, then our IRS reporting may look similar to this:

Gain	$6,625
- Depreciation Expense	$9,545
Net Loss to IRS =	- $2,920

For most new investors, it can be crazy to think that you can make actual cash flow from your rental, in addition to principal paydown, and still *possibly* take a loss on your taxes, according to the IRS. As your cash flow increases over time, this depreciation amount stays the same unless you add in capital expenditures/improvements that you may have to make, and that could increase the deprecation amount of $9,545 we've been using. This may seem too good to be true, and in some regards, it is. The IRS also has something called Depreciation Recapture that we'll talk about next.

Losses, Depreciation Recapture & Taxes

Depreciation recapture, losses, and taxes are individualized to each investor. Also, the tax code is ever-changing, so the scenarios I'm showing here are samples based on today's tax code and should only be used as examples to learn the concepts.

The first thing to look at includes the *losses* we just showed after taking depreciation. There are a few things to consider.

Since our homes are considered "Passive Income," our losses are also considered "Passive Losses." The passive losses are to be taken against passive income during the ownership of the home. So, if you have passive losses but no other passive income, you may not be able to take those losses *in the year they occurred*. Those losses don't disappear if you can't take them in one year just because you didn't have enough passive income. They become suspended losses to be incurred in the future against the passive income you may earn in years to come. If you sell the property and have suspended losses, you can usually apply those against the gains you may have on the sale of the property. For example, if you have two rental properties and one has a passive loss and the other has a passive gain in the same year, then you should be able to utilize a portion of the losses to offset a portion of the gains on the other. This works since both assets are considered passive.

There are some 'exceptions' to being able to write off those losses. If you "materially participate" in the rental properties, such as operating as a property manager or full-time real estate professional; or your job is to own, operate, and manage your rental properties on a level of at least 750 hours per year, then you may have a case to take those losses in the year they occurred even if you don't have enough passive income. The reason is that they aren't necessarily considering these losses/gains as *passive* because you are *actively* involved in them on a daily basis. But if you only own 2-3 homes and aren't in real estate full time, it will be tough to claim that it is taking 15-20 hours per week of active management.

Another possible passive income loss exception is your income level. Currently, if your Modified Adjusted Gross Income is $100,000 or less as a single person ($150k if married), you may deduct up to $25,000 in rental real estate losses if *you are actively participating in the rental activity.* Once again, that comment is not black and white in its meaning. If you're involved in meaningful management decisions and have at least a 10% ownership interest in the property, you may qualify for this exception.

I cannot stress enough how important it is to discuss all tax decisions with a CPA prior to purchasing rental property, especially if you feel that taking a passive loss would be beneficial to you. These rules can be tricky, often change, and not be very clear. I only point out these notes about losses because many investors talk about the tax benefits with real estate, and I want to make sure I'm at least touching on some of the most common benefits. Since the ability to write off some losses are tied to the level of your income, which can fluctuate, in one year you may be able to take a particular loss, and the next year, possibly not.

On to *Depreciation Recapture*. Do you remember that depreciation you took, the one that helped create that passive loss? You didn't think the IRS was just going to give you that because they were nice, did you? Well, they are gonna want some, if not all, of that back when you sell. As far as the IRS and rental properties are concerned, it's legal to forgo taking the depreciation. However, if you don't take it, you will still be charged the recapture tax in the future. In essence, you would be charged the tax on the benefit of the depreciation even though you chose not to take it. I'm not a tax pro, but I can't think of any reason why the vast majority of investors wouldn't take depreciation.

So, what is depreciation recapture? Essentially, the IRS says that when you sell a property that you have been depreciating, and you make a profit, that they are entitled to some of the expense write-offs you have taken due to depreciation over the years. It is recaptured because, during the life of the asset, it was used to offset income. Personally, I always consider depreciation as a loan from the IRS. During ownership, I get to use depreciation as an expense to help save on my taxes that year, and then when I sell it and depreciation recapture occurs, I pay it back to the IRS. Of course, the tax savings taken over the years may not equal the exact amount of taxes owed on the depreciation recapture, and that is because the expense savings over the years, as well as the depreciation recapture, are all taxed at your ordinary income rate, and that can change from year to year. Depreciation recapture is different from Capital Gains taxes. Capital Gains are based more on the appreciation factor and growth in value of that asset, while depreciation is based on the Adjusted Cost Basis after depreciation. Let's look at an example that may help.

Purchase price of our home: $375,000

Value at time of sale in 5 years: $435,000

Depreciation we took over those 5yrs: ($9,545 x 5 years) $47,725

Adjusted Cost Basis (Purchase Price - Depreciation) $327,275
($375,000 - $47,725)

Realized Gain (Final Sales Price - Adjusted Cost) $107,725
($435,000 - $327,275)

Of that Realized Gain, it is broken down into 2 parts:

1. Capital Gains: (Realized Gain - Depreciation) $107,725 - $47,725 = $60,000

2. Depreciation Recapture: 5 years of $9,545 per year of depreciation = $47,725

These two types of realized gains are taxed differently. Typically, capital gains that are considered long-term, i.e., you've owned the property for longer than 12 months, range in the 15-23% range. That range is based on income and other variables. Keep in mind that these are the rates at the time of writing this book, so they may adjust. Depreciation recapture is typically taxed at your ordinary income tax rate. Of course, you'll incur costs to sell the property, such as real estate commissions and possible state transfer fees that should all be deducted from your gains as they are expenses you incurred.

You may pay 15% on the $60,000, or $9,000 in tax for capital gains, and pay 28% on the $47,725 of depreciation recapture, or $13,363. This right here is why having a tax pro on your side is so important. Not only should you be prepared for the possible tax consequences of selling a property, as well as the annual rental income/loss part, but you'll want to have a long-term strategy in place when selling the properties. It may not always be wise to sell multiple properties in one year, or maybe you choose not to sell during time periods where your ordinary income rate may be at its peak. Being a smart long-term investor means having a tax component within your goals and plan.

Let's recap our cash flow analysis for our sample property over 1 calendar year:

Rents collected per month: 11 of 12 months of collecting $2,800 = $30,800

- Utilities I carry during that month of vacancy = $250
- PITI paid for the 12 months of that year: $2,096 x 12 months = $25,152
- Repairs throughout the year = $2,240
- General maintenance = $485
- Capital Expenditure savings: $169.00 x 12 months = $2,028***
- *Between tenant upfit = $300*

  Gross cash flow: $345

+ Add back in our capital expenditure savings that we didn't actually spend: $2,028

+   Mortgage Principal paid by the tenant: $4,252

Taxable Cash Flow before depreciation: $6,625

-   Depreciation of Cost Basis for 1 year: $9,545

Tax Reporting Cash Flow Gain/Loss: -$2,920

There are a lot of numbers and concepts to understand when running a true cash flow. Some are easier than others to forecast and understand, and some may need the help of a professional, such as a tax accountant. However, none of them should be so difficult that you can't grasp the main concept of them. I'd strongly recommend you go through this chapter thus far again to really understand the ins and outs of these cash flows.

Common Investment Calculations

There are other ratios and calculations that you will encounter along the way. Luckily, these shouldn't have anything to do with your taxes! Each investor is different, but having a basic understanding of these is important as you grow. There are many, many formulas in investing, but there are a few that are most common.

Net Operating Income (NOI), Capitalization Rate (Cap Rate), Gross Rent Multiplier (GRM), and Debt Service Coverage Ratio (DSCR) are the ones we're going to look at.

Net Operating Income - NOI is an easy way of looking at gross profitability. It's all of our revenue for a property minus the property's expenses within a year, except any mortgage or debt service.

First, add up your revenue. Computing the revenue portion is relatively easy - how much did you collect in rents during that year? If the home is rented for $2,000 per month and it was rented for 11 of the 12 months of this year, your revenue should be $22,000.

Second, add up your expenses. Operating Expenses can be fairly easy to calculate as well. However, there are a few things not added as expenses in the NOI calculation that you may still be paying. These are some of the items not included:

- ❖ Principal & Interest payments

- ❖ Capital Expenditures

- ❖ Depreciation

- ❖ Amortization when applicable

What is included in our Operating Expenses? Here are a few examples of common expenses included:

- ❖ General repairs such as fixing a running toilet, broken appliance, or dripping faucet

- ❖ General maintenance such as gutter cleaning, HVAC servicing, and trimming back the trees

- ❖ Property insurance

- ❖ County/City property taxes

- ❖ Property Management fees, if applicable

If we were to add up all those expenses for the property with $22,000 in collected rents and they added up to $8,000, then that would be our Operating Expenses.

The actual formula for our NOI is very basic:

$22,000 in Revenue

-$8,000 in Operating Expenses

= NOI of $14,000

When evaluating the NOI that someone else may have put together, analyze it very closely. There are ways a savvy investor can move numbers around into different classifications that may not show up in the operating expenses but probably should and could artificially inflate the NOI. Also, since things like capital expenditures aren't included in the NOI, it's important to find out about those items, as they may have an impact on your decision making.

Capitalization Rate - Commonly referred to as the Cap Rate, this measurement is used to compare how much Net Operating Income a property may produce compared to its current market value. It's helpful when comparing multiple properties at the same time for a quick glance at *which property is the most profitable?* If the property example that produced $14,000 in NOI was currently for sale for $280,000, then we'd have a Cap Rate of 5%. Again, it's a relatively simple calculation of $14,000 / $280,000.

When the value of that asset increases, but our rental revenue does not, then our Cap Rate may decline over time as our rental income is the same, but the price it costs us to get that income has increased. Cap Rates are a commonly used formula, but if you choose to use this as a decision tool, please don't forget about the items that aren't included in NOI expenses. Those items, when factored into future expenses, could affect our decision. For instance, we don't include Capital Expenditures, such as new roofs or HVAC, into the NOI, so we may buy a home that shows a decent rental income, and that could make a Cap Rate look great in comparison to other homes for sale. However, if you have to invest tens of thousands of dollars for large expenses in the near term, you may end up with a cash thirsty rental house that appears to have a high Cap Rate, but the reality of the property is that it is taking way more cash than anticipated.

Gross Rent Multiplier - Commonly referred to as the GRM, this is the comparison of price to rents collected. It may look like a Cap Rate in some regards, but this formula removes the expense portion. For instance, if we take the $280,000 home that rents for $2,000 per month, my GRM will be 11.6. Here is how we got that:

Purchase Price: $280,000 / **Rental Income:** $24,000

($2,000/mo x 12 mo) = **11.6**

If I had the choice between this $280k property and a $325k property that rented for $2,400, which would have the more desirable GRM?

Purchase Price: $325,000 / **Rental Income:** $28,800

($2,400/mo x 12 mo) = **11.3**

Typically, the lower GRM presents a more profitable deal. This formula is used because it helps compare various price ranges with different rental revenues. As with any of these formulas, none is one size fits all, and you must examine all of them closely. Consider future implications with capital expenditures, rentability, and possible appreciation.

Debt Service Coverage Ratio (DSCR) - This formula may be one of the lesser-used in residential rental portfolio analysis from an investor standpoint, but it does come into play in various situations. Especially when securing financing or opting for certain types of refinancing where a lender may want to examine a singular home or, more importantly, your complete rental portfolio. At the end of the day, this formula is used to see if the rents you collected will cover your debt service (mortgage payment/PITI). This ratio is used by comparing two factors. The first is our Net Operating Income, which we already know how to do. The second is just as easy, and that is our total debt service.

If we use our NOI of $14,000 from before, then we only need to figure out our total debt service (principal, interest, property taxes, insurance). If our monthly PITI for that $280,000 property was $1,250 per month, then our annual debt service would be $15,000 ($1,250 x 12 months). Here is the formula:

NOI: $14,000 / Total Debt Service: $15,000 = .933

If a lender requires a DSCR of 1-1.25, then we have not quite met their requirements. In order to get that DSCR in line for this property, we'd have to either try increasing the NOI (reduce expenses or increase rents) or decrease the annual debt service (higher down payment to borrow less or get a lower interest rate). If you don't get within the ratio the lender wants, don't panic. They may look at other assets you have, your creditworthiness, or other factors for final approval. As an investor who plans to grow their portfolio, having an understanding of your Debt Service Cover Ratio, especially as you add more homes, is important.

In concluding this chapter, it's important we look at factors that impact the returns on our rental property that are challenging to accurately measure, especially within some of these more rigid formulas we looked at. There are investors, mainly on the larger scale, whose decision-making process lives and dies by some of these formulas. Personally, I think there are other factors to consider that don't necessarily show up in those formulas.

Some other tips on 'Returns'

Future Appreciation/Growth - If we only base our purchase decision on the values of today's market and don't consider long-term growth and appreciation, we're doing ourselves a disservice. I always advise that when looking at cash flows and cap rates, etc., you should take the time to ask yourself, *"which property is going to appreciate at a faster pace?"* Sometimes, investors get so focused on the cash flow that they miss out on opportunities that may have less cash flow today but could potentially appreciate in value much faster than the high cash flow property they're so focused on today. Appreciation is one of the staple pillars of building a valuable, long-term real estate portfolio, so don't undervalue or ignore that.

Capital Expenditures & Initial Upfit Costs - Many times, the asking price of a property is tied to the work that it needs to bring it up to par. If we plug a low price into some of the equations we just looked at, we may produce falsely higher return rates than they really are. The expenses may be things that are needed on day 1 of owning the property, such as replacing a deck or a kitchen that is totally outdated. However, they could also be things that are going to need replacing in the near term, say 2 to 3 years. For instance, things that may be functioning today, but we know they are working on borrowed time, such as a really old HVAC. If we evaluate the current purchase price but ignore these other items, once again, we could be making a weak financial decision without considering all the factors.

Ease of renting/tenant turnover - This one can be tough to estimate, and your experience over time will greatly assist in this factor. When I evaluate purchasing a rental property, I ask myself a few questions:

❖ Would I want to rent this home, and if no, then why not?
And can I fix those reasons and still make the home profitable?

❖ If I'm open to renting the home, is there something that
would prevent me from signing a long-term lease? Some
examples of such problems include a non-functioning layout
on the inside, the neighbor's loud dogs, a difficult-to-navigate
entrance/exit to the neighborhood. These are things that may
not stop a tenant from renting the home, but once they come
to discover these things, they may not extend their lease. Is
there something that could create unnecessarily repeated
vacancy?

❖ Are there amenities within the neighborhood that appeal to
the tenants or things close by that may be tough to find in
other parts of town, encouraging a tenant to want to stay longer? What makes the area appealing or not appealing?

These are just a few of the items that I consider when buying a
rental property. There is no real place to plug those into a formula, but
I can't ignore these factors. They could directly impact how much the
tenants enjoy a home, and that enjoyment directly impacts their desire
to stay longer or leave sooner. Either way, their decision to stay or go
impacts my revenue & expenses.

Future Resale Hurdles - I wish this was more obvious to more
investors, but once again, some investors get lost in the rates of return
and not the total package of the property. Sometimes there are things
about a home that impact the future sale, but maybe not the rentability.
Some of these items are the same that I just mentioned when talking
about the tenants above, but a home purchaser may be more discern-

ing than a home renter. Things like a severe slope to the lot, being the biggest house in the neighborhood, having a really small yard, or future development nearby may not bother a tenant too much but could bother a future purchaser. Even on my longest-held rentals, I always consider resale hurdles. No home is perfect, but some homes and lots have disadvantages, and I want to go into any real estate purchase with my eyes wide open to the future.

Sweat Equity/Expansion Opportunity - While I don't require that homes I purchase have the opportunity to expand or gain sweat equity, it sure is nice when that opportunity presents itself. There have been many times when I purchased a home that possibly looked overpriced for its current state but presented growth opportunities. I sometimes overpay today for what I think tomorrow will bring. I like to look for ways to *add value.* Do I see something that maybe others are overlooking? Could I possibly put an addition on the property to increase value and cash flow? Do I see a flaw with the home that could be corrected easily to instantly increase value, such as knocking down a wall or two and opening up the layout? There's no reason that you can't purchase a solid rental home with an amazing future opportunity to expand upon resale. When we only focus on one aspect of real estate and don't give much consideration to all of the aspects, we may leave money on the table.

We need to continually train ourselves to evaluate all the benefits of real estate when making a purchase rather than convincing ourselves that a singular benefit, such as cash flow, is the most important to our portfolio success. I know not putting cash flow on a pedestal can go against the grain of other successful investors' teachings, and I'm perfectly comfortable with going against that grain.

As I conclude this chapter and move on to other lessons, I would strongly encourage you to read this chapter at least one more time, even if you feel you have totally understood everything in it. You cannot underestimate the value of truly understanding the numbers, as well as the other factors that can come into play but are harder to calculate.

I can assure you that nothing in this chapter is too complicated for anyone to truly grasp and understand. It may take a few times to go over it, try a few examples and do some more digging, but I promise it's not rocket science. I know many, many successful investors, and just about all of them are far from rocket scientists - myself included. It's time and dedication to really learn these concepts that make the difference.

Chapter 7 - *Building a Portfolio for the Future*

THIS NEXT LESSON IS probably one of the most rewarding because we stop talking about individual concepts and examples and start to pull them together in a way that bears results. Up until now, we've talked about important factors needed to create a successful portfolio. We're now going to bring these things together. We're going to complete a goal-setting profile for our sample investors we mentioned in chapter 3 - James & Cindy Smith. Before we dive into James & Cindy's life and put together their plan, I do recognize that people are at different stages in their lives and have different long-term goals. I know some people may make more or less money, have more or less saved, and have higher or lower price ranges in their markets. These investors we're going to go through are meant to give you the framework on how to combine everything we've learned so far and start to structure your own goals and portfolio. It's less about every penny here and there or what their particular goal is and much more about laying out a path that you too can begin to work on.

The first thing we need to do is set our goals and financial targets. As we do that, we'll approach it from two different perspectives. Are we going to play offense or defense? If we think back to the barrel analogy, the hoses coming into the barrel were our *offensive* moves. We were going out and trying to create more income. In thinking about reducing the number and size of the holes in that barrel to preserve our current money, we were more *defensive*. I think the best investors and financially secure people realize the benefit of being offensive **and** defensive. But that doesn't mean they are always split 50/50. Sometimes, you may be saving more and other times; you may be more aggressive with your investments to increase income. Most people would agree it takes more time to save it than it does to spend it.

In the setting of our goals, **we need to figure out how much money we will need to live the life we want and for how long we still have to live** (guesstimate). In order to do that, we need to answer a few questions:

1) What is it we want for our futures?

2) What expenses will we have in the future?

3) What do we already have saved or working for us?

4) What type of growth do our current investments get us on average?

5) How short will we be of our goals if we don't do anything different from what we're doing right now?

There'll be more questions as we move forward, but we really need to start at two points and fill in the gap.

FILL IN THIS GAP
(WE NEED TO KNOW WHAT THIS GAP LOOKS LIKE IF DON'T CHANGE OUR CURRENT PLAN)

What we currently have   What we want to have

As we start to really work through some actual numbers, I would suggest you stop after each mini section and think about your own situation, then scratch down some notes about your personal situation. These examples always start off relatively easy, then grow and morph into something longer. So, taking it step by step, section by section usually produces better end results. STOP HERE and get a pen and paper. As we go through this example, start to track the numbers as we go. It will help so much more than flipping back and forth between pages to reference these numbers as we move forward. <u>You really should do this</u>!

Section #1 - Setting the starting point and evaluating our ending point

What is James & Cindy's Background?

James Smith is 52 years old, earning $52,000 per year as a private school teacher in Northern Virginia. He averages a 2% pay raise every year. Cindy Smith, his wife, is 51 years old and is earning $58,000 per year as an insurance broker. Her average pay raise is 3% per year. Combined, they are making $110,000 this year. They have $135,000 saved in cash and their 401k currently is $126,000. They have 2 children and 3 grandchildren. By nature, they are relatively conservative investors. They live by themselves in a single-family home with a mortgage.

James & Cindy have given us the basics about themselves. While there is much more to learn about them, we don't want to overwhelm ourselves with unnecessary details too early in the goal-setting process. This is a marathon, not a sprint, so we want to build layer upon layer to try and ensure our end goal and plan are accurate.

Task for you: *What is your background?*

❖ What is your family dynamic in regards to marriage, children, grandchildren?

> Do you see that changing in the next 2, 5, 10 years?

> If so, how might that change impact you financially?

❖ What is the total amount of your household income?

> Is that pretty steady, or do you have a commission or sales job where that fluctuates?

> Do you get steady pay increases?

> Do you like what you do?

> Do you foresee any near-term or long-term changes to that income?

❖ Are you a more conservative or risky investor?

> Do you have money in the stock market?

  ○ If yes, what kind of risk tolerance do you have?

> Do you keep a lot of cash in the bank, or do you invest most of it?

> When an investment drops in value, are you quick to sell or wait it out?

> Do you lose sleep at night over your current investments?

> Do you think you have room in your risk tolerance to invest in different asset classes?

❖ Have you ever owned a real estate rental property?

> If yes, how was that experience?

- ○ How could you have improved on it?
  - ➢ If no, why not?
    - ○ What were the top 2-3 reasons why you haven't?
    - ○ Could those items be overcome with more education and experience?

What is James & Cindy's long-term goal & timeframe to reach it?

James and Cindy have a goal to retire in 16 years, but they don't want to wait until retirement to start to enjoy some of the fruits of their labor. James loves to golf, and Cindy has always dreamed of having a place near the ocean to visit. Their goal is to buy a small condo in a golf community on the South Carolina coastline. Upon retirement in 16 years, they plan on moving there full time. Until that point, they are comfortable with renting it out for some short-term rentals. The average price is $400,000 in the area that they are looking at. They are planning on receiving a combined $1,300 per month for social security upon retirement. During retirement, they still want to travel to visit their grandkids for holidays, graduations, birthday parties, and all the other fun stuff that Grandparents enjoy. They have given themselves a life expectancy of 25 years from the time they retire.

By nature, James and Cindy are more *conservative* people and want an investment strategy that matches their personalities. This point is critical to understand when setting up any sort of financial plan for real estate investing; the plan should match who you are at your core, or else the odds of completing the plan will reduce greatly and may cause unnecessary stress.

James & Cindy have done a good job of laying out the foundation of their bigger picture goals. They haven't yet identified the amount of money they will need to hit their targets, but they have set out their big picture target and some preliminary timelines.

Task for you: *What is your bigger picture and time frame?*

- ❖ When you envision your future, what do you see?

  - ➤ Are you living in the same house you are now?

  - ➤ Are you moving, and if so, where?

    - o What are the prices of that area?

    - o Would you sell or keep your current home?

  - ➤ What do you want to do with your time during those years?

    - o Do you plan on traveling?

    - o When you travel, are you staying relatively close by or planning on big excursions far away?

  - ➤ Will any part of your income continue into the future beyond retirement?

- ❖ How long of a life expectancy, past retirement, do you estimate for yourself?

What are James & Cindy able to save every year?

James and Cindy have a combined income of $110,000 this year and put 6% into a 401k retirement plan. Only 3% comes from them, as the remaining 3% comes from their employers as their 401k match. They are also able to save a total of 7% of their income for their savings. Between the 3%, they personally put into their 401k and the 7% into their savings, a total of 10% of their income is set aside to savings annually. Their 401k averages a conservative 5% return annually, while their interest earned on their cash savings is minimal.

As time progresses and they earn more, they will save more. Here is a sample of how their <u>savings</u> may look over the next 16 years:

Today   Earning: $110,000   Saving: $7,700

In 5 years   Earning: $121,566   Saving: $8,509

In 10 years   Earning: $137,821   Saving: $9,647

In 16 years (Retirement Year)   Earning: $160,347   Saving: $11,224

As James and Cindy earn more, they save more, but still at the rate of 7% of their annual income.

As time progresses, and they earn more, they will invest more as well, including with their employer's 401k match. Here is a sample of how their <u>retirement account</u> may look over the next 16 years, earning 5% per year with a total of 6% of income invested:

❖ Their current balance: $126,000 + 6% of Income Invested = $132,600

➢ $132,600 that earned 5% rate of return = $139,230

❖ Year 2 Balance = $139,230 + 6% of Income Investested (on next years income) = $145,997

➢ $145,997 that earned 5% rate of return = $153,296

As James and Cindy calculate their 401k, they add the 6% of that year's income *(3% from them and 3% from their employers)* to their retirement portfolio, then apply their 5% average rate of return. When they do that process over 16 years, their 401k total is $469,135.

At this point, we know the basics of their end goal, and we're starting our early stages of forecasting. We do have how much money they make, how much they are saving, and how much they are investing currently.

Task for you: *What do you earn and save?*

* ❖ How much cash do you save per year?

  * ➢ Is that amount consistent, or does it fluctuate?

  * ➢ Can you save more, even if not always consistent?

  * ➢ Is your cash savings earmarked for retirement or something else?

* ❖ Do you have a retirement account?

  * ➢ Are you the only one that funds that, or does your employer participate?

  * ➢ What are your average returns annually?

  * ➢ Would you be open to adjusting part of your retirement funds to earn a potentially higher rate of return if the risk was also higher? If yes, what percentage of that would you be open to adjusting?

* ❖ Start your early steps of forecasting for just savings and retirement if you stay on your current track. This is just a place for you to start thinking about this in more depth.

What do James & Cindy currently have?

We already know they have $135,000 saved in the bank and a combined 401k of $126,000. Their current home that they have lived in for 10 years is worth $575,000, and they still owe $346,000 on their mortgage. They have 23 years left on the mortgage, which is financed at a 4.25% interest rate. They originally purchased the home ten years ago and refinanced it 7 years ago, thus giving them 23 years remaining on their 30-year mortgage. At the time of the refinance, their mortgage amount was $400,000. Their principal & interest payment is $1,968. Their property insurance is $1,500 per year, and property taxes are $6,800. Their total mortgage payment (with taxes & insurance) is $2,660, with about $740 of that going towards principal every month at this time and increasing as time goes on.

They currently don't own any other real estate besides the home they live in. They have 2 small car payments, but those will be paid off in the next 12 months.

At this point, we know what James & Cindy's long-term goal is, as well as the time left before their main source of income stops. They have also laid out what they currently have in place and what they can currently contribute to those funds consistently each year.

Task for you: *What are your assets, debts & expenses?*

* ❖ How much have you saved in total thus far?

  * ➤ How much cash is in the bank?

  * ➤ How much in retirement savings?

* ❖ Do you own a home?

  * ➤ What is it worth?

- ➢ How much do you owe?
    - ○ What is that monthly payment?
    - ○ What are the mortgage terms? Is it fixed or Adjustable?
    - ○ How quickly are you paying off that mortgage balance?
- ❖ Do you have any other significant monthly debt payments?
    - ➢ Do you have car loans? If yes, how much and what is the monthly payment? When will they be paid off? What interest rate are you paying?
    - ➢ Do you have student loans? If yes, how much and what is the monthly payment? When will they be paid off? What interest rate are you paying?
    - ➢ Do you have any other miscellaneous financial obligations, such as medical bills or child support? If so, how much?
- ❖ Start to look at your disposable income.
    - ➢ Where does your extra money go?
        - ○ Do you eat out a lot?
        - ○ Do you have a large cable or streaming services bill?
        - ○ Do you buy new clothes a lot or have expensive hobbies?
    - ➢ This is the section where you really have to start to dig deep into your past financial, bank, and credit card statements to really see where your money is

going. *How many holes do you really have in your barrel? Take your time on this, don't just guess. Actually, look at your real numbers for the past few months.*

Before moving forward, we should recap and plan out where James & Cindy would be if they continue on the same track for the next 16 years until they retire.

RECAP - Section #1 - Setting the starting point and evaluating our ending point

❖ **Savings** – Currently, they have saved $135,000. They are saving 7% of their income per year while they are working, which we know is increasing annually. They are getting raises on that income; 2% for James and 3% for Cindy.

➢ *How much should they have saved in 16 years?* They started with a base today of $135,000 in savings. As they save more and more every year, at the end of 16 years, their 7% of annual income saved should equal a total savings of $284,684.

➢ This is what they would have with no changes, but remember they may use some of this to leverage their future real estate investments to reach their goals or to pay for part of their South Carolina condo now.

❖ **Retirement Accounts** – Currently, they have $126,000 in their 401k. They add a total of 6% each year (split 3% from them and 3% from their employers) and are earning an average of 5% growth on those investments.

> *How much should they have in their 401k at the end of 16 years?* Their total 401k, at the end of the 16 years, should give them a balance of $469,135. Remember, they will continue to earn 5% on average on this into retirement as well.

> *Most people don't liquidate everything they have upon retirement, but rather keep the investments going and draw on them as they need. As you start your road map, start to think about what items will be liquidated at the time of retirement, such as a home sale, versus what items will still be earning a return through retirement, such as a retirement account.*

❖ **Primary Residence** - Their current home is worth $575,000. Over the past few years, their area has appreciated in the range of 3-5% per year. Since James & Cindy are conservative by nature, they are choosing to use only 2% per year for their forecasting. In 16 years, their presumed home value will be $789,351 with a remaining mortgage balance of $142,760. These numbers all came from a simple amortization of their $400,000 30-year fixed mortgage at 4.25% that they have 23 years remaining on. They plan on selling their home when they retire and, per their forecast, should net $591,337. *This speaks to the power of owning a primary residence as well.* This is what their net would look like:

Sales Price:	$789,351
- Mortgage Owed:	$142,760
- Costs to Sell:	$55,254*
Net to James & Cindy:	$591,337

Approx. 7% of sales price for selling fees

James and Cindy now have a solid base upon which they can start building a plan. They don't yet know what their future expenses will be, nor do they know how much money they will need to reach their goals yet. However, they do know <u>what they currently have</u> *and* <u>what they will have if they don't make any adjustments</u>. *If we look at the below image again, we can see that James and Cindy have started to work on their path from left to right.*

Task for you: *Recap your situation and your future forecast?*

At this point, you should lay out the following:

- ❖ What is my end goal?

- ❖ How long do I have before I plan on retiring?

- ❖ What income streams do I have, and how are they structured?

- ❖ How much do I currently have saved and invested?

- ❖ If I stay on my current track, what should I have by the time I reach retirement?

Just as we did with James & Cindy, you should put together a full recap of all of these items to create your base.

Section #2 - What will James & Cindy's condo cost?

Next, we need to look at the details surrounding the condo in South Carolina that James and Cindy want to purchase now. There are 3 parts of this we need to look at and identify:

1. How much is the condo going to cost James & Cindy to purchase, and where will those funds come from?

2. How much will the condo cost between now and their retirement?

3. What expenses will be associated with the condo once they move in full-time during retirement?

Part 1 - What are the purchase stats?

The condos that they are looking at cost $400,000, and at the time of purchase, mortgage rates are at 4.5% for this type of purchase. These condos have appreciated in the past at a rate of about 2-5% per year, so James and Cindy are using a rate of 1.5% per year to stay within their conservative view. In 16 years, when they retire, they forecast their $400k unit will be worth $507,594 if they get an average of 1.5% per year. They plan on putting down 20% ($80,000) and have about $5,000 in closing costs. They are also setting aside $7,500 to furnish the unit. Their initial total budget is $92,500.

James & Cindy had $135,000 in savings today, and they need at least $92,500 for their purchase and upfit their new condo. That will leave them with $42,500 in savings now. That will put their new estimated savings, after 16 years, at $192,184, which is down from their original forecast of $284,684. *This is the first time in their planning that their future forecast has changed. If James and Cindy didn't do their original forecast, they wouldn't know how the purchase of the condo would affect their plans.*

They are going to get a mortgage on the SC condo for $320,000 at the previously mentioned 4.5%. Property taxes on the home are $3,600, property insurance is $1,200, and the HOA's are $350/month. That gives them a complete monthly payment of $2,371 that is going to start once they buy the home, presumably this year. Using an amortization chart, they should have a mortgage balance of $201,822 in 16 years upon retirement. The first month of their mortgage, $421 will go towards their principal, but by the time they reach retirement, $861 will go per month as they will pay less and less interest as time goes on.

Part 2 - How will the condo affect them between now and retirement?

The condo payment of $2,371 is a new <u>hole in their barrel</u> (expense), and as to not impact their current savings rate or 401k contributions, they plan on doing short-term rentals over the next 16 years at this property to help offset that expense. They will still use the condo throughout the year, but they realize that utilizing it as a short-term rental will assist in offsetting the mortgage expense.

Short Term Rentals on the condo - As for the short-term rentals, they have spoken to a local property manager in SC and have been presented with off-season and peak season rental figures. They plan on renting the unit out at a 60% occupancy rate and are calculating the other 40% as normal rental vacancy, and for the time they will be visiting the property. Here is a snapshot of what their short term rental will look like <u>during a peak season month</u>:

Rental Income		**Expenses**	
Average per night:	$225	Management Fees (15%):	$607
# of nights per month:	30	Utilities:	$250
Vacancy Rate:	60%	Misc. Repairs/Cap. Ex. Savings:	$350
Gross rents:	$4,050	Taxes on Gains/After Expenses:	$125

During peak season, James & Cindy should make gross rents of $4,050 on the condo, with expenses of about $1,332. That would net them $2,718 during the peak season before their mortgage payment. After paying their mortgage of $2,371, they would have a positive gain of $347 per month. During the off-season, the estimated net will reduce by about 30%. Therefore, after paying their mortgage during the off-season months, they would actually take a monthly loss of $560. James and Cindy conservatively estimate the condo will cost them about $2,500 out of pocket annually after the short-term rental. They feel they can absorb this cost by reducing some of their current travel and disposable income plans. This $2,500 will not impact their current plan, but they will continually re-evaluate. Keep in mind that these are estimates from a property manager *prior* to purchasing the condo. After a year or two of ownership, they may find out they are making more or less than they thought and need to adjust accordingly.

Part 3 - How will the condo impact James & Cindy in 16 years when they retire?

James and Cindy want to pay off their condo mortgage balance of $201,822 when they move in full time. Even if their mortgage is paid off, they will still have continual expenses with the condo. Here is their estimate:

Utilities:	$3,500
Repairs/Cap. Ex.:	$3,000
Property Taxes/Insurance/HOA:	$12,355
Property Taxes Increase/Yr:	2%*
Property Insurance Increase/Yr:	2%*
HOA Dues Increase/Yr:	2%*

* *James & Cindy know their property taxes, insurance, and HOA dues will increase over the years. They are planning for a 2% increase per year. In doing so, they forecast their total property tax/insurance/HOA expense in year 16 will be a total of $12,355 using the 2% per year based on today's expenses of those items.*

James and Cindy plan on the condo costing them $18,855 in year 16 when they move in full time after they pay off their mortgage balance.

We have now put together a forecast for their dream condo and how it will affect them today, over the next 16 years, and when they move in full time during retirement.

Task for you: *What is your end goal cost?*

James and Cindy have a goal that involves moving into a new home at a location they love. That doesn't mean it is your goal. Your goal may be location or property-related, but it also may not be. Maybe you want to open up a charity for something that you're passionate about. Maybe you want to pay for your children's college or wedding. Maybe your goal is to stay in your current home and travel the world. The list of possible goals anyone may have is endless, but most likely, they all will come with some sort of cost or expense. Here is what you need to answer to figure out the cost:

❖ What is the overall cost?

❖ Is it a one-time cost or recurring?

❖ Will any of the expenses increase over time? If so, at what estimated rate of increase?

❖ What could possibly affect expenses in the future?

❖ If you're starting on your goal today, what costs will you incur starting now?

Some of these will be estimates, and that is fine. You should always be re-evaluating these costs and expenses as you move forward. As the numbers change, either in reality or forecasted, you should adjust your game plan accordingly. James and Cindy would be silly if they just forecasted numbers today for their retirement in 16 years and never looked at them again. They will need to evaluate these at least annually to see what has changed, either positive or negative. You should do the same.

Section #3 - What will James & Cindy's expenses be through retirement?

We need to start figuring out James & Cindy's expenses after they retire in 16 years and live the lifestyle they plan on living. What are some of the things James & Cindy should be considered outside of the expenses for their condo? As we go through this list, start making notes about your own personal questions that may apply.

❖ How much are they going to want to travel to visit friends and family, along with some other trips?

❖ What will supplemental health insurance, medical costs, prescriptions, etc., cost?

❖ What will their social security benefits provide, if anything?

❖ Every day living expenses such as food, gas, utilities, etc.

❖ Miscellaneous spending allowance for disposable things, such as going to the movies, nice dinner, or a sporting event

These are all things James and Cindy need to figure out, or at least estimate for, so they can see how far their savings & 401k will go. Remember, they are planning on a life expectancy of 25 years beyond their retirement.

Task for you: *What are your future estimated living expenses?*

For most people, the easiest way to forecast your *future* expenses is to start with your *current* expenses. By starting with all your current expenses, you can then decide which of those, if any, won't be applicable in the future or possibly reduced. For instance, if you're not driving to work, you may have a smaller fuel budget or have one less car payment. On the flip side, with more time in retirement, you may pick up more hobbies or travel more, all of which will have a price tag. Really go through all your expenses and write them down. No matter how small or minor they are, write them down. Once you have those, start asking yourself some of the following questions and assign estimated values:

❖ How much am I going to travel per year during retirement?

❖ Do I want to pick up new hobbies or expand more on current ones?

❖ What are my future medical expenses going to look like?

➢ Health Insurance or supplemental to Medicare (if applicable)

- ➢ Prescriptions

- ➢ Co-Pay's

- ➢ Specialty visits as you get older

- ❖ What will my disposable income look like? How often will I spend money on the following:

  - ➢ Movies, sporting events, dining out

  - ➢ Grocery or fuel bill

  - ➢ Car payments

  - ➢ Spoiling the grandkids

  - ➢ Fancy coffee drinks

  - ➢ Start to think about all these little things that may expand from their current expenses to a higher number when you have more time in the future

When doing this exercise, it's fine to use today's prices for these items and not worry about what they may cost in the future. We'll add a buffer later for possible future inflation.

What are James & Cindy's estimated expenses during retirement?

After mulling these things over and running some real-world estimates based on their current lifestyle, James and Cindy have come up with the following annual retirement expenses:

- ❖ $8,000 per year for travel after they retire

- ❖ $6,000 per year for supplemental health insurance

- ❖ $2,500 in prescription & co-payments

❖ $22,000 per year in miscellaneous expenses - groceries, gas, car repairs, dinner dates, etc

❖ $5,000 to their annual retirement budget for the 'unknown' that could be there - unexpected expenses, bigger house expenses or traveling a little more, etc.

❖ Their condo expenses we already mentioned of $3,500 for utilities, $3,000 for possible repairs, and $12,355 for the property taxes, insurance & HOA dues

The total per year they estimate they will need is $62,355.

Here is a visualization of where their money will be used during retirement. *Having a chart or graph of your own streams of income (hoses into the barrel), as well as one of the expenses (holes in the barrel), is sometimes easier to see where to improve than just listing them out. Here is James and Cindy's pie chart of their holes in the barrel upon retirement **as they forecast it today.***

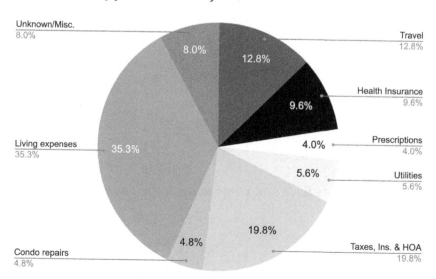

James & Cindy have now determined what they think they will need per year during retirement. Now, let's see how that stacks up over their 25 year life expectancy beyond the start of their retirement.

Estimated per year needed: $62,355

# of years saving for (25):   x 25 years

= $1,558,875

Hopefully, you are starting to really see James & Cindy's plan coming together with real numbers and targets. Since we're estimating expenses that won't start until 16 years from now and then will possibly run for an additional 25 years after that, there is obviously room for error. Even though James & Cindy should continually evaluate these figures, we need to add some margin of error to be as accurate as possible. Also, we realize that over time, prices of items have a tendency to naturally increase (inflation), so we also want to add some inflation to these figures. James & Cindy have decided that they are going to add a 10% margin of error, plus a ½% per year adjustment for inflation.

Base Amount Needed:	$1,558,875
+ Margin of Error (10%):	$155,888
Total:	$1,714,763
+ Inflation (½% per year/next 16 years):	$142,447
Total:	$1,857,210

James & Cindy have now come up with their targeted savings goal of $1,857,210.

You should now have the baseline for how to build a plan step by step, including room for error and unknowns. There is no doubt a lot of detail and thinking involved, but once you set your initial plan, any tweaks are typically easier to make. Most people just never invest the few hours of critical thinking it takes to really see what they have, what they will have and what they need.

Task for you: *What is your total number?*

Formulate your total number. You now have the tools, along with this example to start to laying out your expenses that you think you'll need and roll that into a total annual amount. From there, you should be able to apply your own margin of errors. You may be very detailed in your expense estimation and thus probably need a lower margin of error, or you may be pretty broad in your estimates and choose to apply a larger margin of error. Before moving on, you should have the following tasks completed:

- ❖ Determine your long term goals and future plans

- ❖ Create your current baseline financials of what you have

- ❖ Discover where your current plan would take you if you make no changes

- ❖ Calculate what your end goal will cost you and if there are any financial implications between now and then

- ❖ Estimate your annual retirement expenses and come up with a total goal amount

Section #4 - Making sure James & Cindy reach their goals?

Part 1 - How short will James & Cindy be of their goal?

Now that James and Cindy have laid out their retirement plans, and started looking at their estimated future expenses, we can start to see where they will end up if they don't change their current path.

Here is a recap of previously mentioned numbers to see what they will have:

Net proceeds from sale of primary home (Cash):	$591,337
Cash savings:	$192,184
Social security: $1,300 per month x 25yrs	$390,000
401k/retirement savings:	$469,135
Total:	$1,642,655

James and Cindy need $1,857,210 as their target, so it looks as if they are about $215k from their goal with an estimated current plan total of $1,642,655.

If you've made it this far on your own budgeting to figure out what you want and need, what you currently have and what you'll be short on your targeted goals, then pat yourself on the back. Few people, let alone investors, truly take the time to do this. Some investors skip this critical step and simply buy on a whim, just hoping that it all works out. That strategy can create more stress, debt, leverage issues and assets to manage unnecessarily. If you can relate to James & Cindy's goals, then you don't need to build a massive portfolio. A few select investment properties can do wonders for you! If you want something much more grand than James & Cindy, that is fine too. This step-by-step plan we have gone through so far is user-friendly for any goals.

We're missing one really important factor in their goal that we have not addressed yet. Remember, when James and Cindy move to SC full time in 16 years, they will want to pay off their mortgage on their condo. As was previously mentioned, the balance will be $201,822 at that time. So, let's fine-tune this…

Total estimated savings:	$1,642,655
- Mortgage pay off in SC:	$201,822
Actual savings:	$1,440,833

Here is a more accurate assessment of their shortage:

Total estimated funds needed to span 25 years post retirement:	$1,857,209
Actual savings James & Cindy plan on having:	$1,440,833
How short will they be of their goal:	**-$416,376**

Part 2 - What variables should James & Cindy reconsider in their estimates?

Before we dive into how we are going to help James & Cindy make up that $415k shortfall, there are a few things that can be a challenge at first when forecasting for the future. James and Cindy had to make certain assumptions, all of which impact their current and final numbers. Here are some of the items that they're estimating and why it's so important to continually evaluate your path.

❖ What rate of appreciation should you use for your primary

residence's future value?

- ❖ What rate of savings are you consistently doing and can continue to do?

- ❖ What rate of return are you getting on your 401k and what is a conservative view to the future?

- ❖ How should you allow inflation to impact your future budget goals?

- ❖ What will your future property taxes and property insurance be at in 10, 15, 20 years?

- ❖ How will you estimate medical prescriptions and health insurance so far out?

- ❖ How reliable is Social Security or the Medicare option?

Questions like this are very common and if you're asking yourself these items, then you are doing some real critical thinking and are on the right path. The short answer is that we just don't know what the future holds in regards to many of these. My typical method is to look back at the last decade and use some historical values to help forecast the future values. However, I lean on the conservative side. For instance, during the 2 year stretch that I wrote this book, real estate values increased at the highest pace we've ever seen in that amount of time. It would be foolish to presume that an above average rate of appreciation would last year after year into the future. For James and Cindy's property appreciation, we used a slightly below average return rate of 2% for their primary house and 1.5% for their condo in SC. In the future, some years may see values go up 5%, while other years may dip 2-3%. It's truly impossible to know what the value will be of any of these items in exactly 16 years. That is partly why we added a 10%

buffer to their overall budget, gave ½% per year for inflation and added some "unknowns" to their future expense expectations. Those are the best things we can do to hedge ourselves against the unknowns.

Task for you: *How did you determine your expense forecast?*

❖ Did you just guesstimate numbers or did you actually try and put real numbers behind your estimates?

❖ Did you err on the conservative or aggressive side while fore-casting?

❖ Did you make presumptions on what you're dreaming about doing in the future or what you're actually working towards accomplishing?

❖ What are you using for your appreciation data to formulate future values?

This is an opportunity to review your numbers again now that we're further through helping James & Cindy. Many times when people do this exercise, if they go back 2 or 3 times through their original estimates, they end up tweaking current numbers, thinking about new possible expenses and trying to firm up estimates using more data. I would encourage you to do the same. Take your time. Remember, this is the base of our plan. A plan that will hopefully change the course of your financial futures. There is nothing wrong with going back and reviewing it a few times!

Part 3 - What should James & Cindy do to accomplish their targeted goal?

James & Cindy have accomplished what very few adults rarely even attempt. They have mapped out the future they envision for themselves using actual estimated numbers and have discovered they are <u>not</u> on track. Truthfully, at this point, many people would think that being short $415k is impossible to make up in 16 years and they would downsize their goals, totally give up, or go back and tweak their future expectations. It would be very easy for James & Cindy to adjust their forecast model and use a 4% appreciation rate instead of 2%. Or for them to presume they'll get a 8% return on the retirement instead of a 5%. Those types of off-the-cuff changes that take you from a conservative view to a more aggressive view may very well just set you up for future disappointment. Wouldn't you rather set up a plan that relies more on you and your efforts than hoping the stock market does something great every year? Only one of those two options is actually controlled by you.

It's important to remember that they don't need the full $1,857,209 in estimated savings on day 1 of retirement. They just need to have that amount over the course of their 25 year life expectancy after retirement. While it may look like they are sizably short, that shortage may not affect them until late into their retirement. For example, that means if they were to buy two rental properties during the 16 years left leading up to retirement, they wouldn't have to sell them on day 1 of retirement. In fact, they can probably hold those properties well into their retirement years and sell when the day comes that they actually come up short with their savings. If they're lucky and they were too conservative in their forecasting, they possibly could even pass on some of that real estate to their children and grandchildren. That is the beginning of what we call *Generational Wealth*. That is where the next generation starts off with a certain amount of wealth or assets that would have taken them years to accumulate if they started from scratch.

I realize that after the last few chapters some of you may be exhausted by all these numbers. Hopefully, though, you now see how they flow in order. We are going to add the last layer to James and Cindy and that is <u>how can they make up the $415k they are short</u>? The answer is with real estate rentals.

Rental Property #1 Purchase Plan

We determined that after James & Cindy used some of their savings to buy their SC condo, that they would have $42,500 of their savings remaining today. Based on their average income, they would save $7,700-$11,224 per year for the next 16 years. Also remember, they just bought their SC home this year, so the idea of them buying another home in the same year might be a little overwhelming. James & Cindy are rookie real estate investors. They are novice beginners just trying to reach their goals, so we need to understand that after every large purchase, there may be a 'cooling off and regroup' period before they are ready to just go out and buy more properties. This falls in line with their more conservative by nature personalities as well.

In 4 years, James & Cindy would have about $80,000 in their savings between what they have saved in those few years on top of the remaining $42,500 they had as a previous balance. At that point, they would be 12 years away from retirement. They would then have enough savings to buy a $250-300k house. If they waited until that time to purchase again they would have given up four years of potential gains by waiting. Instead of waiting to save more money for a traditional down payment, I'd actually suggest they tap into their primary home's equity sooner and buy a rental home the next year after the condo purchase. **They can do this by opening a Home Equity Line of Credit (HELOC) leveraged against the equity in their primary home.** That would leave them 15 years of potential gains versus 12 if they waited.

Here is how that rental property would look.

<u>Prospect House #1</u>

Estimated Purchase Price:	$300,000
Down Payment (20%):	$60,000
Estimated Closing Costs:	$6,000
<u>Estimated Upfit Funds:</u>	<u>$5,500</u>
Total Cash to Buy:	$71,500

One year after buying their SC condo, they will only have about $50k in their savings. The $42,500 balance after they bought the SC condo plus about one more years worth of savings. That obviously isn't enough, and it would drain all of their savings if so. They are conservative by nature, so draining their savings is not really an option. *Please note, I keep going back to James & Cindy's conservative personalities and investment style. We don't want this portfolio-building process to be filled with anxiety and overwhelm them. Moving forward, we want to use the investing options and tools that are more inline with their personalities. Ideally, we'll use a relatively easy plan, without too much risk or many complex financial strategies.*

In order to see if the HELOC would work, we need to look at the equity in their primary home. We noted their primary home was worth $575,000 today and they owed about $346,000, so there is approximately $230,000 worth of equity in the home that they can leverage against using a Home Equity Line of Credit as we explained earlier. They will have $50k in savings, but don't want to drop too much below that as their safety net. If the rental home is going to cost them $71,500 cash out of pocket, plus a few extra thousand dollars for an early vacancy, James and Cindy plan on needing $75k total. They will need that from the HELOC. Since they have equity in their primary home, that is no issue. Here is how that HELOC would look:

Today's Home Value:	$575,000
- Mortgage Balance:	$346,000
= Potential Equity for HELOC:	$229,000
Bank's max LTV for HELOC:	x 80%
= Max HELOC available amount:	$183,200
How much do they need?	$75,000*
Interest Rate on HELOC:	4.75%
HELOC Payment Amortization:	30 years
HELOC Balloon Payment:	20 years**
Monthly Interest Payment Due:	$297

* *They may open the line of credit for the full amount of $183k but choose to only borrow the $75k for now. Their payment is based on the $75k that they actually borrow*

** *While their payment is calculated by using a 30yr amortization schedule, their HELOC requires it to be paid off within 20 years. For James & Cindy, that is fine as they plan on retiring and paying this off with their primary home sale in 16 years.*

Using these stats on the HELOC, James & Cindy make a few assumptions about moving forward:

❖ They plan on paying off this HELOC when their savings reach that point to have the extra or when they sell their primary home. Since this HELOC is an Interest Only loan, they will owe $75k in the future when they go to pay it off

❖ The complete mortgage payment *on their primary home* is $2,660. That will increase with the HELOC payment to $2,957

❖ Since they already increased their expenses when they bought the SC condo by a few hundred dollars a month, they want to be cautious in adding another $297 in HELOC payment. They'll want to make sure that the rents they charge on the rental property they are going to buy will offset most, if not all of this increase.

Now that we know where they are getting the $75,000 from, let's look at the actual rental property and what it can produce. We know they are looking at a $300,000 rental home with 20% down. Here are some assumptions James & Cindy are making about the new property:

❖ Same level of appreciation that we've used on our previous examples of a modest 2%. If the rental property they buy was purchased for $300,000, in 15 years when they retire the value is estimated to be $395,843 *(remember, they are buying their first home 1 year after the condo, so they own it 15 years until they retire.)*

❖ Their mortgage on this house would be $240,000 *($300k purchase price with 20% down)*. They will have a 4.5% interest rate, $2,700 in property taxes and $1,500 in insurance. Using an amortization schedule, their total monthly payment would be $1,566 and after 15 years, their mortgage balance would be down to $158,961 from the $240,000 they borrowed.

❖ They can rent this home for $2,400 per month, which on the surface leaves a cash flow per month of $537.

Rental Amount:	$2,400
- PITI Payment:	$1,566
- HELOC Payment:	$297
Gross Cash Flow:	$537
- Estimated Vacancy, Repairs, Cap. Ex. & Taxes:	$387*
Net Cash Flow Per Month/Year:	$150/$1,800

* *Estimates using the financial models from the previous cash flow chapter*

If James & Cindy keep this one rental house for 15 years, until they retire, the profit from this house will be broken down into 3 categories:

1. Sale of the property/Appreciation Gains:

Value in 15 years:	$395,843
Purchase Price + Closing costs/upfit:*	$315,000
Estimated Costs to sell (7%):	$27,709
Gross before taxes:	$53,134
Estimated Taxes (25% of gains):	$13,383
Net Gain on Appreciation:	$39,751

* *Purchase price was $300,000, but $15k in closing costs, upfit and vacancy that came out of the $75k HELOC*

They should roughly net $39,751 in appreciation profit.

2. Mortgage Principal Paid Down by Tenant:

The tenant, over the course of 15 years, has been in essence paying their mortgage for them, reducing it from the original $240,000 to

$158,961, *for a gain of $81,039.* The tax on this tenant's principal paid down is actually paid during each year and not at the end of the sale, and we already accounted for that previously in the cash flow analysis that showed a gain of $150 per month/$1,800 per year.

3. Annual Cash Flow from rental:

As per the earlier cash flow calculation on this property, James and Cindy should net $1,800 in actual cash per year on this rental. $1,800 per year for 15 years = *$27,000 net cash flow gain.*

The money they should earn on this house should be as follows:

1. $39,751 in appreciation net profit

2. $81,039 in principal paydown

3. $27,000 in cash flow

   $147,790 net gain after owning the home 15 years*

* We are working under the presumption that the tax savings on depreciation that James & Cindy received over the years is the same amount of depreciation recapture owed at the time of final sale. We did not add in any tax savings from the rental property depreciation taken over the years and therefore are not including depreciation recapture at the time of final sale for this calculation.

If you notice in the approximate $148k gain, that there is no mention of getting their down payment back. That was the difference between the $300,000 purchase price and the $240,000 mortgage. That $60,000 would traditionally come back to you and go into your pocket. However, in this case, that money should be applied against the HELOC to help pay it off at the time of sale. Had they used their cash savings to purchase this home, instead of using the HELOC, they would have gotten that money back as well. It wouldn't have been calculated as a *gain*, but would have come back to them nonetheless. Since they used the line of credit, when they sell the rental property or their primary residence, the HELOC will be paid off. Please note, that the downpayment was $60k, however they took a HELOC for $75k and the difference was used for closing costs, upfit and vacancy, which was noted in the gains calculations we previously used to get the $39,751 (we used $315k instead of $300k purchase price to account for that extra $15k in costs when they purchased and is what raised the $60k downpayment to a total of $75k they drew from the HELOC). *The remaining HELOC payoff of will be paid with the proceeds from the sale of their primary home. As you'll come to see, James & Cindy may actually hold this rental property well into retirement and not sell it right away. Due to the HELOC's balloon payment, previously noted of 20 years, they will need to pay off the HELOC even if they continue to hold rental property #1.*

How does this Rental Property #1 impact James & Cindy's goal shortage?

If we go back to what James & Cindy had which showed us they were short $415k and we add in the extra $148k, they would still be short $267k at the time of their retirement.

What are James & Cindy's options at hand to continue to chip away at the $267k shortfall? Before answering that question, there are a few points we need to talk about with respect to rental house #1, which may impact their future decisions. Some of these points show the beauty of holding real estate long term:

❖ James & Cindy's cash flow should actually increase every year beyond the $1,800. Remember from previous lessons, we should be working to *decrease vacancy* and *increase rents* at a faster pace than the increase of property taxes & insurance, or our operating expenses. So, the $1,800 used above should increase year after year and thus reduce that shortage. To remain within their conservative view, James & Cindy used year 1 rental figures to come up with their gains at the end. They were hesitant to make presumptions about annual rental increases and expense decreases, which should occur as their experience grows.

❖ When James & Cindy retire, they should have about $1,440,833. Of that, $591k was from the sale of their primary residence. If they decide not to sell this rental property at the beginning of their retirement, the amount they get from their primary house sale will be reduced by the $75k to pay off the HELOC. While that will reduce their $1.44M savings in the beginning, they will get most of it back via the sale of the rental property whenever that occurs. Also, there is the difference between the purchase price of the rental house ($300k) and the mortgage ($240k), which leaves the $60k down payment. That $60k will come back to James & Cindy at time of rental property sale, whenever that may be. After the HELOC of $75k is paid off, their estimated $1.44M savings will reduce to $1.365M.

On the day they retire, do they immediately need all that $1.365M?

Would this extra $148k from this rental house sale really do anything for them at that particular time? They really don't need this extra $148k until they've eaten through most of the $1.365M they already have. Therefore, they should actually *consider holding this house* further into retirement. Here is an example of what happens if they hold this house an *extra* 10 years into retirement. The rental home would be worth $482,531 and their loan balance would then be $65,228. Using the same formula set up as before, the following amounts would be forecasted:

1. $100,315 in appreciation net profit - Still using the conservative 2% appreciation

2. $174,772 in principal paydown - remember, more principal gets paid as time goes on

3. $45,000 in cash flow over 25 yrs (15yrs until retirement, hold an extra 10yrs into retirement, and still only use $1,800 per year)

Total: $320,087

The $320,087 would be an overall return from this house if it was held for 25 years instead of only 15. If James & Cindy decide at the time of retirement that they have plenty of money to last them for at least a decade, they should actually hold this rental house and not sell it at the time of retirement. Their estimated return of $148K at the time of retirement could increase to $320,087. If they do that, now their shortfall of $415k is reduced down to about $95k ($415k - $320k from rental property #1). Also, keep in mind that at the time of retirement, they are going to pay off the HELOC, which has a payment of $297, so the money that was once coming from the rental income to pay that expense will now go into their pocket. That amount of extra income will be over $3,500 per year once that HELOC is paid off.

James and Cindy don't know quite yet if they really want to manage any rental properties after they retire. They are leaning more towards selling the rental property #1 when they get to retirement, but they just aren't sure yet. To be safe, they will probably want to buy one more rental property prior to their retirement to ensure they hit their goals. They don't want to wait 15 years until they retire only to find out they should have bought one more property to ensure they hit their goals. If they waited a few more years after purchasing rental property #1 and got used to being landlords, they would have enough of their own cash saved for another down payment. They could also use some of the remaining equity on the HELOC they have *(remember, they only borrowed $75k, but the line of credit was approved for a much higher amount)* or do a cash-out refinance on their rental property #1.

After completing a forecast for their assets, they see the value in buying residential rental properties as a way to hit their goals. On the other hand, they don't want to end up owning 5 homes to hit their goals. Due to their conservative nature, they aren't big fans of leveraging a whole lot of debt to grow and they can only save so much money at a time. There are many investors who have a higher risk threshold than James & Cindy and could grow much faster or expand on their end goals financially by adding in a few more rental properties.

If they want to buy one more property, what are their best options?

1. They can actually wait until they can save enough money to buy another rental home in probably 5-7 years. They are saving $7-11k per year in cash and already have some in savings. If they bought their 2nd rental property in another 5-7 years, that would put them about halfway into their 16-year path to retirement. They could once again sell that property at the start of retirement or hold it deeper into retirement, as we looked at for property #1.

2. They can use the *equity* in their rental property to *leverage* another down payment via a *cash-out refinance*. Depending on rates & values, they could even opt for a cash-out refinance on their primary property. In doing so, that would pay off their 1st mortgage and the HELOC, then give them the cash for the down payment on rental property #2.

3. Since a few years would have passed since they got the HELOC to help purchase rental property #1, and we noted their primary house would appreciate at 2% per year and their mortgage balance will continually be going down, they may be able to draw more on the original HELOC to help with the down payment on rental property #2. Originally their HELOC was approved up to $183k, but they only used $75k of that.

These 3 options are easily viable. By this point, they will have purchased their SC condo and had it running some with short-term rentals. They will also have purchased their first true rental property, so it will be up and running for the last few years. Their experience in doing these things has increased and buying another property is probably not as scary to them. Each of the options above has its own pros and cons, as well as the number of steps involved to complete. Either way, James and Cindy can purchase their second rental property through the traditional savings or leverage strategies we've talked about!

Let's try and pull this together:

❖ Without buying rental properties, James & Cindy would be short of their goal by $415k

❖ If they bought just one property and sold it on the day they retired and did nothing else, they would be short $267k.

- ❖ If they held that first rental property for an additional 10 years into their retirement, they would only end up being short $95k

- ❖ If they bought a 2nd rental property and held it into retirement, using similar numbers as property #1, they should have no problem making up that $95k shortfall. They could even hold that property well into retirement as well to ensure they end up with a surplus.

I've been teaching similar lessons to groups of people for years and I know some of you have arrived at this part of the book and are probably thinking one of several things. Some are sitting here confused by the numbers and feeling overwhelmed. Some of you are analyzing every part of James & Cindy's situation and picking out differences between their situation and yours. Hopefully, there is also a group of you that realizes this is totally possible to achieve. *And yes, you can fit into multiple groups!*

For the group confused by the numbers please know that for the most part there are only 3-4 financial concepts used to reach James & Cindy's end goals. There are also only a few tools used to map out the gains from the properties. The first step in your journey is not to worry about the houses, but solely focus on what your end goal is with an actual number. Sitting down for a few hours and really going through your expenses now and what you may have in the future is a huge head start that most people never do. Adding in things like margin of error or inflation is actually not nearly as important as just coming up with some actual numbers. Before you ever think about your first home, start putting this together.

Whatever you do, do NOT give up here and toss in the towel. Force yourself to sit down and write some numbers on paper. I sometimes compare this exercise to going to the gym (which is not my favorite thing to do), and the hardest part for me is just getting to the actual gym. Once I'm there I'll do what I need to. Same thing here, the hardest part is just trying to start. Once you start, you'll see some progress!

For the group comparing themselves to James & Cindy please stop doing that now. This isn't a comparison of person to person, or goal to goal. James and Cindy are just an example of how to lay out your goals and hopefully reach them. Some of you will save more money than others, some will get higher or lower returns on their retirement investments. Some homes will appreciate more or cash flow less. Some of you may only have one income or more or fewer years until you retire. This is about YOU. *You* need to do the work to figure out *your* goals. Every single person who does this exercise should have different numbers, different goals and different gaps to make up. I'm not pretending to say that owning a few rental homes will get you a private jet to a secluded tropical island to retire, but what I am saying, with the utmost confidence, is that owning residential rental properties can completely change your financial future. As with any investment, it may go up and down, but if you stay focused and diligent in your path, then you can hit your targets.

For the group that seems to understand the numbers. It is great that you understand the numbers, but sometimes having certain knowledge can create complacency and laziness. Even as you get started and gain success, try not to lose the urge to continually learn about the subject matter. Try not to take a 'know it all' mentality and miss some of the finer details. I've been doing this for over two decades and I still continue to learn more.

Try to make sure you don't get *paralysis by analysis* with all these numbers we went over. And more importantly, try not to doubt yourself.

Doubt and fear will kill your dreams faster than actually failing will. The numbers used in this chapter could have been made even more detailed or even more generalized, but I tried to find a happy balance between the two. More than anything, you need to take action. You can look at these goals and game plan for months on end, even years, finely tuning them for every change that occurs in your life, or every market shift. If you do that, you'll just end up with a spreadsheet full of numbers and watch the time you have to reach those goals pass you by. Setting up this game plan is critical to your success, but this plan and your numbers will continually change, so get to it and start taking action. That is just how life works - it changes. There will never be a perfect time to start. There will always be something in your life that you'll want to use as an excuse for why not to start. That is just fear and anxiety whispering thoughts in your head. Shut that junk down!

1. Set a goal

2. Forecast your numbers

3. Buy a house

If you rinse and repeat that process continually, I promise you'll start to see the light!

Chapter 8 - *Tenant Management, Day to Day Operations & Business Structure*

UP TO THIS POINT, we've talked a lot about tenants from the perspective of collecting rents, but we haven't talked much about how to manage tenants or qualify them. Since this book is written to assist novice and intermediate investors, I want to talk about tenant management, especially because many smaller investors choose to self-manage their properties instead of using a property management company. If you're going to use a property manager, you should still become familiar with these items as you'll want to be informed on what they are doing and have the ability to ask educated questions. You may have heard the saying, "you don't know what you don't know." The best investors know when it's wise to hire people to do certain things. You might hire a CPA to do your taxes, even though you can do them yourself. You may hire a painter to paint a room, even though you can do it yourself. The same goes for property management. With all of those examples, even though you may be hiring someone else to do those items for you, it's wise to have at least a grasp on what they are doing. After all, it's your responsibility to protect your business.

There is no set way to qualify tenants. There are some relatively common practices that most investors use. I have learned some valuable and expensive lessons in my investment career regarding tenants. Within the first three years of purchasing rental properties, I had a tenant selling drugs out of one of my homes and subsequently raided by authorities. I had tenants that had continual domestic situations that resulted in the police, and myself, getting calls. I had a tenant smoke about three packs of cigarettes a day in a property that had a non-smoking policy. The first few years had some trials and tribulations with my tenants. In the beginning, I just thought most tenants must be like this, and if I wanted to be in this business, I just had to get used to this. The issue wasn't my tenants - it was me! The tenants were pretty terrible too, but the real problem was that my qualification process was very weak. I was so nervous about having a vacant home for too long that I was giving too many people the benefit of the doubt.

Once I made a conscious decision to refine my qualification process, things changed. Developing my mindset from *finding a tenant* to *finding the right tenant* made a big difference. I realized that the right tenant would end up costing me less in the long run, even if I needed to have additional vacancies to find them. It was one of the best business decisions I made. We've talked some throughout the book about little tips on working with tenants, but I want to give you some tips on qualifying tenants next.

Here are a few things I do with every tenant, along with a brief explanation:

Rental Application - This is a basic document to gather information about the prospective tenants, their background, employment, rental history and various other important items. These are all things that are common for any rental application. It should also include information about anyone else who may be living in their home, along with if anyone has pets. I also request information about their financial obligations and even social media accounts. There are tons of rental application templates available online, and after you do a rental application process or two, you'll probably tweak your version. My application is always a work in progress and sometimes is property specific. For instance, if one of my rental properties has an HOA that does not allow you to park more than two cars out front or doesn't allow boats or trailers. That info is part of the application, so applicants don't miss it and know that up front.

Credit, Background & Eviction Reports - These three reports are commonly available from several online companies specializing in tenant qualifications. A quick internet search of 'tenant screening reports' will show you multiple options. There are a few nice things about using these companies. The first benefit is that the potential tenant pays these companies directly, online. I do not pay for these reports; the tenants do as part of the qualification process. The benefit is that I have zero monetary risk if I deny the tenant's application. The second benefit is that I never hold on to any information that could lead to the potential tenant's identity theft. I never get any payment information directly, as the reports I receive from these screening companies do not share social security numbers or account numbers. They provide information about the credit score, accounts reported, and other pertinent information. One of the risks with personally qualifying tenants is receiving personal information about those people. And if not handled correctly, you could be putting them at risk of identity theft or fraud. From these three reports, this is what I want to gather:

❖ **Credit Report** - There can be a plethora of valuable information on a credit report, but it can also be misleading. For example, I may have an applicant who has a high credit score but is held down by a lot of monthly payments. They may have auto loans, student loans, furniture loans, department store credit cards as well as regular credit card payments. They may be making all those payments on time and have a high credit score, which makes them prospective applicants. But with all those monthly payments due, I may want to check if their income will support all these expenses, plus the rental amount. This is not always the case, of course, but when you run into an applicant that charges everything on their credit card, including clothing, groceries, gas, etc., sometimes they might not have a large safety net of savings to fall back on. My initial concern would be that if the applicant lost their job, even for a short time, could they still make rent? You can have an applicant who could be the exact opposite as well. Someone who has a low credit score but doesn't carry much debt or doesn't have many payments. Their low credit score could be the repercussion of a past incident or a time in their life when they weren't fiscally responsible. I like to say your credit score is like sledding in the snow - it can take a long time to walk up the hill and only seconds to slide down. It's easier to destroy credit than build it, so things like being late on payments or financially overextending yourself can hurt your credit score. However, you may be a different person, financially, today even if the score shows otherwise from past events. It's important to discuss this report with your potential tenant if you have questions. Occasionally, you may need to request supplemental documentation to support answers to your questions, and sometimes their explanation will line up perfectly with certain information on the report. This is a great example of not judging a book by its cover - the credit score should not be your only determining factor when reviewing the report.

❖ **Background check** - In my experience, the vast majority of these background check reports come back with nothing to report or minor items such as a traffic violation. I don't worry about traffic tickets unless I see a pattern of careless behavior. For instance, getting a speeding or parking ticket once or twice a year is not a big deal to my qualification process, but if you're getting five speeding tickets each year, that may be something worth considering. I know this may seem silly to have speeding tickets impact your qualification but remember we're looking for the <u>right</u> tenant. And part of that process is trying to get a better idea of this person as a whole, not just their finances. For anything more serious, such as a felony, or other crime, I take each of those on a per case scenario. Typically, these scenarios can be too complicated for you to have a universal decision. I'm also a believer that people deserve second chances, so in the few circumstances that I had concerns about something in a background check, I have had an open conversation with the tenant. I either believe them, or I don't. In the end, my gut has to make that decision. Most of these reports check registrations to the Sex Offender lists as well, although it's always a good idea to check that on state and federal websites.

❖ **Eviction Reports** - While this type of reporting has not been around for as long as credit or background reports, it can be very helpful. Eviction reports typically include court records reported to particular credit agencies and can come from various sources. If there was a court judgment issued against a potential tenant applicant for property possession, judgment for rent, or even writ of possession, those things might end up being reported to various credit bureaus. Therefore, they will show up on this report. Be careful with giving too much weight to this report if it does not show any results. That does not mean that the tenant has never been evicted or had a judgment against them. With many eviction/rent/payment judgments, it is up to the landlord to report them to the various credit bureaus, and if they don't, they may not show up or be reported. It doesn't mean those judgments aren't there or are invalid. It just means they didn't find their way to this report. This type of report is getting better as time goes on and more information is collected, so I'm hopeful that it will soon become more reliable and in-depth. Until then, we need to use all the other information we can gather.

The next part of my qualification process is references and past landlords. Most people don't put references on their applications that won't give them a glowing review. For that reason, I don't put a lot of stock in them, but I am always curious to see who they put as a reference and maybe how long they have known those people. I do call the references and try to ask generic questions about the applicant, but again nothing typically comes up. Every once in a while, the reference contact will say something that catches my interest and thus be helpful, but not too often. What I am most concerned about is the past landlords. The applicant gets to pick and choose who they put down as a reference, but if I'm paying attention, they won't have that luxury with the past landlords. The reason I say I have to be paying attention is that every once in a while, an applicant will put down false dates on their application in an attempt to skip a particular landlord. You must ask the landlord what dates they stayed at their property and ensure they line up with their application information. Getting ahold of past landlords and getting anything worthwhile can be a challenge, especially when the landlord may be a corporate owner like an apartment complex. That challenge may also apply when a property management company manages the rental property. Even when the applicant grants permission to those corporations or property managers to speak about their time at their properties, many have internal corporate restrictions on what information they will pass on. There are a few things I would like to gather. While I may not get all of this information, hopefully, I get enough information from landlords to make an educated decision. We just have to make the best decision we can with the information we have at hand. Here are some things I'd like to find out from the landlords:

1. What were the dates they lived there?

2. Did they pay on time?

3. Did they leave the property in good condition?

4. Did the neighbors have any complaints?

5. Did they have any pets on the premises?

6. Would you rent to them again?

Some landlords can be more chatty than others, but if I only get the opportunity to ask a few questions, I'd push for #1 and #6 above. The first helps me determine if they are skipping landlords per their application dates, and the last one sums up numbers two through five pretty effectively. If a landlord wouldn't rent to them again, that red flag needs to be addressed.

Since some landlords don't give any real valuable information, I request at least three contacts of past landlord's information from the applicant so I have a better chance of reaching one of them. If they lived in the same place for the past few years or only had one landlord ever, I will consistently try to reach that contact. If they move every year, having three landlords' info should suffice to reach at least one, if not more. Again, this is not an exact science, and on occasion, I will request more information.

Next, I ask for certain documentation from the applicant. Here are some of the pieces of documentation I request and why:

- ❖ **Pay Stubs/proof of employment** - Typically, I want to see two months' worth of pay stubs. If someone is paid weekly, like in a restaurant or service industry, I may not request a full eight weeks of pay stubs, but if someone is paid monthly, I certainly will want to see two pay stubs, if not a third. Furthermore, if there is anything on those paystubs that looks inconsistent to me, such as line items for bonuses or commissions, or if the gross pay or hours vary by more than about 5-10% between the pay stubs, I'm going to probably request an explanation, along with probably another month worth of statements. Coming from a sales and commission background myself, I know that income can vary greatly from month to month, and as more of the workforce turns to contractor positions versus traditional employment and as more jobs turn to flexible payment options, having more income information can be very helpful.

- ❖ **Bank Statements** - I used to only rarely ask for bank statements as I felt it might be a little too invasive, but over the past few years, I've grown my process to always ask for them. I have the applicant cross out any personal info, such as account numbers, individual purchases, and deposits; however, I want to see your bank balance over two months. In my industry, I've seen where people will keep a job just to qualify for rental, home loan, or a new car, only to quit that job a week later, and there is nothing that can be done. That money in their bank accounts gives me a level of security that if they did quit next week or even get fired or laid off, they at least have some funds to pay rent (or not) still.

❖ **Copy of Driver's License/ID** - Having a copy of their ID is always good, if nothing else, for safety reasons. If you need to show the authorities what your tenant looks like, that copy may be the easiest option. The other reason I like to have the copy is that it shows an address on it. And since no one likes going to the Department of Motor Vehicles, I can feel confident that whatever address they have on their driver's license is probably a place they lived at for a while, or at least they were planning on it. Based on that address and where it falls in their application timeline, I can see how many times, if any, they have moved since last changing the address on their license. If they have lived in 2 different places since last changing their license, that is interesting to me. Why have they not adjusted the address after moving a few more times? It may not raise a red flag but certainly raises a yellow one. I always look to see if their license is expired or has any sort of additional vehicle classification, such as a motorcycle or commercial truck. If the license is expired, I want to see how long ago it expired. Again, I know going to the DMV is never an enjoyable experience, so if it's been expired for a few weeks, I'm probably not going to worry, but if it's been expired for months, I'm going to ask some questions. If they have a classification for a motorcycle or commercial truck, I may want to know if those vehicles will be stored at the property. Remember, the vehicle that someone shows up in to look at the property does not mean that it is their car, nor does it mean it's their only car. This knowledge is more so to set an expectation with parking, neighbors' expectations and any HOA restrictions for parking, etc.

Can the applicant afford the rent? That question can be subjective, although there are some common calculations that many investors use. Some people out there make quite a bit of income, but burn every penny. On the other hand, some people don't make much money, but manage it extremely well. A good source for financial rental housing qualifications is to mirror the requirements that lenders use for people who are looking to purchase a home. Lenders use the Debt-to-Income ratio (DTI), which we discussed earlier in the book. Landlords and lenders alike typically like to ensure that the rents don't account for more than 30-33% of the applicants' gross income. Let's presume we have an applicant that makes $60,000 Gross per year and is applying for a $1,500 rental home. Here is how that DTI would look:

Proposed Rental Amount of House:	$1,500
/ Applicant Monthly Gross Income:	$5,000 ($60,000 / 12)
DTI ratio for rental payment:	30%

That ratio is good on the surface since the rental home is only charging $1,500. What about all their other expenses? What if they also own two cars, both with car payments, have student loans, and a credit card bill every month? That is why the best landlords also add in the second DTI ratio that factors in *total household expenses,* and we want that cap to be around 45-50% of gross income. Here is how that DTI would look with their sample expenses:

Car Payment:	$400
Student Loans:	$120
Credit Card Payment:	$150
Proposed Rental Amount of House:	$1,500
Max Rental Amount:	$2,170
/ Divided by their Gross Income:	$5,000
= DTI Ratio for total expenses:	43.4%

In this scenario, the applicant has come in under both DTI max ratios we use.

Qualifying a tenant is a blend of objective facts and subjective influences. For instance, if they give me two bank statements showing $10k in the bank, along with several pay stubs showing $5k per month, those things are relatively factual items. However, the feedback I may have gotten from past landlords or references will be subjective. I never discount my gut feeling on people either. Even if all the facts seem to check out, I still need to feel *good* about them. We're also at the mercy of not having all the details. When applying for a home mortgage, the lenders get years of tax returns, require more detailed bank statements, and require loads of other information. Hence, their decisions are pretty secure for that particular applicant. As landlords, we gather quite a bit of information, but we typically don't get tax returns and other detailed info. Once again, we have to make the best decision with the info at hand. Lenders are loaning hundreds of thousands of dollars, so a more detailed process would be expected compared to the person looking to rent a $1,500 home for 12 months. Since we don't gather as much information as a lender may, you must do all the due diligence with the info at hand. Don't presume that the information they provide is 100% accurate - go and verify it. And if it can't be verified, ask questions!

For novice investors, sometimes asking some of these personal questions and requesting so much information can be intimidating. I can assure you that you'll want to do your research *before* signing a lease. You can wait for a bad experience yourself to learn some of these lessons, or you can take the lessons learned from others' mistakes to start in a better position.

Day to Day operations

After your tenants are in the property, the day-to-day operations should be relatively quiet and smooth, especially if you took your time and qualified the right people to move in. Also, if you have taken my previous advice of having the home in great shape, that will make the initial few weeks even easier. There are a few things I'd like to address specifically because I think they may be helpful.

The first item is how you are going to manage your properties. Many '*mom and pop*' investors are pretty informal about how they run their properties, and while that may work for some, in today's day and age, I think it's much better to run these properties just like you would any other business. That means keeping detailed financials and any communication you deem important, especially anything regarding the terms of the lease, condition of the property, or any agreed or denied adjustments. What may seem innocent at one time could be important later. Whenever I have a phone conversation with a tenant, I email them recapping what we discussed, so there is at least a written record. If you just own a few properties, I don't think you need to spend a lot of money on bookkeeping programs, but you do need to use some sort of system. I've been using excel spreadsheets for almost 20 years, and they have worked great for me. I'll admit, the bookkeeping programs do a much better job of keeping track of expenses/income and putting together nice percentages with pretty graphs, but you don't need to buy the most expensive. I keep all my receipts and label what they were used for. Between my receipts and spreadsheets, my accountant has a pretty easy time doing my taxes. I would use whatever you're most comfortable with, just as long as you use something.

Remember how I've mentioned you need to think of your rental properties like a business? This is another example of that. If you think of your rental home as a store that sells widgets, you will keep good documentation of how many widgets you bought, how much they cost, and how much money you received for the widgets when they were purchased. You'd keep track of the utilities, taxes, and insurance of the storefront that you sold the widgets out of. You'd analyze which widgets were most popular and profitable, as well as what time of year you're more likely to sell the widgets. If you run your rental properties like they are individual businesses, not only is the paperwork and taxes easier to keep track of, but you'll start to find inefficiencies that may exist. Thus you can work on making the property more profitable. The more profit you're able to squeeze out of each home, the fewer homes you may need to own to hit your goals. Those last few sentences are often misunderstood when I teach them. I'm not saying skip out on repairs and don't invest in the home. I'm saying the opposite. I think investing in the homes, as I've previously mentioned, and making the homes nice and well-maintained increases rents and reduces vacancy, all the while inviting more interested tenants to apply and thus giving you a better pool of rental candidates to choose from.

Everyone has different methods for collecting rents and handling repairs, so there is no set path, but I'd like to pass along some tips.

Collecting rents - Some landlords still collect checks or even cash, while most have moved to electronic payments. I'm ok with collecting a check upfront for the security deposit or first month's rent as long as the check has time to clear before giving the keys. After all, on the checks are typically their address and bank information, two items that I hope I have seen before that moment during the application process and gives me another opportunity to cross-reference. For electronic payments, there are many online resources that will process those payments for free. I've used several different ones and never paid a penny for them. The tenant simply pays through the online company portal, the company processes the payment, holds it for a few days to have it clear, then deposits it in my account. The nice part is it removes me from once again handling too much of their personal information that, if lost, could be harmful to them. Some landlords also set up direct deposit from the tenant to their account and bypass the 3rd party sites altogether. I do think handling most of the payments electronically is best. No more "check is in the mail" type of excuses either!

Handling Repairs - During every investor's time as a landlord, there will be rare circumstances that require an emergency repair. For me, I've only had 3 or 4 over two decades. One of the emergencies was weather-related when a part of a tree had fallen onto the home and did some damage. In that case, the first priority is always tenants' safety and property preservation. Once the tenants are out of harm's way and the property is secured to prevent further damage, you can turn your focus on actual repairs, shopping for contractors, working with insurance company processes, and getting temporary housing for the tenants, if needed. I only mention that situation to point out that you will have an emergency from time to time, but 99% of all other repairs will be easy repairs that may be time-sensitive, but are not dangerous in nature. Every once in a while, you may have the heat go out during the winter, or air conditioning may stop working during the summer.

Luckily, you can typically resolve these items with a few phone calls. For all your other basic repairs, such as dripping faucets, falling towel bars, jamming door handles, or broken appliances, I traditionally call one of several handymen or mechanical contractors to fix the issue. Sometimes, getting someone out there can take a few days, and while tenants may not always understand that, it's important to keep open lines of communication with them. If I can't resolve the issue for a few days for whatever reason, as long as I'm continually updating the tenant, even if there is no real update to give, they are usually more relaxed. By just sending them a quick text once a day until the item is fixed, they know that I haven't forgotten about them. A single text per day can go a long way to buy you some time to get the item fixed, especially if you want someone you've previously worked with to address it. I have my favorite handymen and know whose services are more affordable, but they can't always be there that day, so in order to use them and buy some time, I use communication with the tenant as a tool to achieve that. If you take good care of your properties, conduct regular maintenance, and service your systems, you may be surprised to know that you don't have to make as many repairs. You'll have to make more repairs when you let the property fall apart or when you do have repairs to make, and you don't fix them properly the first time just to save money.

There are a few other tenant/rental questions I get often, so I'd like to dive into those real quick as well. Things like how do I handle pets, what is a good process for a move-in walkthrough, how often do I check on the property, and if I do anything with the neighbors. This isn't a book on property management, but I feel some of these items are important for any investor to think about.

Pets - Some investors are strict against pets as their personal preference, and for those investors, that is fine, although I do think it reduces your pool of qualified tenants. There are some places where having certain pets can be more problematic than others, such as having a barking dog in a townhome or condo property. There are some HOA's and property insurance companies that limit the type of breeds of pets, irrelevant of whether the property owner is ok with them, so always check the HOA covenants, as well as check with your property insurance company. For investors who are open to pets and don't have any above-mentioned restrictions, I would suggest a few things:

- ❖ **Take an extra pet <u>deposit</u>.** In addition to a normal security deposit, I typically take an additional $250 *pet deposit* per pet. I also usually cap the number of pets at 2. If the rental home is $1,500 per month and I am approving one dog and one cat, their total security deposit would be broken down as one month of regular security deposit of $1,500 plus an extra $500 for the two pet deposits, for a total of $2,000. The extra deposit is purely for the extra risk I take on as an owner of a property with pets on the premises. If the home has pets, I always ensure my property insurance company knows that and notes the file. I also make sure the tenants' renters insurance company has provided me with some sort of acknowledgment of the pets as well. Basically, any insurance company that has an interest in the property is notified, just so they know.

- ❖ **Charge a pet <u>fee</u>.** In addition to the pet deposit, which can be refundable based on the condition of the property, I take a *non-refundable pet fee.* Once again, it is $250 per pet, and I make sure they know it is non-refundable, as well as I make it crystal clear that this does not give them permission to allow the pet to damage the property in any way, nor does it alleviate any of their lease obligations. The pet fee is because, as an owner, I am incurring more risk, as I mentioned, but also because *a pet will naturally decrease the life of my flooring and may require extra deodorizing/deep cleaning for my next tenant.* Whenever there is a pet involved, I require the tenants to have the carpets professionally cleaned with a pet deodorizer and provide me with an invoice upon the end of their lease. Even though tenants do that, they sometimes choose the cheapest company for the services, and I've had to have it done afterward as well. Some landlords prefer to spread their fee out monthly by an increase in rent, so instead of $1,500 per month, they may charge $1,525 if you have a pet and still require a larger deposit upfront. When possible, I prefer to have all of the money on the front end, but there is that option.

❖ **Type of Pet and documentation** - I am a pet owner and pet lover, so I consider myself a reasonable property owner when it comes to allowing pets, but I never let my love for pets come before the business part of this. I always use some sort of pet addendum which clearly lays out the dog's details and requires a picture of the pet. On occasion, I request to meet the pet myself. I usually only require to meet the pet if I feel they could end up interacting with my neighbors closely, such as in a townhome or condo. In those cases, I want to ensure that the pet seems relatively friendly and that I'm not putting anyone at unnecessary risk or annoyance. In a townhome or condo situation, the neighbors of your rental property can be your best friends or your worst enemies, so I do take them into consideration. A pet addendum should require the breed, size, age, color, and name of the pet. It should be very detailed so that one approved dog can't be swapped out for another unapproved dog. Having a 13-year-old yellow lab in the home is different from having a 6-month-old yellow lab in the house. If I approve of 'one yellow lab,' I have opened myself up for potential issues if the first older lab passes away and is replaced with a puppy. If the tenant says the dog is a 'mutt' or 'mixed breed,' I really want some sort of documentation from a veterinarian to confirm that. Sometimes, mixed breeds are mixed with certain breeds that an HOA or my insurance company may have an issue with, so the more documentation, the better. For cats and such, I'm more concerned about if they are declawed or not, indoor or outdoor cats, or are they cats that just hide under the bed all day or are out and about. Cats can sometimes leave an odor behind that is tough to get out, so just like dogs may cause damage, cats may have their own issues. Traditionally, I don't allow more than two pets approved at any given time. I have no requirements for things in containers, such as fish or small hamsters, etc. I get asked all the time what about snakes, and I take them on a per situation basis - is it a 15" long, non-venomous snake or a 100lb boa constrictor???

One last note about pets. Some of my longest-standing tenants have been people with pets. Since some rental places are very restrictive about pets, when a tenant finds a place that allows their pet, they have a tendency to stay longer and not move around as much. It decreases my vacancy on some of those properties. Plus, since most rentals charge a non-refundable pet fee, if they move, they will probably incur another non-refundable expense at their next rental too. I've even had some properties that I was planning on adding fences to for particular reasons, but held off until I had a potential tenant that had a pet. I would tell them that I'll add a fence if they sign a 2 or 3-year lease. I was going to add the fence anyway, but I used it as leverage to lengthen the lease terms, and the lack of vacancy helped pay for some part of the fence. Little strategic moves like that can make a real difference to the overall bottom line over time.

Security Deposits – As for the amount of security deposit I require, I typically follow state laws. In my area, it is legal and most common to request a security deposit amount equal to one month's rent if the lease is for an initial 12-month term. If it is a shorter-term lease or a lease of several years, the amount allowed to be collected in security deposits may vary. No matter what is allowable per state laws, I usually require the maximum allowed. I don't want to dive too deep into when and by what amount security deposit deductions can be made; however, I will note that I follow what the lease agreement states, and on a rare occasion, I will consult with a real estate attorney for their opinion before making certain deposit deductions. Each tenant, lease, and state is unique for these deductions.

Move-In Walkthroughs - When your tenant moves into the property, it is a golden opportunity to ensure the condition of the property is up to par. It also sets the standard upon which the security deposit will be based in the future. If the home has a bunch of cosmetic issues and needs repairs, then there is an easier opportunity to create a dispute about future deductions from the security deposit. However, if the home is in good condition, there is less chance of that happening. This helps set the tone of your expectations in regards to maintaining that condition. Here are a few tips I have found very helpful over the years:

❖ Do a video walkthrough of your property prior to the tenant moving in and share the video with the tenant. I do a video with my phone and walk the property room by room, around the entire property and even turn on lights/appliances/test smoke detectors in the video. I talk during the video, pointing out any cosmetic flaws to the home or anything else that I think could be of importance later. The video has all but eliminated any disputes over security deposit issues.

❖ I also give the tenant a move-in form to fill out within 72 hours of getting the keys. That is their opportunity to point out anything that they see as a flaw or concern with the house. It may be repetitive to what is on the video, but this is to ensure that the tenants have their own opportunity to express what they feel is an issue, and we will all sign it. From time to time, tenants can notice something that I did not.

❖ Beyond the walkthrough video and form, I also do the following to the homes:

> Change any burnt out lightbulbs

> Ensure the carbon monoxide detector works and replace the batteries

> Replace the batteries in all the smoke detectors, even if not dead, and ensure that it's operational

> Write the date on the replaced smoke/carbon batteries

➢ Supply a new or non-expired fire extinguisher

➢ Supply a container of ice melt (may not be applicable per your part of the country)

➢ Replace the HVAC air filter, write the date on the filter and supply 3-4 extra filters

➢ Ensure HVAC has been serviced recently

➢ Have the yard cleaned up and well maintained

➢ Change the locks from the previous tenant and any other code/accesses

➢ Notify the HOA if applicable and my insurance company of new tenant (and pets if applicable)

➢ Ensure all utilities have been transferred into the tenants' responsibility

➢ Confirm that any of the landlord requirements per the lease have been met and documented

All of those things noted usually take less than 1-2 hours to complete at every tenant turnover, so it's relatively easy too.

Dealing with neighbors - The last few tips revolve around the neighbors and checking on the property throughout the year. As for the neighbors, I try to notify at least two surrounding neighbors about the home being a rental property. I typically only do this when I first buy the property or see a neighbor move out. I don't typically do this at every tenant turnover unless I have a specific reason to do so. If the neighbor is not home, I will have a pre-written note with me to leave at the door. Basically, I just want the neighbors to have my contact information in case they see something of concern or something bothering them about the home or tenant. I would prefer that they call me before calling the HOA or city authorities if they have a minor concern such as yard maintenance or too many guests parking cars, etc. Those are the most common complaints, and many neighbors can feel helpless in trying to contact a landlord. Consequently, they end up getting more upset and can become a thorn in the side. Some neighboring property owners, for a particular reason or no reason at all, may feel they don't want to live near a "rental property." If I can let them meet an actual owner behind that "rental" and give them my information, as well as explain to them that I intend to ensure the property is kept in equal, if not better, condition as most in the neighborhood, then I usually have very few issues. The little extra benefit to doing this is that you simply end up with another set of eyes and ears on the property. Just like forming a relationship with the tenant is important, developing one with the neighbors can be equally important. There have been several instances where I've had a neighbor help me out with a property, whether it's that they noticed a garage door accidentally left open on a vacant home or notified me of something going on with tenants that I may not have known about. Yes, some will get a little too nosey, but I'd rather have that than the neighbor who sees something suspicious or negative going on and not let me know.

Property Inspections - It's important to check on the properties throughout the tenants' lease period. If everything is running smoothly and I haven't been called for any issues or repairs, I try not to bother my tenants or their privacy, but I still need to perform a property inspection every so often, especially if they have large pets or the yard seems unkempt. I will typically drive by each property once every 60-90 days. This is not on a set schedule – I just swing by when I'm in the area. I just want to give the yard maintenance a quick glance and see if there's anything glaring that needs immediate attention. As for the inside, I usually change the HVAC air filters every 3-4 months *(don't forget to write the date on them when you do)*, and that allows me the opportunity to come into the property to do so. I tell my tenants that I do this upfront before they sign the lease, and I typically give them about a week's notice before the day I want to come by. I very rarely do surprise visits. I've learned that with a week's notice, sometimes, the tenants will clean up, so the version I see is typically their best version of the property. I'm ok if the tenants are messy, but I do want to keep an eye on future expenses that may be incurred based on how they live day to day or things that may cause bugs or mold, etc. Over the years, I've worked with the same HVAC contractors, so typically one to two times a year, when I have them service the HVAC, I will ask them to be my eyes and ears inside the property when they service the units. They will also replace the HVAC filters for me and take a look around. They know to report back to me if they see anything of concern, and typically, they do a great job. They are in hundreds of homes per year, so they have a good point of reference for how various people may live in the homes and know what may be a concern. If during the year, I have a handyman or contractor go by to fix something, I'll ask them to take a glance as well. The more eyes on the property, the less risk of incurring issues or a major expense. It also saves me from going to the property in person as often and thus, has created another efficiency for my business. If you do a great job of qualifying the tenants upfront, you'll have less risk of an issue during these property checks.

Business Structure

Structure - Up to this point, we've talked some about qualifying the tenants, managing their move-in process, how to manage repairs, dealing with pets, and how to check on the property. Next is to evaluate your business setup strategy for the property. The business structure (Limited Liability Corporation - LLC v. Personal ownership), insurances, banking, lease structure, and identifying the right rental property are all factors that are important to at least have a basic understanding. To help reduce possible personal liability, investors will sometimes look towards the relatively easy Limited Liability Corporation option for ownership, an LLC. These Limited Liability Corporations, especially where there is only one managing member, typically yourself (or multi-member with a spouse/business partner), have become popular over the years because they are relatively easy and affordable to create. Even though they are recognized by the IRS as a company, you typically don't pay corporate business taxes on the gains *plus* personal taxes. Rather, just personal taxes. LLC's allow you to open and operate a company, but without the double taxation that many corporations incur where the business pays taxes, then they pay the employee (you) and then you pay taxes. The IRS views LLC's, with certain member structures, such as single-member, as *pass through entities* for the purpose of taxes. That income *passes through* the LLC directly down to the shareholder to be liable for the taxes.Business structures for owning rental properties are very similar to taxes in that everyone's situation is unique. There is no black and white answer, and if you ask 10 investors, you'll probably get close to 10 different answers on how to set up your business structure. When evaluating the options for how to deed/own the property, you really should have a conversation with your CPA for any tax implications, as well as a business attorney for liability risk discussions. You should also have a conversation with your insurance broker to see if owning the real estate in a company name will affect the type of property insurance policy they will require. Finally, the mortgage company involved in your loan will have input as to whether an LLC can own the property or it must be in your personal name.

Since there are so many different situations that are unique to each investor, I'm going to just give you some general information that will hopefully help you in starting that decision process. Usually, there are two main options that investors consider when it comes to how to take title/ownership of the property. Those are either owning the property under your personal name *(commonly like your primary home)* or in the name of a company *(commonly an LLC set up)*. Many investors feel that if they own the property in their personal name instead of a business entity, they open themselves up to more liability in regards to being sued or losing personal assets in a litigation situation. That may be somewhat true, but it also depends on your state laws. Each state has different laws when it comes to repercussions from lawsuit judgments and what assets can and cannot be at risk. Those are State-based questions for your business attorney. You just need to be aware that owning an investment property in any titled name is not cut and dry in regards to risk and liability. I should also point out that there are various types of risks with regard to possible litigation. For example, take a *slip and fall* incident at one of your rental properties. Did someone slip and fall because the front stoop was icy, or did someone slip and fall because you failed to provide a solid handrail on the front stoop? Both are slip and fall injuries, but in one, you seem more *negligent* as a property owner. When it comes to law and lawsuits, there is no one-size-fits-all. My business attorney once told me, *"a good attorney will sue everyone, regardless of who is on the title of the property. They'll throw it all against the wall and see what sticks!"*

The other concern with thinking an LLC will give you this overwhelming liability protection is that many investors innocently *pierce the corporate veil.* If an investor, who is the managing member of an LLC, gets sued, they want to claim that their LLC is totally separate from themselves as an individual personally. However, many times, there can be a direct link between the LLC and you that may contradict that claim. For example, let's say the property is owned by your LLC, but when the home is vacant, you pay the electric bill from your personal checking account for that single month. Didn't you just tie that house to you personally and bypass the LLC? Something as minor as that could technically connect you personally, and therefore, your attempt to claim that you have no personal involvement in the property could be tested due to the fact you *pierced the corporate veil.* Keeping your LLC completely separate from anything to you do personally is critical. Of course, your LLC can pay you, and you can personally fund the LLC, but any business transactions should be done strictly through the LLC.

The last point of interest is how the mortgage company may receive the idea of putting the deed of the home into an LLC. If you don't have a mortgage on the property, there should be no restrictions in titling the home into an LLC. However, if you have a mortgage on the property and that mortgage was approved based on you personally, i.e., they looked at *your* W-2/income, *your* debts, *your* assets, and *your* credit, and not the LLC's, then they are probably going to have an issue with you changing the title of the home into an LLC. It could make it more difficult for them to take action if you stop paying the mortgage because they have another entity involved. Most mortgages have a "Due on Sale" clause which says that if you sell the home, you owe the mortgage company the remaining balance of the loan. By transferring the deed from you personally to an LLC, even if you're the only member of that LLC, and even if your LLC didn't pay you for the home, technically, you have sold the property. Will the mortgage company take action if you do this? Will they call the loan due? Will they take legal action? Honestly, there is no way of knowing, but there is always that possibility. When investors do make that deed change, they typically do so through what is called a Quit Claim Deed (QCD) and have the deed recorded at the courthouse. There is no money exchanged from you personally to the LLC and no sales price; just a title change of who the owner is.   Some investors have asked me in the past, "How would the mortgage company ever know if I do that QCD?" Truthfully, most investors are the ones who unknowingly tattle on themselves, and here is how. When you change the title to the property, you also change your homeowners insurance policy because you are no longer the owner, right? The LLC is. The LLC should be the name on the insurance policy. Well, when you bought the home, a requirement was for the mortgage company to be listed as an *interested party* on your insurance policy, which means every single change that is made to your insurance policy, a notice gets sent to the mortgage company. When that title change occurs, and you adjust the insured party on that policy from you to the LLC, the mortgage company gets a notification letting them know that. The same thing happens with the county tax assessor's office. When the title changes, they change who will be paying the property taxes from you to your LLC, and once again, the mortgage company is notified. Innocently enough, by simply making the name change, the insurance company and county revenue department inform the mortgage company. Investors still do it all the time, and there was a time when no one really thought twice about it. The mortgage companies typically took the stance of "as long as we're getting paid, we're ok." When the financial crisis happened in 2008, and there was an influx of foreclosures, some of which were owned by investors, the banks quickly realized that there was a legal headache in trying to obtain the houses as collateral in court proceedings when they were no longer owned by the individual, but rather their LLC's. Now, mortgage companies keep a much closer eye on those types of things. If you do this, you need to understand that it comes with a risk. There are some mortgage companies that will allow you to title the property in the name of an LLC. However, they may require you to obtain a commercial mortgage even though you're purchasing a residential property. That qualification process can be more strenuous and comes with a higher interest rate or costs.

Overall, I do think having an LLC is a smart idea when possible. Checking with a business attorney and your CPA is critical prior to starting an LLC. As your portfolio grows, you may choose to open several LLCs, so no single one has too many AUM (Assets Under Management). There are some investors who even create an LLC for each and every property they own. Each investor has its own unique situation and risk threshold, so there are many different options and theories available. One thing is sadly true, though: as you own more properties and people think you have more to give in a lawsuit, you have a tendency to become more of a target for some people trying to take advantage of you. The more liability protection you have, whether with insurances or corporate structures, the better off you will be. I usually tell novice investors that starting an LLC and understanding the ins and outs of it may be a little much to take on when they are also buying their first investment property, so I don't stress too much on the first or second property. After owning 1-2 homes, I do strongly recommend that you seek out a business attorney to work alongside your CPA to figure out the best long-term tax and liability strategy. You can never eliminate all risk – that is common for any business – but being smart and proactive can go a long way!

Banking & IRS Registration - Banking is relatively easy for rental properties, whether you own it under your personal name or an LLC business name. Even though each state is regulated differently, if you're opening an LLC, you'll need to get an Employer Identification Number (EIN) number from the IRS (easily done online). You'll also want to set up some business bank accounts. Once you have your state LLC certification and an EIN number, setting up a bank account and business credit cards is typically pretty seamless.

Regardless of how you own the property, personal or LLC, you'll want to have some sort of financial system in place. If you're planning on growing your portfolio into several homes, the banking part becomes even more important. I've dealt with many investors who utilize a haphazard type of accounting where everything is jumbled together. Ideally, you have one account that holds tenants' security deposits with no other transactions. Then, another account accepts rents and pays out expenses. For me, each of my homes has those 2 accounts. It may seem like overkill, and when you log into your online banking, it may look like you have a ton of accounts despite owning a few homes, but the year-end accounting is very simple, and very little gets lost. Using a debit card or check for those property expenses once again allows you to track things pretty easily within those accounts. I will also use a business credit card based on the situation. It is much easier to start out being very organized, even if you only own one property, so when you grow, your habits and documentation process are already in order.

Insurances - One of the less-often talked about topics is insurance policy options. Interestingly, investors will pay top dollar for a great CPA to save taxes, and they will invest in a business attorney to help form their companies, yet when it comes to proper insurances, they simply shop for the lowest rate and move on with the day. Do not underestimate the value of a really good insurance broker. Someone who is well versed in investment properties, responds quickly and tries to find the happy blend between premium costs and proper insurance coverage can be extremely valuable to you. Most investors are going to be familiar with the two basic types of insurance policies – Homeowner/Landlord and Renters.

Homeowner policies are typically broken down into 2 subcategories - Primary Homeowner and Landlord. Both of these policies are going to cover the structure itself, but the main difference between the two is the coverage of the contents and possessions inside, such as the furniture, TVs, etc. When you're a landlord, unless you're offering furnished rentals (Air Bnb, corporate rentals, etc.), the possessions inside the home are owned by the tenant, not you. Therefore, you typically don't need coverage on those items. Your landlord policy would traditionally not cover the tenant's possessions. However, that policy may offer other items that a primary homeowner may not necessarily need, such as lost rents during tenant default or property damage, etc. Make sure to review these policy options, and if you're offering any furnished rentals, ensure that your insurance company is aware of that too.

As for the tenants, I require that they provide me a copy of their renters insurance policy with two important items noted. The first is that I require them to have a minimum amount of coverage. Some states may set the minimum, but I usually require at least $300,000 in coverage and sometimes more if they have pets on the premises. The cost to the tenant is usually $150-250 per year based on what posses-sions they own and what company they use for the policy. The second important item is that they must have me or my LLC as an "Interested Party" on their policy. This is very common, and insurance compa-nies do it all the time. It means that any piece of mail that's sent to the tenant, such as cancellations, renewals, claims, and other important information, also gets mailed to me. Even if they try to remove me as an interested party, I will get a notification of that too. This is critical to ensure that they always maintain coverage. Lastly, don't forget what I mentioned previously about approved pets. I require at least an email from their renters' insurance company, noting they are aware that the tenant has a pet on the premises and that they are covered under their policy – it's just one extra layer of protection.

If you own several properties under an LLC, there may be an option for a multiple property commercial policy. Even though they are resi-dential properties, some insurance companies will open up the option of having a commercial blanket policy, so one policy will cover several properties with one annual premium. It could be a way to effectively earn some cost savings without having to give up on liability coverage. Each insurance company is different, but worth investigating based on your situation. You may also want to consider some sort of General Liability policy for any LLC you operate (GL policy). The policies are typically generic business policies with limited coverage, but may help protect the LLC if it gets sued. As with any insurance policy, there are limitations to the coverage, so do your research first.

Two other optional policy types to discuss with your insurance broker are a Vacancy policy and a Builders Risk policy. These poli-cies are used in particular situations, and you may never need them, but they are good to be aware of. When a home is vacant, whether it be while making updates or in between tenants, there is usually a grace period during which your insurance policy will still cover you if the home was broken into or vandalized while vacant. That grace period only goes so long, typically 30-60 days. If the home is vacant beyond that grace period and is vandalized or broken into, you may be surprised to find out that your insurance policy may not cover that. For that reason, during periods of extended vacancy, they have what is called a vacancy policy. If you find yourself in that situation, review your policies to explore those options. The Builders Risk policy is considered for situations when you're doing sizable renovations to the property. Some properties that we purchase need a lot of work before being habitable, but our intention is to turn them into rentals. During those times of rehab, we may have materials in the home that are not installed yet, such as appliances, lights, and plumbing fixtures. While we try to limit the amount of uninstalled material at a job site, it's impossible to always have watchful eyes on everything. Sometimes, those materials magically grow legs and walk off. This policy is to help with larger-scale theft of materials during renovations. Even when you have to pay a deductible for a claim, these types of policies can give you more overall coverage during a rehab than a traditional landlord or homeowners policy, so be sure to explore it if you find yourself in that situation.

The last policy we want to dive into is what is called an Umbrella policy. It's my opinion, as an investor, not as an insurance broker, that every person should have an umbrella policy. The name is derived from the image it implies - an umbrella over you and your assets. Take your auto and homeowners insurance policies, for instance. Both of these provide you with a certain amount of coverage for each of those categories, right? What happens if you have a claim that exceeds that coverage? That is where the umbrella policy comes into play. It is there to cover claims that exceed your coverage. You could just increase the minimum coverages on all your policies, but if you did that, all of your policies would get quite expensive. The alternative is this policy which can, with just a single premium, increase the coverages of all your individual policies. So instead of paying increased coverage premiums on all policies, you just have this one extra blanket policy. They are typically sold in $1 million dollar coverage additions, so you can have policies starting at a minimum of $1M up to much, much more extensive coverages. As you own more assets, you have an increased liability concern and, therefore, would want an increased amount of umbrella coverage. Again, I cannot stress this enough - if you don't have an umbrella policy, I would suggest discussing it with your insurance agent at the very least. The cost is relatively minimal and is one of the best types of protection you can get!

Lease Structure and Finding the Right Property

Lease Structure - Now that we've discussed the various ways to structure your business itself, we should look at ways to creatively structure your lease and things to consider about the property itself. Obviously, longer-term leases, more than 1 year in length, can help quite a bit with your cash flow and make life easier so you don't have to find new tenants every 10-12 months. What is sometimes overlooked with investors as they grow is the vacancies that occur at the *same, or similar time*, as other properties you own. As landlords, we typically think of lease terms within the mindset of years and not months, which I don't like. I think of leases in terms of months with a minimum of 12. What I mean by that is that I have no problem with a 14-month lease or a 19-month lease, etc. In my area, homes rent quicker and easier in the Spring months than in the winter months or over the holidays. If I have a tenant who wants to sign a year lease on November 1st, I'll give them some sort of incentive to actually sign a 15-month lease instead of 12 months. Therefore, instead of having a vacant home the following November and through the holidays, I will get that home back for re-renting before February 1st as we move into the Spring market. If the next tenant that moves in wants to sign a 1-year lease, I'm more inclined to do that because if they sign a lease in February, I'll get the home back the following February/March; again in the early stages of the Spring. That little tweak may save me an extra 30-60 days of a vacancy during our slower months, and on a selfish note, it doesn't force me to deal with that property over the holidays when I want to enjoy more family time. As you build your portfolio and start to gain more financial freedom, your personal and family time becomes more of a driver for your decisions than the actual dollar or return on investment.

Another lease structure tip is to try and not line up too many vacant homes at one time. If you're self-managing, it's a little more of a headache to show multiple vacant properties, qualify tenants, and look after vacant homes at the same time. I want to be careful here not to contradict my previous tip of structuring leases to clear the slower months and holidays. Even so, I try not to end up with too many vacant properties at once. For instance, if I were to own 5 homes, I don't want 3 or 4 of them to all be up for rent again in February or March simply because that is a lot of running around between properties, showing the homes, qualifying possible tenants, and outflow of carrying costs consolidated into a short time period. I'd prefer to spread that out if possible, both for sanity and cash flow purposes. So, I may structure a 15-month lease on one home to come up for rent again in February instead of November, and then on the next property, I may do a 17-month lease to have it become vacant in April, etc. What I'm doing overall is trying to clear the slower rental months in my market and, at the same time, not overload my total property vacancy at one time. When you reach a certain number of properties, that is next to impossible to do all the time, but as a novice investor, reducing the outpouring of carrying costs at one time while creating an opportunity for the home to rent easier is just smart business.

"Not every dollar is equally earned." This is a quote I tell my new students quite often when we talk about real estate, and this is a good time to explain it. It doesn't matter what your profession is, I'm sure you have some days at work that are great and some that are brutal, but within those days, you may have made the same amount of income. Those dollars, while maybe taking the same amount of time to earn, take different tolls on you, both mentally and physically. *Those dollars were not equally earned.* As you progress through building and managing your portfolio, thinking outside of the norms, even something as minor as tweaking a lease length by a month or two, can make your life easier, and thus, those dollars earned to become a little easier.

Finding the right property for you - Let's talk about finding the right rental property for your situation. For most people, this book is not their first foray into trying to learn about real estate investing. From the thousands of books that have been written on the subject to seminars, classes, programs, podcasts, blogs, online videos, social media, and just about every other forum available, people have been giving their two cents on real estate investing for decades upon decades. In some regards, I guess this book is no different. That overload of information creates the perfect situation for *paralysis by analysis* and may force you to create an imaginary property in your mind that checks all the boxes but, in reality, doesn't exist. And if you do find it, you may have wasted so much time that you may have lost a tremendous amount of money in *opportunity cost* with other properties you passed on in the meantime.

No podcast, blog, social media post, seminar, or book (yes, even this one) will replace actual experience. Yes, it's very important to be educated in this field, and some resources are more fruitful than others, but at a certain point, you just need to go try it. With real estate, time has a tendency to fix your mistakes if you just give it long enough. If you hold a rental property long enough, it becomes difficult to lose money overall. Stop getting so many opinions from people who aren't cutting the check. We live in a world where people easily hate on other people's success, so while you may ask a friend, colleague or family member their thoughts on a potential property, I'd take some of it with a grain of salt. They may have something of value to add or see something you don't, and that's great; however, make sure you are able to read between the lines with what they say. I once heard someone say, "Most of the people who say money is bad don't have any." Just be careful about whose opinion you let impact your decisions.

I hope you have seen how each person's goals and path to getting there are going to be different, which means the homes that an individual investor chooses to plug into their portfolio may work for them and their plan, but possibly not work for yours. One investor may be looking for pure cash flow, while another may look for a long-term appreciating area and not be as concerned with the cash flow. Someone may be looking for a property with the potential to add some sweat equity and leverage it later to build their portfolio. Personally, I've even purchased properties to rent for a few years with the long-term plan of moving one of my parents into the home. The point is that the home that works for my plan may not fit into yours, so don't get caught up in following others too closely. Work on identifying what next property will fit into your portfolio for your goals. Remember when we talked about building your real estate portfolio similarly to how you build your retirement portfolio - you plug and play various funds and stocks to reach your overall goals. It's the same thing with real estate.

There will be parameters to starting your initial search. Price is typically the first and foremost restrictor of your search criteria. Here are a few different ways to view pricing and affordability:

❖ How much do I have for a downpayment and closing costs?

❖ How much debt am I comfortable with?

❖ Do I plan to buy more homes in the future and if so, how does this purchase impact those plans?

❖ What amount of a loan will I qualify for?

❖ What carrying and vacancy costs can I manage?

In addition to price, you may want to consider some other factors or personal preferences. I've noticed that when novice investors buy something they are more familiar with, it can be an easier experience for them. For instance, if you've always lived in a townhome where an HOA cuts the grass and maintains the exterior, you may be more inclined to look in that direction for your first rental home. If that makes you more comfortable, then fine. Some people will tell me they'll never buy a home with only 1 full bath, and if that is their preference, that is fine too. Moving outside of your comfort zone takes time and if having some of those criteria in place assists you in taking action sooner, then do it. I think it's important to consider a few other factors about the property itself:

❖ Location of the property - of course, certain locations create certain levels of desirability, but they can also cost more. A great place to start your search is a place that you know very well, and that is typically closest to where you live now. You typically have a good grasp on that area, who may want to live there, what is great about it, and what neighborhoods seem to always sell quickly and be more desirable. If you can't afford to purchase rental property in your hyper-local area, then expand out and try to learn as much as possible about the surrounding areas. I would encourage you to only focus on 2-3 areas at first. Trying to grow familiar with too many areas at the same time can be overwhelming. You'll have plenty of time to explore new areas and expand your reach later on.

❖ Size of the home and yard - considerations with regard to the size of the home will have you asking, 'does it fit within the averages of that neighborhood,' 'would it work for a large rental pool of possible tenants' and 'what would the costs be on a continual basis for items such as new flooring/paint, etc.' Some people think bigger is always better, especially if the price seems like a better value. Keep in mind that the bigger the house, the higher the maintenance & utility costs. As for the lot size, remember that most tenants will do the bare basic yard maintenance, so if you have a large yard and want it maintained at a certain level, that may end up costing more on your end. Plus, a larger-sized yard can encourage a tenant with pets, and possibly more of them, and of a larger size. I'm not discouraging you from a large yard, but you'll want to think a little deeper about some of the aspects of the property and what it could mean to you down the road with both the possible tenant and costs. The power of efficiency is important to remember.

❖ The style and type of home or neighborhood may weigh into your decision as well. Some people have preconceived notions, and maybe some justifiable, about the style of home or neighborhood as it relates to desirability in your particular area. Some people are against townhomes or condos because they are directly connected to a neighbor. Some are against neighborhoods with an HOA (Homeowners Association) due to their costs or regulations, while others may love some of those regulations or reduced maintenance responsibilities that can come with an HOA. Much of this is a personal decision, and for novice investors, as I mentioned, I think it's ok to explore any option that gives you more comfort. However, as you grow, I'd encourage you to put less weight on your personal feelings and more weight into which may present the best investment opportunity for you.

Another common question I get all the time, especially in markets that have lower inventory levels, is "where do you find some of your deals?" Many of the homes I've bought came directly from open market sales, such as a seller hiring an agent and that agent listing the home for sale to the general public, typically via the Multiple Listing Service (MLS) or the major real estate websites. They weren't hidden secrets. When market conditions exist where demand is high, and inventory is low, sometimes real estate can be tough to obtain at a reasonable price. That is where your networking skills come in handy. For most novice investors, trying to buy a few homes over a few years is really not a major challenge, and most of the time, you'll simply find a home on the open market for sale. For those investors reading this who want to expand faster, own lots of homes, or are in a market where there always seems to be a lack of inventory, then here are some tips on other places to explore for leads:

Local real estate investor groups. Most decent-sized cities have one, and if not, you can hop on to other cities' investor groups virtually. Meeting other investors, lenders, wholesalers, and contractors that are well versed in what you're trying to build can really be invaluable. Build relationships with local real estate agents who focus on investment properties.

Reach out to various attorneys specializing in situations where real estate may need to be disposed of, such as divorce or estate.

Reach out to local real estate wholesalers who specialize in finding homes that are off-market, then connecting them to buyers, such as investors. *Tip: Some wholesalers will require that the deal be completed with cash, but there are options for how to make that happen with what we call Hard Money converted into a traditional loan via a Cash-Out Refinance.*

Driving for Dollars is another popular way that you may find an 'off market' property. This is a method in which you actually drive around particular areas and search for homes that look like they are vacant or distressed, and try to reach out to the owner.

Mass Mailings is quite popular but expensive, so many novice investors choose the previously mentioned *driving for dollars* method as you pay less in postage, data list purchases, and printing. As a tradeoff, you spend more time. Mass mailings are like using a commercial fishing net tossed in the ocean, trying to see what you can catch, while *driving for dollars* is like using just one fishing rod searching for a particular type of fish; it's much more targeted.

Courthouse foreclosures can be another way to purchase a property. However, each state's rules are different. They can be riskier, so make sure you do your research prior to placing any bids.

Various national companies offer property finding services. There are a few large, well-established companies in the US that, for a fee or membership/franchise, offer to help find properties. These may be on the pricier side, but will have a larger marketing budget, more refined system and save you time.

Reach out to landlords who are marketing their properties for rent. I've always enjoyed reaching out to other landlords who are marketing their property for rent to simply ask, "would you consider selling?" You can expand this to local property management companies and even landlords who already have tenants in place. You don't know if you don't ask.

Bandit Signs can be useful, although many cities have regulations against them. These are the smaller signs you may see stapled to a telephone pole or as you exit a strip mall that simply says "We buy houses" or anything of the such.

Social media has become a great place to interact with other investors, both in your local market as well as nationally. These platforms have grown rapidly with various investors groups, as well as groups promoting off-market sales. Even if you aren't personally on social media, it could be a good asset for your investment growth. However, as we've spoken about many times, be careful what and who you listen to!

Utilize the power of word of mouth with your friends, colleagues, and especially neighbors. And we're not just talking about the neighbors who live next door to where you live – we also include neighbors who live near your rental properties. Word of mouth can be very valuable, especially if you're well-liked by the people spreading that word. These are just some of the ways I would suggest that you start if you're looking to grow and expand your portfolio size. For investors who only want to own a few homes, which is the majority of people, I'm not so sure you really need to dive too deep into any of these unless they personally pique your interest. The open market is probably the best place for you, but I wanted to at least share some options.

As I conclude this chapter, I want to acknowledge the fact that some of what I've spoken about, from various lease terms to LLCs, business setups, banking, and other comments, may be state-specific, as well as many may require more in-depth professional advice from a CPA, or an attorney. At a minimum, I hope it has created a base knowledge that you can use to ask further questions when you get that advice. Many investors are looking for the singular *right answer,* and if you're one of them, I think it's important to understand that there may be several different *right answers* for your situation!

Chapter 9 - *Long Term Strategies, Investment 'Rules' and Lessons Learned*

OVER THE YEARS, AS I've taught more and more potential investors, there are always a few recurring questions that spring up. But none of those questions seem to fit seamlessly into any particular section of this book. So, I thought I'd dedicate this chapter to all those questions. We will go over them individually, and I hope you find it helpful, either now or in the future.

QUESTION: Should I pay cash for an investment home if I can do so?

As with most investment questions, there is rarely a black or white answer. This is very specific to your situation, so there are a few questions you need to ask yourself before making this decision:

1. What percentage of the cash needed to buy the house is coming from the total cash you have? For instance, if you have $300,000 saved up, I'm not so sure using all of it for one house is the wisest long-term financial decision. If you have $2M saved up, using $300k of it shouldn't impact your long-term financial risk.

2. Do you want to continue buying properties, and if so, how do you plan on financing those purchases? Many times, the people that ask this question are using a majority of their saved funds in order to pay cash for one property. If that is the case, and you want to buy more homes in the future, the question now is, how will you fund those? For the person looking to grow their portfolio, acquiring debt (mortgages) and spreading out their

saved cash over several homes is probably more effective than using all of it on one home. As we've discussed, once that cash is in the home, the only real ways to get that cash back is by selling it, a cash-out refinance, or possibly a line of credit. There is a real opportunity cost you may incur if you plan to grow but can't because you don't have the funds due to investing too much into a single property.

3. Where do you think interest rates will be in the future? If you're planning on growing your portfolio, and you think interest rates will go up in the future, then there is a case to be made to save your money and use it when those rates are higher. That way, you can borrow less in the future at higher interest rates and finance more now while rates are lower. If you think the opposite and that rates may decline in the future when you go to buy your next home, then that may not impact you too much.

At the end of the day, this decision usually comes down to what you currently have and what you hope to do in the future. Some people feel that if they take the risk of buying investment rental property, they need to pay in cash or put down a huge down payment for the cash flow or to reduce possible risk. It's odd to me because many of those same people carry mortgages on their primary homes, but are considering paying cash for an investment property. I inquire with them, "So, you're going to buy a home to put a stranger in it and not carry any debt as to reduce your financial risk, but the home that you and your family live in, you're going to keep a mortgage on it?" It implies that if you're ever going to reduce any risk, it should be focused on the property you live in and the one that may be easier to leverage in the future. On that note, their *reduced risk* consideration is about having to pay a mortgage payment during vacancy times, or if the market suddenly dropped, they wouldn't be upside down on what they owe. I explain to them that if you finance the house and keep your cash, you still have that safety net in either of those situations. Just because you don't have a mortgage doesn't mean you don't have vacancy carrying costs (insurance, property taxes, utilities, maintenance expenses). For the people out there that have extraordinarily higher income levels and can save vast amounts of money in a short period of time, paying all cash for your properties may be a good option. It still gives you the ability to purchase with cash and grow your portfolio in the future through your high income. For the majority of people who don't fall into that category, focus on your future plans before spending all your money on your first or second home!

QUESTION: *What are all these investing "Rules" I hear about?*

There are so many 'rules' in real estate investing that, if you tried to find a home that fit all of them, you might be looking forever. And even then, you may never find one that checks all the boxes. There are 4 *rules* that I hear more often than others, so we'll touch on those. These rules are more theories that some investors prescribe to. I would not let the rules affect your purchase decisions, but rather your forecasting, goals, and plan should be the leading decision-making factors.

The 1% rule is one of the most common of them all for rental properties. It states the rents you charge for a particular property should equal 1% of the purchase price + costs. Here is an example:

Purchase Price:	$250,000
Closing Costs:	$5,000
Upfit Costs:	$10,000
Total Investment:	$265,000

In order to meet the 1% rule, the home would need to rent for $2,650 per month.

These types of blanket *rules* can do more harm than good for a variety of reasons. The first is that when novice investors repeatedly hear this, they feel like their investment may be a poor one if it doesn't meet that ratio. If this home is rented for $2,300 per month, it may still be an amazing investment. I don't think the rule is useless, but each market is different. In my market, for instance, meeting this 1% can be very difficult, but investment properties still sell all the time without it. There is so much more to real estate investing than just the rents collected as it relates to the price.

The 65% rule, typically associated with properties that need a lot of work and may be used for a fix-and-flip, is a quick way to evaluate a home. That equation states that 65% of your After Repair Value (ARV) should not be more than your purchase price + repairs. Here is an example of a house that needs $40,000 worth of repairs:

After Repair Value:	$345,000
x 65% rule:	$224,250
- Repairs:	$40,000
Max Purchase Price:	$184,250

Using this equation, the max I should spend would be $184,250. If the seller wants $200,000, does that mean I should pass on this deal? Does it mean it's not a good deal? Maybe, but very well, maybe not. There are a lot of other factors and variables to consider that you can't determine in this simple math exercise. This rule is meant for a very quick, surface-level decision without diving into the details. If the seller wants $200k, it may be worth doing some deeper analysis. If the seller wanted $280k, it might not be worth spending too much time on it.

Cap Rates are sometimes exclusively used to make investment decisions. Earlier in the book, when we spoke about Capitalization Rates, I mentioned some of the flaws that this equation can present when using it as the sole determinant of a good or bad investment. However, some investors, typically on the larger scale and national level, have a tendency to use this as their main deciding factor. When you're on the level of owning 50, 100, or even 1,000 homes, then putting more weight into this calculation can be useful. After all, when you own so many properties, you have to be able to act quickly and can't do the same level of due diligence that a novice investor may do on their first few properties. For those groups, using a Cap Rate as a leading indicator for purchase is fine. As a novice or intermediate investor, it's important to consider that rate of return, but also take a step back and evaluate all the due diligence data you gather. Things such as possible appreciation levels, long-term growth rates of the area, future vacancy issues, and steady increases of rents are all factors to consider outside of today's Cap Rate. Those items don't have a place within the Cap Rate formula. Therefore, they aren't considered.

You must make your money in real estate on the front end. That saying, while still widely popular, has seemed to lose some ground over the years, and thankfully so. At its core, that saying is expressing that the real money in real estate is made by getting a great price when you purchase. You're building in your protection automatically on the initial purchase versus waiting for time to help mature the asset with the other benefits. Typically, the less you pay for the home, the lower your short and long-term risks may be. It can also help increase your cash flow if you pay less and thus borrow less. All of those things may be true. There's no disputing that paying less for a home is always better when possible from an investment standpoint. The issue with the saying is that it can paralyze the newer investors from being able to actually purchase anything, especially at market value, because they feel that if they don't get a *deal*, they aren't doing it correctly. Some of the best investment purchases I've personally made have come on homes that I paid fair market value for, and even occasionally, a little more than I thought they were worth at that moment. There was no immediate equity on the front end, but rather all baked into the long-term potential of the home. The underlying point is that finding a deal is great, but if you only search for a discount, you may end up buying a terrible investment home with no real long-term potential or incur a lot of opportunity costs along the way by passing on other great properties at market value.

QUESTION: *What is a 1031 Exchange?*

There is a tax code called *1031 Like Kind Exchange*. Before going into this, please note this rule is applicable at the time of writing this book, and every once in a while, this tax code comes up for review. There is often talk about adjusting it.

In essence, the 1031 tax code allows you to *defer* taxes due, not *forgive* taxes due. For purposes of this book, the rule states that if you sell a residential rental property and, within 6 months, buy another residential rental property, then the gains from the first home (*called the relinquished property*) can be applied to the next property (*called the replacement property*) and the capital gains tax due, as well as the depreciation recapture tax due, would be rolled over into the new property. You wouldn't have to pay those taxes in the year of the sale of the relinquished property. They are deferred. The idea is that you'll have extra money to use and, therefore, have more leverage to buy something more expensive and possibly have better cash flow on the replacement property. As with any IRS code, there are many rules, and some of them are not always crystal clear. In order to complete the 1031 exchange in its purest form and not have to pay any of those taxes in the year of the relinquished property sale, you have to do the following:

❖ The purchase price of the replacement property must be higher than the sales price of your relinquished property.

❖ The amount of your debt (i.e., mortgage) on the replacement property must be equal to or higher than the debt balance you had when you sold the relinquished property.

❖ The two properties must be like-kind exchanges, residential rental for residential rental.

❖ You must identify 3 possible properties that you entertain purchasing for the replacement property within 45 days of selling the relinquished property.

❖ You must close on the replacement property within 180 days of selling the relinquished property.

❖ At the closing of the relinquished property, you cannot receive or benefit from any of the proceeds, and they are to be managed by and held with a Qualified Intermediary.

You can do a partial 1031 if you don't meet the debt & purchase price rules above. In that case, you may owe partial taxes on the unused part, called a *boot*. Entire books are written on this subject, so just know that this is an opportunity if you're looking to sell one property and, within a near-term time projection, buy another similar property. If you're considering a 1031 exchange, you should certainly talk to your CPA, as well as a Qualified Intermediary, to discuss the rules and how it fits into your particular situation.

There are some pros and cons to doing a 1031, and many may be exclusive to your particular situation; however, here are some general thoughts on it.

The most glaring pro of a 1031 is simply that you're deferring taxes due to the IRS and, therefore, can use that money to buy more real estate. With your real estate purchase, you can, hopefully, earn more cash flow and better long-term gains. For instance, let's say I sold a property of mine and had a gross gain of $125,000 with an overall tax liability of $35,000 on that gain. After I paid the IRS the $35k, I'd only have $90k to invest into my next property. Would I rather have $125k to invest or $90k? I'd much rather have the $125k, which is what the 1031 allows you to do. That money remains in my new asset and not in the hands of the IRS. If you start the 1031 exchange process, but don't complete it, the IRS does not punish you for that. You just have to pay the taxes due. You may incur fees from the Qualified Intermediary who is holding your funds and has done all the paperwork and possibly some CPA fees, but probably nothing earth-shattering cost-wise.

There are some cons to consider. The first is with regard to the time constraints for completing a 1031. There are some timelines that you need to hit along the way. The toughest one for most investors is that you need to close on your new replacement property within 180 days of closing on the relinquished property you're selling. It's actually 180 days or the common tax day of April 15th. If the 180 days are not over by April 15th, most investors just file a tax extension so they can get the full 180 days. In some market conditions, identifying properties within 45 days and closing within 180 days may be no issue. However, if inventory is low, or demand is high, it can become a challenge to identify a worthy replacement property. In those hotter market conditions, you may have to overpay some just to secure a property. You also need to purchase "like-kind" properties as to what you just sold. There is a tad bit of a gray area here, but here's an example: if you're selling a long-term residential rental property, you need to replace it with another long-term residential rental property. There could be issues if you sold a long-term residential rental property, but replaced it with commercial real estate in a strip mall, for example. Also, since the root of the 1031 exchange is to defer taxes due on gains and depreciation recapture, you'll want to ensure you have enough actual gains to make it worthwhile. If your depreciation recapture is relatively low, you can inquire with your CPA about a possible *Cost Segregation Study* to help increase your allowable depreciation in a shorter period of time.

This tax code rule, when used properly, can be a great tool for investors to grow quicker. However, it's imperative that you pay close attention to the rules, so you complete it properly as it was intended. Doing a 1031 is not always the best path for all investors. Sometimes it's better to pay the IRS what is due versus trying to complete the 1031, especially if it could negatively impact you in the long run by being rushed into your next purchase. The 1031 option should certainly be understood by investors of all levels as another possible growth tool.

QUESTION: *What is the BRRRR Strategy?*

This acronym stands for Buy, Renovate, Rent, Refinance, Repeat. The core of this strategy is pulling out the money you put into a property and then being able to roll that money into another property. At the end of the day, you could purchase two homes using the same single lump sum of money if this strategy is done correctly. Many investors say they are doing this strategy, but they aren't pulling out their entire initial investment and thus can require funds to purchase the second property. That is considered a partial BRRRR. If you're trying to grow at a fast pace, you would want to complete a BRRRR within 6-12 months of buying the first property. Let's go through each step quickly:

Buy – typically, you have to purchase a home that needs a significant amount of work or buy a home at a large discount. However you get there, there needs to be a good amount of equity potential in a short period of time in order to fully make the Refinance part work down the line.

Renovate - since it's usually easier to find a home that needs a lot of work than find a seller willing to sell a decent home at a big discount, the renovation step is used to quickly increase the value. Of course, the renovation numbers need to work so you can put in the money to fix it up, but in turn, the end value needs to be significantly higher than the money you just invested. If you put in $25k in repairs and the value has only gone up to $25k, you really have the equity you need to do this strategy properly. A better example would be that you invested $25k in repairs, and the home value was now worth $75k more. In the latter, you have created the equity portion critical to the strategy.

Rent - this is a very important step. In order to refinance with the best rates and not have a huge amount of your income covering mortgage expenses, the bank that's refinancing the property will want to see the rental income on it. Most banks will want to see about 6 months of rental income, although some banks have workarounds on this. Either way, having the home rented by a tenant will make this strategy easier to complete and more effective.

Refinance - this is the linchpin to the whole process, as this is where you do a Cash-Out Refinance. If you did this correctly, you should be pulling out the money you have put in during the process. This can be accomplished because if you found a home that had the equity opportunity in it and you did the renovations correctly, then the new value of the home should be significantly higher than what you've invested. Now, when you complete the new mortgage, you should be able to borrow more. This allows you to pay off the first mortgage, but more importantly, get your cash out to go and apply to your next property. You are borrowing more on the first property, so you will most likely have a higher mortgage payment and, thus, less cash flow, but this strategy is about growth and quantity of homes. Cash flow will be built in the long-term by owning more homes. The real money maker in this is the ability to buy more homes for all the benefits we've talked about previously, but do so using the same money over and over.

Repeat - this is pretty simple. If you're growing your portfolio, continue to do this strategy over and over.

At the end of the day, this is just a cash-out refinance, as we've talked about, but it's sped up to a much quicker timeline and is meant to expedite your growth. The most successful BRRRR properties are ones that get all of your initial funds back, not just a portion, although investors do utilize partial BRRRR's all the time *(Those are simply considered Cash-Out Refinances)*.

QUESTION: *Should I turn my primary home into my first rental home?*

Simply answered, yes! For many novice investors, turning your first primary home into your first rental home is a great step in the right direction. For most primary homeowners, you'll start off by getting a better interest rate with lower down payment requirements than an investor may get. If done properly, there are even some tax advantages to transitioning their first primary home into their first rental home. When I bought my first two primary homes, both of which ended up being investment properties, I focused more on the long-term investment and rental options for those homes and less about if I would personally like them. I was in my 20s, single and with no children, so where and what I lived in was less important at that time. I knew I would never live in them that long. The length of time you live in the home in relation to when you rent or sell it can impact your gains and taxes, so as usual, chat with your CPA. Living in a home for 12 months as your primary residence before turning into a rental property is usually the line where your mortgage company is less likely to cause you any grief about renting it out. However, if you get a mortgage on your primary residence, and 90 days into purchasing it, you turn it into a rental home, you may have an issue on your hands. The mortgage companies care about your intent at the time of buying the home. You can probably safely convert a primary residence into a rental property twice, if not more, without too many lender questions. If you have a 20% downpayment saved for a property, but don't own a primary residence yet, you may consider putting down 10% on a primary residence, living in it for a year, then purchase another primary residence with the remaining 10% and turn the first property into a rental. Instead of using the 20% on a single property, you'll end up with two properties because of the lower down payment restrictions on primary residences.

QUESTION: *What is 'delayed financing'?*

Delayed financing, in its simplest form, is paying cash for a property and then obtaining a mortgage on the property shortly thereafter. At first, it may seem odd to pay cash and then get a mortgage, but as an investor, there are a few reasons why you may consider this. First, remember that the cash does not necessarily have to be your cash. You may take a loan from a friend or family in the form of a promissory note or even get a private lender to loan you the cash using what is commonly referred to as 'Hard Money.' If a property needs to close very quickly, such as in a week or two, and a traditional mortgage cannot be completed in that time frame, paying with cash will allow you to secure the property. Another example would be if the home needs a lot of work and the mortgage company won't give you the loan because the home is uninhabitable. In that case, you could pay cash, fix it up, and then finance it after with a traditional mortgage using a cash-out refinance. Timing, condition of the property, and convenience are typically the reasons why an investor would want to pay cash to purchase, then approach the financing after.

QUESTION: *What is hard money?*

Hard Money is another term for a private loan from a non-mortgage licensed entity that is secured by real estate. The security usually comes in the form of a lien against the property until the money is paid back. Since this type of loan is not considered a consumer loan, but rather a business loan, it is lent from company to company, not person to person. In order to receive hard money, you would need to have an LLC or other business entity set up. Hard money is notorious for being relatively expensive. Meaning, that the interest, points, or percentage of profit agreed to as payment for the loan is usually much higher than a traditional mortgage. This type of loan is also meant for short-term lending, usually less than 6 months in length. Hard money started to gain popularity when wealthy individuals would lend their private money to real estate investors to purchase, renovate, and resell properties for a profit, what we call a *flip*. As time has gone on and investors have gotten more creative and savvy, hard money has been utilized in many other ways as well. You might consider hard money as a way to purchase using the delayed financing method or BRRRR strategy we talked about previously. Hard money is ideal if you don't personally have the cash to purchase but do have a real estate opportunity at hand. More importantly, it's especially useful if you need to act quickly. Private lenders have their own parameters as to what they will lend their money on. Some solely focus on the property's numbers itself, while others will consider your personal creditworthiness, experience, and ability to pay back the loan. Most hard money lenders will charge a monthly interest fee, along with upfront *(time of purchase)* and back end *(time of final sale/refinance)* fees, called points *(1 point = 1% of the money borrowed)*. Other hard money lenders prefer to just take a percentage of the profits. Since you're working with a private lender, the terms can be negotiated.

QUESTION: *What is Owner Financing?*

The easiest way to describe owner financing is that the seller of the home you are buying will, in essence, become the mortgage holder. When a seller does not have a mortgage on a property they are selling, they may sometimes consider doing the financing for you as well. It makes them more money by collecting interest from you on the money they lent to you and, at the same time, may help you forgo some of the lending requirements and costs that a traditional mortgage lender may impose. For example, if you buy a property from a seller for $300,000 and you give them $60,000 in down payment, you still owe $240,000 to complete the sale. The seller may offer to do a mortgage (owner financing), where instead of them getting that $240,000 right now, it is broken up in mortgage payments you make directly to them at an agreed-upon interest rate. That way, they still get their money, just over the course of time instead of immediately. This can be a great tool when the opportunity arises; plus, the closing costs are usually lower with seller/owner financing. The trick is to find a seller who can offer owner financing, and it should be on a property that you want. Don't purchase a property just because there is an owner financing option if it's not the right property for you or your portfolio.

QUESTION: *How can I create efficiencies within my portfolio?*

Newer investors have a tendency to fix up their rental properties too nicely. Now, let me be clear as I've talked about this throughout the book - I make all of my rental properties decently nice to beat most of my competitors, increase rents, decrease expenses, and entice a higher level of tenants to want to live there, but I don't make the rental home nicer than my own home. Novice investors go one of two ways. First, they buy a dump of a house and leave it a dump. Or, they buy a house and over-improve it by pouring unnecessary money into it. Understanding what, when, and where to invest money in a property is something that comes with experience, and while there are a lot of tips out there, you will slowly learn as you grow. Creating efficiencies within your portfolio will help you get there faster and save you money.

For instance, every one of my rental homes is painted with the same color on the inside. I never have to wonder what color a room in a house is because I already know. I buy kitchen cabinets from the same company, so I can interchange parts or doors much easier. Except in rare circumstances, I use one of two backsplash tiles or bathroom floor tiles. If I have a tile break, no sweat because I've got 25 replacement tiles that are extras from other homes. Those types of things will make your life so much easier as you grow your portfolio. I try to pick colors and materials that have stood the test of time. If you choose to own and run a few furnished rentals, short or long term, have the same size beds and sheets between the homes. Purchase the same coffee makers, TVs, and kitchenware. Being able to have your cleaning crews swap one for another between all the homes creates efficiencies that save you time and money. You're not living in the home, so don't worry about what you want. Worry about what feeds the investment side. Think about those types of details as they add up over time. A fellow investor once explained it to me like this - "Don't just be a doctor, be a specialist." In essence, he was saying, don't just be a real estate investor, but be a specialist at it and analyze all the small details that can add up over time. If you're going to start off by focusing on rentals, then be the very best at that part of real estate investing and don't try to master it all at once.

QUESTION: *What is a Subject-To?*

Truthfully, I debated on including this question in this book because Subject-To's are a little more complicated and risky than most novice investors initially want to get involved in. I only bring it up because this topic is one that swirls around the investment world a lot, and I didn't want to ignore it. These are when you buy a property from someone *subject to* their mortgage. That means the deed gets changed to you as the new owner; however, the seller's mortgage stays in place, and you make the payments. This is not a *loan assumption* because, typically, the seller's mortgage company has no idea this is going on. From a buyer's perspective, doing a subject-to can allow you to obtain a property, even if you may not have the credit, loan qualifications, or funds to actually purchase that property in traditional fashion. From a seller's perspective, this can help them if they are late on mortgage payments or trying to prevent foreclosure, and want to remain in the property. There are a lot of risks on both sides of this transaction, from property insurance liability issues to due-on-sale clauses to a whole host of other items that could happen. While many of these subjects-to's are performed on a shorter-term basis and not usually intended for a long-term ownership method, they can be high-risk, and you should definitely involve an experienced real estate attorney to advise you and create any documents needed.

QUESTIONS: *How can I 'renovate & flip' homes while also having rental homes?*

When I teach various courses, I usually get people who want to invest in real estate in one of two ways - rentals or flips. I immediately tell both groups not to ignore the other. Some deals you may come across are better suited for a flip, such as a home that requires a ton of work to maximize your profits, and you may not want to risk putting a tenant into a home that you just invested significant renovations in. Even with the best tenants, I'd be cautious to risk that. For some homes, there's not enough *meat on the bone* in regards to profit, to renovate and sell, so they are better suited for a rental. However, there is a large middle ground between the two groups that I think is often missed, and I really enjoy properties that fall in that gap. Those properties are the ones in need of a good amount of work, but there's not enough profit to flip it today. Those homes fall into the portion of my portfolio I call the *Future Flip Pipeline*. They are homes that I'll probably hold on to for a shorter-term, such as 2-5 years, and I will plan on doing a large renovation and sale at the end of that time frame. They aren't typically long-term rentals due to the amount of work they need. I will invest just enough to get a tenant in the property, and I will adjust my rents for the quality of the home at that time. Then, after a few years of rental income, I'll do the big renovation and sale. That usually gives me a few years of cash flow, principal paydown, market appreciation and puts me into a Long Term capital gains tax bracket with the IRS, which is lower than the Short Term capital gains bracket I would be in had I just renovated and flipped the property initially. Remember, you may have to invest some money upfront to make it safe and decent enough for a tenant for those few years. It's a great way for investors to build their future pipeline and reduce the stress of trying to find the perfect deal right now. If there isn't necessarily enough profit in the deal to flip it today, the extra time you're holding the property, while renting it, can allow the profit portion to evolve. It's a great way to prepare for the future and try to stay ahead of the investors solely looking for flips, as well as the investors who don't want to take on any work for their rentals. It's a great space between the two investment strategies.

QUESTION: *How do I know when to buy and when to sell?*

Trying to time the market can be very difficult, and any investor who has tried enough times has probably lost once or twice. This all reverts to early in the book when we talked about setting forth your goals and identifying what each home needs to do for you over a particular period. I think it's very important to set an estimated time of ownership of each property when you initially purchase it. By doing this, you can continue planning and forecasting for the future. If you never implement an exit strategy for your homes, it becomes difficult to figure out how many homes you may need to own and where the cash to do so will come from. Plus, without some sort of exit timeline, it becomes difficult to make accurate financial decisions. I'll be the first to acknowledge that I have set ownership time frames on homes of mine, and when that time came, I decided to hold them longer for one reason or another. I've also had homes that I have sold earlier than expected. One of the things that I think is important to realize is that real estate, just as any other investment, may not increase in value at an incremental, equal rate each year. Some homes may earn the bulk of their gains early on, and some homes will have to wait around and earn that bulk later down the line. If you have a home that earns a bulk of its gains early, there is something to be said for exploring the options of selling, capturing those quick gains, and rolling it into another similar project that can earn higher gains moving forward. Just like I compared houses to stocks earlier, the same thought process applies here. You may not hold each of your retirement stocks forever. There may come a time when the bulk of those gains should be realized and placed into another investment that can repeat itself at another high rate of return. Another factor to consider is the market conditions when you're buying or selling. A fellow real estate investor once said, *"I sell when everyone is buying, and I buy when everyone is selling."* If tons of people are buying, demand is high, and supply is squeezed, therefore giving higher prices. When the opposite occurs, prices may deflate or increase seller competition giving opportunity to fish around for better deals. The tough part with this mentality is that if everyone is buying and prices are increasing, greed can get in the way, and many sellers hold on too long and try to time the peak of the market. If you're a buyer, and inventory increases and prices are softening, you may hold off buying too long because you're waiting for a bottoming. You will never know the peak or valley of any market until you have passed them and look back in time. There is nothing that pinpoints that exact time while it is occurring. I always believe money in real estate is *fake money* until it's actually *realized*. You can have a portfolio that, on paper, is worth a large amount of money, but until you sell something and realize some gains, it's all on paper. For some people, that is their goal - not to realize any gains until later in life, and for them, that is perfectly fine. If you fall into the group that is planning on realizing some gains throughout your investment career, then you'll have to realize some gains at some point. At the end of the day, I let my goals and plan dictate when I'm going to sell or buy something, and while I don't ignore the market conditions, I don't necessarily let it dictate what I'm going to do all of the time. There have been instances where I let certain market conditions or continual media stories influence my decisions, and as a repercussion, I probably sold some assets too early and deviated from my plan. Unfortunately, you may not see those results until later down the road, and you use them as lessons learned. There is a quote about greed that I like to use, and this may be a good place to share it, "Pigs get fat, hogs get slaughtered." I'd rather leave some possible extra gains on the table and be on the safer side than push for greed, but that is who I am at my core, so I follow that.

QUESTION: *Is it ok to have cash and not invest?*

This question relates to the investors who like to hold on to a little extra cash and not invest every dollar as it comes in. There are plenty of successful investors who subscribe to the mantra, "cash is trash," which means that just having cash in the bank doesn't earn you more money, so it's useless unless put to work. On the other hand, I prescribe to a different mantra, "Cash is king!" When you're getting started, you'll probably need to put the vast majority of your money into your first property or two to purchase it, but as your portfolio grows, and so do your cash savings, I think keeping a healthy nest egg to the side is important. This topic is highly debated upon – invest everything or save more than you may need for any realistic emergency. The reality is that it's a very personal question, and there is no right or wrong answer. If you ask me, I'm a little more of a conservative investor by nature, so I like to be more particular about what properties I buy. Consequently, I hold on to more cash than most investors. Having that nest egg lets me sleep better at night, not worry too much about changes in market conditions, and best of all, I'm always ready to easily pounce on a good opportunity because I have the funds readily available to do so. By holding more cash and being more particular, I accept the opportunity cost involved by not continually investing. That path works for my family and me, and you should pick the path that works best for you and your risk tolerance!

QUESTION: *What if a price is too good to be true?*

Another expensive lesson I learned early on, and have even repeated once or twice along the way, was letting the price dictate if the deal was good or not. Let me clarify that. Of course, the price is a driving force in determining a good deal or not. However, in getting a property at a certain price, I believed all the other issues with the home could be explained away. For example, homes with a steep driveway, terrible layout, or location next to a busy road are all examples of properties that, with a lower price and more time on the market, will find a buyer. The issue comes in that even if you get a discount on the front end for that property, you may have two issues on the backend to contend with. The first is that you should be planning to sell the home for more money in the future and as prices go up, the buyers have a tendency to be more discerning. If I purchased a home for $300k with a steep driveway, I may say, "The driveway is terrible, but for $300k, how could I go wrong?" Fast forward ten years, and I want to sell it for $500k, and that higher-priced buyer may say, "For that much money, I'd rather wait for something with a better driveway." The discount I may have to give to the $500k buyer may be more than the discount I received when I purchased it at $300k. Price points sometimes impact what buyers will or will not ignore, as well as the percentage of discounts needed to overcome some property hurdles. The second issue to consider is the market conditions you're in when you go to sell. If you happen to be selling when inventory is low, then it may not impact you at all. However, if you're selling during a buyers' market with loads of surplus inventory, it may be very difficult to sell that property in a timely manner, or at least, not without a larger than an expected discount. When you're buying that home, you never know what the market will be when you go to sell it, so you weaken your exit options when you purchase a home with issues that you cannot fix. Lastly, those items will impact a tenant too, and even though you may offer lower rents as a counter, you may incur higher vacancy rates and overall lower cash flow. At the end of the day, don't let price be the only deciding factor, especially when something looks too good to be true. Even on the homes you plan to hold forever, always look at the exit strategy when you're buying it. No one has ever gone through life without having to use their Plan B from time to time.

QUESTION: *Why can't I find the right home?*

In over 20 years of doing real estate, I've never once been in a *perfect* house. I've been in some pretty awesome houses and even owned a house or two that seemed to check almost every box, but never have I seen the perfect one. Just like stocks or companies, there's no perfect one. Searching for perfection is a futile task and a great exercise in wasting your time. Instead of searching for the perfect investment home, just start with the one that would work *good enough* to get you going. It doesn't have to be amazing. It doesn't have to earn you double-digit returns. It doesn't need to be a home that you brag to your friends about. It doesn't have to do anything except *safely house another person at a fair rate and appreciate close to market levels.* That's really it. When you look at it from that perspective, there are tons of possibilities out there for investments. People get so caught up in the overloading of information, intense amounts of research, and fear of making the wrong decision, that they just face longstanding indecision. There's also no perfect market. I've bought and sold homes in hot sellers' markets, hot buyers' markets, all-around mediocre markets, during the uncertain phases of the COVID pandemic and during the years of the Great Recession. Real estate is typically treated as a longer-term investment and there will always be a new news cycle or market impact right around the corner. Stop looking for the perfect house and perfect market conditions. Some will be amazing investments, and some will be average, but until you start to actually take action, your rate of return will always be 0%.

QUESTION: *Should I partner up with people when just getting started?*

I'm all for building wealth as a team. After all, there's no point in having a little extra if you can't share it. And, there's plenty to go around. My concern with novice investors creating companies and partnerships very early on in their investing careers is pretty simple. It can get pretty muddy pretty quickly. You don't have to look far or ask too many people, and you'll hear stories about family, friends, colleagues, and strangers who have started out with the best of intentions, only for things to quickly turn sour. Or investors who created partnerships with contractors and built rental portfolios, only to have arguments over anything from the color of countertops to missing funds. It's not all doom and gloom, of course. I do have some suggestions and tips for teaming up in a partnership. First off, there are many ways you can *be in business* with someone and not have to *create a business* together. There are also ways that you can have an interest in a property without being a technical owner. For instance, let's say you and your best friend want to go and buy a rental house together. Your friend will be supplying most of the money, and you're running the operations, management, etc. They could provide you with the money via a deed of trust and a promissory note. You would be the owner on the title, but because your friend's money is recorded as a lien against the property, you would not be able to sell the property without the terms of the promissory note being met. It's just like if you went and got a mortgage. The lender has a lien against the property, even though they have no actual ownership stake in the property. In addition to the promissory note path, you can look into joint venture agreements that are drawn up for a specific property between specific parties, whereas one party may be the owner of the property, and the other party's interests are protected by that agreement. In none of those examples was there a need for the various parties to join together and create a single company, nor was there a need for both parties to be on the title. When you start to explore multi-member LLCs and various business structures, consult an attorney who specializes in that field. Creating businesses, partnerships, LLCs, and any other business structure certainly has its time and place. There are certainly reasons for why they may be warranted, but I would suggest that you complete a few deals with the said party prior to going out and incurring a lot of expense and becoming so ingrained with them in a formal business.

QUESTION: *How can I build something for my kids to have?*

I love the idea of generational wealth, and it is a great way to look at your exit strategy for your portfolio. Generational wealth is not about leaving your heirs a lump sum of cash but rather leaving them physical assets that produce continual income for them. Instead of receiving a chunk of money at the closing of your estate that they can go out and do anything with, I'm in love with the concept of leaving them those real assets. You can even have those assets placed in a protected trust so that it's difficult to immediately sell those assets upon your passing. If your goal is to leave your heirs your portfolio and to help the next generation start off with a certain level of wealth, then it is wise to start early on with the estate and tax planning of it. How you structure the financing, titling of the property, and tax consequences could all have a real impact on what is reasonable to leave within the estate or trust. When looking into the future about what you plan to leave behind, remember there is a difference between leaving physical assets that are cash flowing or just selling the properties and leaving a pile of cash behind.

My Final Thoughts

WHEN I STARTED THIS book, I really had two goals in mind, and neither of them was monetary-based. I wanted to share my passion for real estate in a way that hopefully gave motivation to some people to get out there and start investing. The second was that I wanted to provide people with realistic, everyday methods to be able to accomplish their goals. Book after book seems to sell this dream of owning many homes, buying apartment complexes, or using complicated financial instruments or partnerships. The reality is that most people won't go down that road. And that's fine. I don't own 100 homes, not even close to that amount, and yet, I still have a solid financial future based on a core of real estate. I have no desire to own an apartment building, and I'm fine with that. I have no desire to take on as much debt as possible and keep buying more homes, and I'm fine with that too. I'm following my goals and path: the one that works for my family and me. If your plan is to own a lot of homes, buy apartment complexes or maximize your financial leverage as much as possible, then go at it 100%. You attack your goals and plans with the deepest of vigor and passion. The beauty of real estate is that it can work for everyone and yet is not a one size fits all type of asset. It can produce this amazing financial stability for so many reasons, yet each home may be unique to each investor in how it fits into their plan or doesn't. The point is, it has to follow your plan, which means ignoring some of the outside influences that don't have direct input on that plan.

As you progress through your investing career, continue to tweak and adjust your plan. But before you can tweak your plan, you must have one. In my opinion, the most critical part of being successful is to lay out your plan with what you want to accomplish and when you need to accomplish it. Really invest some time to lay out a solid foundation with that plan, then tweak and adjust as you move forward accordingly. I cannot stress how important this is.

We know real estate gains are typically created over time. If it feels like you're not making tons of cash every month, or the loan balance is slowly getting paid down, or even that the home isn't appreciating as fast as you would like, just be patient. Real estate can be like a seedling that needs to sprout and grow roots before it can become a strong tree. But once it becomes that tree, it can serve as something steady and strong for your future.

Enjoy your success as you gain it over time. Don't wait till you've hit all of your goals to take a little time to reward yourself. I think it's perfectly fine to every once in a while, take some of your gains and treat yourself. Now, I'm not talking about renting a private jet to cruise to a tropical island you rented out, but more along the lines of a little trip somewhere or treating yourself to something you've wanted for a while. Even paying off a nagging debt, like a student or car loan, are all things that can give you some joy. Whatever it is you want to do, as long as it's within reason in relation to your gains, go ahead and treat yourself. We never know what tomorrow will bring, so *don't wait till you have everything to spend anything.* When I tell people to enjoy the fruits of their labor, I think about Yvon Chouinard, the late founder of the clothing brand Patagonia. He had a policy with all of his employees that when there was a swell in the ocean, his employees could leave work to go surfing, no matter what they were working on. He understood that when an opportunity for pure joy is in front of you, you seize that opportunity. Enjoy it, as you never know when the next swell will come ashore.

In order to enjoy some of your success, you will need to have the financial gains to do so. That means that every once in a while, you need to take some profits off the table. It's fine to *clean up your balance sheet* from time to time. As the musician, Kenny Rogers famously sang, '*You've got to know when to hold 'em. Know when to fold 'em. Know when to walk away. And know when to run. You never count your money when you're sittin' at the table. There'll be time enough for counting when the dealin's done.*' Greed can cloud your vision and steer you away from your well-laid-out plan. So, when making decisions on exit strategies, decide if you're holding for <u>greed</u> or <u>opportunity</u>; sometimes, they look alike, but are disguised by the appeal of more money.

I've referenced a few times to aim for wealth, not riches, all while valuing your time, and I'd like to reiterate those. In my opinion, there is a big difference between being *rich* and being *wealthy*. Both revolve around money to some extent, but I view the rich as people who still **have to work** to maintain their level of income and lifestyle. I view wealthy people as people who **choose to work** because they want to. Wealthy people make money while not actually being at work, and they do so through multiple streams of income and assets that produce residual cash over time. Wealthy people have freedom. Freedom from being tied to a job. Freedom from worrying about what their retirement stock account does. Freedom from worrying about future income. Freedom from having a boss. At the end of the day, when people say *money doesn't buy happiness*, they are right. Money can't make you happy, but money can buy you freedom, and that freedom sure can help make you happy. The reality is that money always has been, and always will be, the currency on which the world turns. You need money to create *financial freedom,* and if that is one of your goals, then real estate should clearly be a part of your strategy. Become an entrepreneur for freedom, not for money.

Value your time outside of work and be kind to others. As I've noted before, you buy things with time, not money. Your time invested at your job earns you a paycheck, and that paycheck allows you to pay for the needs and wants of your life. If you didn't spend that time at work, you wouldn't get that paycheck. Keep that saying in the back of your mind as you move forward and have to adjust your time spent in a way that allows you to embark on this real estate journey further. When getting started, there is a fine balance between becoming so absorbed in this stuff that you push everything else to the side and have a singular vision of real estate investing. It can consume you. The common consequence to that is there is less time to spend with your family and friends, and you become so tight with your money that you forget about others along the way. Never put a house before your family. Never give up an opportunity to experience something new or wonderful with your kids. Don't pass up that opportunity to have a beer with a buddy. Just like you shouldn't ignore great financial opportunities, you shouldn't ignore great personal opportunities, either. *Don't allow your family and friends to become an opportunity cost of your success.* The last thing you want is to amass a certain amount of wealth and have no one around to share it with. And if you don't succeed or don't like real estate investing, you certainly don't want to lose your friends and family over it.

A personal note unrelated to real estate - be kind and give back. Do it when you only have a little to give and do more when you have more to give. Do it when no one is looking. Do it for the pure act of giving with nothing expected in return. The world isn't fair, and to some, it's less fair than others. That's just the way it works, unfortunately. Do your part. Heck, do more than just *your part*. If you don't have the time to help, open up your checkbook. If you don't have the money to help, give some of your time. Never feel guilty for your success, but also don't convince yourself that it's all because of you. Appreciate the fact that along the way, things had to work in your favor from time to time. Nobody's success is 100% attributed to just hard work, and nobody's success is totally attributed to just luck, either. People who help others are the wealthiest people around. The residual effects of when you help another person goes on well beyond any dollar earned. When in doubt, remind yourself that it's just that little bit extra that can make all the difference to someone. From time to time, we all have a pebble in our shoe that no one sees. Just because someone's problems aren't visible to you doesn't mean they don't exist. Create the desire to climb to the top, not so people look up to you or you look down on them, but rather so you can help others get a better view.

And finally, I'll leave you with this: <u>Plug the holes, fill the barrel</u>.

Plug the holes of your expenses and fill the barrel with income.
Plug the holes of your time wasted and fill the barrel with time valued.
Plug the holes of the naysayers and fill the barrel with belief.
Plug the holes of the excuses and fill the barrel with opportunity.
Plug the holes of procrastination and fill the barrel with action.
Plug the holes of greed and fill the barrel with giving.

Writing this book has given me a wonderful opportunity to share my thoughts with people like you. Love it or hate it, I hope the book added some sort of value to your future endeavors, and I sincerely thank you for giving me this opportunity.

Now, go buy some damn houses!

THANK YOU for reading!

We'd really appreciate your feedback
by leaving us a review here

Made in the USA
Coppell, TX
12 April 2022